Streamlit for Web Development

Build and Scale Secure Python-Powered Apps with Streamlit

Second Edition

Mohammad Khorasani
Mohamed Abdou
Javier Hernández Fernández

Streamlit for Web Development: Build and Scale Secure Python-Powered Apps with Streamlit, Second Edition

Mohammad Khorasani
Melbourne, VIC, Australia

Mohamed Abdou
Cambridge, UK

Javier Hernández Fernández
Madrid, Spain

ISBN-13 (pbk): 979-8-8688-1825-7
https://doi.org/10.1007/979-8-8688-1826-4

ISBN-13 (electronic): 979-8-8688-1826-4

Managing Director, Apress Media LLC: Welmoed Spahr
Acquisitions Editor: James Robinson-Prior
Editorial Project Manager: Jacob Shmulewitz

Cover image by padrinan on pixabay

Distributed to the book trade worldwide by Springer Science+Business Media New York, 1 New York Plaza, New York, NY 10004. Phone 1-800-SPRINGER, fax (201) 348-4505, e-mail orders-ny@ springer-sbm.com, or visit www.springeronline.com. Apress Media, LLC is a Delaware LLC and the sole member (owner) is Springer Science + Business Media Finance Inc (SSBM Finance Inc). SSBM Finance Inc is a **Delaware** corporation.

For information on translations, please e-mail booktranslations@springernature.com; for reprint, paperback, or audio rights, please e-mail bookpermissions@springernature.com.

Apress titles may be purchased in bulk for academic, corporate, or promotional use. eBook versions and licenses are also available for most titles. For more information, reference our Print and eBook Bulk Sales web page at http://www.apress.com/bulk-sales.

Any source code or other supplementary material referenced by the author in this book is available to readers on GitHub (https://github.com/Apress/Streamlit-for-Web-Development-2nd-ed). For more detailed information, please visit https://www.apress.com/gp/services/source-code.

If disposing of this product, please recycle the paper

To my parents and my departed grandparents.

—Mohammad Khorasani

To my family, friends, and the open source community.

—Mohamed Abdou

To my family and friends for their support.

—Javier Hernández Fernández

Table of Contents

About the Authors

 **Mohammad Khorasani** is a hybrid of an engineer and a computer scientist with a bachelor of science in Mechanical Engineering from Texas A&M University and a master's degree in Computer Science from the University of Illinois at Urbana-Champaign. Mohammad specializes in developing and implementing software solutions for the advancement of renewable energy systems and services at Iberdrola. In addition, he develops robotic devices using embedded systems and rapid prototyping technologies. He is also an avid blogger of STEM-related topics on *Towards Data Science*—a Medium publication.

linkedin.com/in/mkhorasani/

 **Mohamed Abdou** is a software engineer with diverse academic and industrial exposure, a graduate of Computer Engineering from Qatar University, and currently a Software Development Engineer at Amazon. Mohamed has built a variety of open source tools used by tens of thousands in the Streamlit community. He led the first Google Developer Student Club in Qatar and represented Qatar University in national and international programming contests. He is a cyber security enthusiast and was ranked second nationwide in bug bounty hunting in Qatar in 2020 among under 25-year-olds.

linkedin.com/in/mohamed-ashraf-abdou/

Javier Hernández Fernández specializes in the area of technology innovation and brings over twenty years of practical experience in overseeing the design and delivery of R&D initiatives on behalf of multinational companies in the field of IT, telecom, and utilities. He currently manages research and technical consulting projects as part of the Innovation team of Iberdrola, working in the smart grid, renewables, and energy efficiency domains. In addition to a B.Sc. in Computer Science from the University of Ottawa (Canada), Javier holds two master's degrees in Energy Management from the University of Zaragoza and Project Management from the University San Pablo CEU/IEP (Spain) and a Ph.D. in Computer Science & Engineering from HBKU.

linkedin.com/in/javier-hernandezf/

About the Technical Reviewer

Vladyslav Haina is an AI infrastructure and MLOps engineer who specializes in building scalable, production-grade artificial intelligence systems. His primary focus is on designing and automating end-to-end machine learning workflows. Leveraging deep expertise in DevOps, DataOps, and Site Reliability Engineering (SRE), Vladyslav skillfully integrates real-time data streaming using Kafka and Flink, orchestrates complex pipelines with tools like Matillion and ArgoCD, and implements robust monitoring solutions with Grafana and OpenTelemetry. His key areas of proficiency include MLOps and AI Platforming, Cloud-Native Architecture across GCP and AWS with Kubernetes and Terraform, and establishing comprehensive Observability for ML systems. Vladyslav is also an active contributor to the tech and research community, with articles published in *All Tech Magazine* and *The American Journal of Engineering and Technology*.

Acknowledgments

This undertaking would not have been possible without the support and efforts of a selfless few. Individuals and entities who, in one way or another, have made a contribution to the contents of this book are named as follows in no particular order:

- *Streamlit:* The visionaries who created the framework itself, empowering countless developers

- *Iberdrola Renewables:* The folks who served as a test bed for our very first Streamlit ventures and had to put up with our constant pitching of Streamlit's resourcefulness—*Daniel Paredes, Nuria Sanchez Sanchez, and Brenno Teixeira Martins*

- *Iberdrola Innovation Middle East:* Our beloved coworkers who were Streamlitized, whether they liked it or not—*Ayman Al-Kababji, Mohd Alomar, Fawaz Kserawi, Mohamed Elwaleed, and Mohamed Elbiba*

- *Dr. Nikhil Navkar:* For being another trailblazing Streamlit user

In addition, a tangible part of our careers and personal endeavors would have simply been inconceivable without the spirit of the open source community. It is therefore in order to give a special tribute to Python and its respective developers, in addition to the multitude of other online forums that are silent heroes. Without their efforts, all-nighters would be every other night, and our works not nearly as neat as they are.

Preface

It was a typical night when, just as I was about to fall asleep, my phone buzzed. Being a millennial, I couldn't resist checking it, only to find another annoying email advertisement for something called "Streamlit." Normally, I'd ignore it, but for some reason, the sleek Streamlit logo caught my eye. In hindsight, I'm glad I clicked on the ad. Since then, my programming life has been closely linked to a framework I had been hoping someone would create—the powerful Streamlit.

Early in my career, I noticed that many skilled Python developers, including myself, excelled in backend and server-side programming but struggled with frontend user interfaces and client-side software. While Flask and Django made efforts to address this, both required significant knowledge of HTML, CSS, and HTTP, making them tough to use. I often turned to Tkinter and PyQt for local desktop applications, but I couldn't deploy anything to the cloud. What we needed was a pure Python web framework with an intuitive API that allowed easy creation and deployment of web applications, focusing primarily on the backend. Essentially, something like ReactJS but for Python. And when I clicked that ad, I found exactly what I was looking for. It was a eureka moment!

This happened in the summer of 2020, and Streamlit had only been publicly released in the fall of 2019. In less than a year, the development team had crafted a framework and API that matched my needs perfectly. Since then, Streamlit has only grown in popularity, and for me, it came at the perfect time. I had just joined Iberdrola and was tasked with developing a Python-based web application. Before Streamlit, I would have hesitated to even consider deploying applications to the web, but now, I was advocating for web applications, proudly showcasing Streamlit's capabilities. In no time, I became a trailblazer within my development team.

As with all great discoveries, it felt wrong to keep it to myself. I decided to share Streamlit's potential with the world, and this book is the result. It's written for developers who, like me, have struggled with creating and deploying web applications. This book offers a comprehensive guide to Streamlit, from simple use cases to building complex, cloud-based applications.

By the end of this book, readers will not only understand how to use Streamlit, but also how to integrate their web applications with powerful server-side infrastructures like MongoDB, PostgreSQL, Linux, Windows Server, and Streamlit's deployment platform. The goal is to empower readers to take their ideas and bring them to the web, possibly even kickstarting their own ventures.

—Mohammad Khorasani

Acronyms

aaS	As a Service
API	Application Programming Interface
BLOB	Binary Large Object
CLI	Command-Line Interface
CPU	Central Processing Unit
CRUD	Create, Read, Update, and Delete
CSP	Cloud Service Provider
CSRF	Cross-Site Request Forgery
CSS	Cascading Style Sheets
DI	Dependency Injection, a coding pattern
DG	Delta Generator, a core module in Streamlit
DOM	Document Object Model
DTW	Dynamic Time Warping
GPU	Graphics Processing Unit
HTML	Hypertext Markup Language
IDE	Integrated Development Environment
ISP	Internet Service Provider
JSON	JavaScript Object Notation
JWT	JSON Web Token
LLM	Large Language Model
MLaaS	Machine Learning as a Service
MVC	Model-View-Controller
NAT	Network Address Translation
ORM	Object-Relational Mapping
OS	Operating System
PID	Process Identifier

ACRONYMS

PV	Photovoltaic
RAG	Retrieval Augmented Generation
RCE	Remote Code Execution
RDP	Remote Desktop Protocol
REST	Representational State Transfer
SaaS	Software as a Service
SCADA	Supervisory Control and Data Acquisition
SQL	Structured Query Language
SQLI	SQL Injection
SSH	Secure Shell
TPU	Tensor Processing Unit
UI	User Interface
URI	Uniform Resource Identifier
URL	Uniform Resource Locator
UX	User Experience
VPN	Virtual Private Network
WSL	Windows Subsystem for Linux
XSS	Cross-Site Scripting

Intended Audience

This book assumes that you have at least a basic understanding of the following topics:

- Object-oriented programming

- Data structures and algorithms

- Python and the following bindings:

  - Pandas

  - Numpy

  - Plotly

- SQL (both relational and nonrelational databases)

- Git version control frameworks

- Cloud computing

To fully benefit from the content in this book, it's important that you have some experience in programming. If you're unfamiliar with the areas mentioned, it's recommended to take an introductory course before diving in. That said, you don't need to be an expert to benefit from the book. Even if you're already able to build applications with more advanced frameworks, you may still appreciate how much time and effort Streamlit saves. It enables you to create a robust web application in hours, something that might have taken weeks with frameworks like Flask or Django.

However, if you're looking for highly customized and intricate frontend user interfaces, Streamlit might not be the right choice at this moment. While it is continuously improving, there may be more flexibility in frameworks like Django for now. But, as mentioned, Django requires more advanced programming skills to develop web applications.

By the end of this book, you should be capable of building and deploying scalable web applications to the cloud, with the ability to handle both backend and frontend requirements. You'll be able to integrate your applications with databases like PostgreSQL and MongoDB and deploy them using cloud services such as Microsoft Server, Linux containers, and Streamlit's own cloud platform.

While this book will go into significant detail on the required concepts, some level of self-learning and research will be necessary. There may be gaps in the tutorials, or some tools might become outdated as you read. You'll need to apply your own intuition and judgment to fill in those gaps. This book will also focus on the practical application of Streamlit and other tools rather than explaining the inner workings of their source code. Each tutorial will present a specific use case or application, with accompanying code. All the code provided in this book is open source, released under the MIT License. You are encouraged to adapt and apply the methodologies shared here to meet your own technical needs.

Additional Material

This book is supported by a wealth of online resources, including repositories, datasets, libraries, APIs, and their corresponding documentation. Where applicable, URLs to these materials will be provided throughout the book. All tutorials and source code featured in this book can be accessed through the following repository: `https://github.com/Apress/Streamlit-for-Web-Development-2nd-ed`. Additionally, any references to the Streamlit API can be found on their official documentation site at `https://docs.streamlit.io/library/api-reference`.

CHAPTER 1

Introducing Streamlit

With the overwhelming influx of data and the speed at which it is generated, traditional computing methods are increasingly unable to deliver results efficiently. In contrast, cloud computing serves as a powerful enabler, helping to overcome these limitations. Offering greater scalability, lower costs, and improved flexibility, cloud migration benefits service providers, developers, and users alike.

As Python remains the scripting language of choice for much of the software development community, it becomes crucial to offer a web framework that bridges the skills gap for developers. While traditional frameworks like Flask and Django require a solid understanding of HTML and CSS, Streamlit stands out as the first major framework to rely entirely on Python, drastically reducing development time from weeks to hours.

1.1. Why Streamlit?

Restricting oneself to local computing is now a relic of the past, as the cloud unlocks a wide array of advantages, empowering developers to make a significantly greater impact on the world. This is precisely why a new generation of developers is wholeheartedly embracing the cloud, and the swift shift toward this computing paradigm underscores its transformative potential. In this context, a pure Python web framework like Streamlit becomes invaluable, offering developers an accessible bridge to make the transition while serving as a powerful enabler for those seeking to harness the full potential of cloud computing.

© Mohammad Khorasani, Mohamed Abdou, Javier Hernández Fernández 2025
M. Khorasani et al., *Streamlit for Web Development*,
https://doi.org/10.1007/979-8-8688-1826-4_1

1.1.1. Local vs. the Cloud

The cloud is increasingly becoming synonymous with data. Wherever there is an abundance of data, cloud computing is often intricately linked. Simply put, harnessing the value of big data without leveraging the cloud is nearly impossible. Gone are the days of relying on Microsoft Excel to create outdated dashboards for datasets. With the sheer scale of data available today, local computing alone is no longer sufficient.

That said, local computing does have its merits. Prototyping an idea is often faster, and latency between nodes and servers is significantly lower. This is why edge computing maintains a key advantage in specific scenarios. For applications where security is critical or regulations are restrictive, local computing may be the better option. However, beyond these cases, the drawbacks of local computing outweigh its benefits. High overhead costs for maintaining infrastructure and limited adaptability to traffic spikes, such as the surge during the Super Bowl halftime, make local computing impractical for many modern applications.

In contrast, cloud computing offers cost-effective provisioning, exceptional scalability, high reliability, and resilience against failure. It allows scaling in two ways: horizontally, with multiple instances of the same resources, and vertically, with bespoke resources like GPUs, TPUs, and advanced database systems. Most notably, the cloud expands possibilities, enabling products to be offered as services on the web. This shift toward the *as-a-service* (aaS) model—spanning software (SaaS), machine learning (MLaaS), and beyond—has redefined how value is delivered online.

This is where a framework like Streamlit becomes invaluable. It serves as a cloud enabler, addressing the skills gap that has kept many developers from deploying their work online. Streamlit empowers developers at all levels, making it easier to bring value to the web and participate in the cloud-driven future of software development.

1.1.2. A Trend Toward Cloud Computing

Cloud computing has become the compass of modern technology, guiding academia, corporations, governments, and even intelligence agencies as they rapidly transition from local systems to the cloud. With legacy software struggling to provide growth and returns on investment, organizations are increasingly turning to cloud service providers (CSPs) for agility, cost efficiency, and access to advanced computing resources. Even CSPs are reimagining their offerings, with Google and Microsoft migrating their legacy applications to the cloud through platforms like Google G Suite and Microsoft Office 365.

From a business perspective, the rationale for embracing the cloud is stronger than ever. Disruptive businesses have fully adopted what many had previously hesitated to accept, making cloud adoption less a choice and more a necessity for survival. Reduced lead times, scalability, lower capital expenditures, and heightened innovation are just a few benefits driving this shift. For CSPs, the advantages are equally compelling: resource pooling, enhanced elasticity, and decreased maintenance costs create a compelling value proposition. Most notably, for consumers, the cloud has become a transformative force, akin to the Internet itself. SaaS models deliver unmatched flexibility, granular pricing, and exceptional value, creating a win-win-win scenario where everyone benefits.

The trajectory toward cloud computing was already strong, but the global pandemic acted as an accelerant, breaking down long-standing barriers to remote learning, online exams, remote work, and more. Decades of effort by the tech community could not achieve what this singular event accomplished in normalizing cloud-based solutions. Moving forward, the growth of cloud adoption is likely to surpass even the most optimistic forecasts. If trends and data serve as indicators, the direction is clear, as illustrated in Figure 1-1.

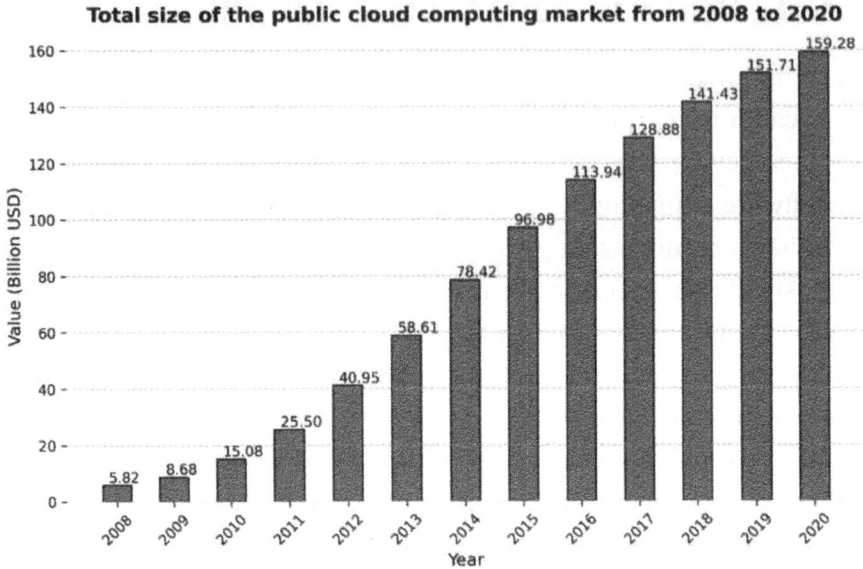

Figure 1-1. *Growth of the public cloud computing market from 2008 to 2020. [13]*

1.1.3. History of Web Frameworks in Python

Web development often requires a multidisciplinary team with expertise in frontend, backend, and server-side development. This demand has led to the rise of full-stack developers, who possess knowledge across the entire development process and are highly sought after, often enjoying competitive compensation.

Historically, web applications were developed using languages like JavaScript, PHP, or Perl, while Python was relegated to local scripting tasks. This was primarily because Python was not natively designed for web development and required a framework to interact with web servers and browsers. Over time, however, the Python community has introduced several frameworks that enable effective web development. Thanks to Python's focus on simplicity, readability, its rich library ecosystem, and open source nature, it has evolved into a popular choice for web development. Major platforms like Google and Instagram have also adopted Python, further cementing its reputation.

Web frameworks generally fall into two categories: full-stack and microframeworks (non-full-stack). Both manage essential aspects of web development, such as communication and infrastructure, but differ in scope. Full-stack frameworks provide comprehensive, built-in solutions for handling tasks like interpreting requests, managing data storage, and rendering user interfaces, making them suitable for complex applications. In contrast, microframeworks offer only basic functionalities, such as routing HTTP requests, dispatching controllers, and returning responses. Developers typically integrate them with additional APIs and tools to build applications. Examples of popular frameworks from both categories are outlined in the following sections.

1.1.4. Flask

Flask, developed in 2010 by Armin Ronacher, originally started as what was reportedly an April Fool's joke. It is a microframework, or non-full-stack framework, that provides an application server but offers minimal additional components. Flask's core is built around two key tools: *Werkzeug*, which supports HTTP routing, and Jinja, a template engine for rendering basic HTML pages. Additionally, it incorporates *MarkupSafe* for string handling and *ItsDangerous* for secure data serialization, enabling session data to be stored as cookies.

Flask is a minimalist framework equipped with only the essentials needed to create a web application. This design gives developers significant flexibility and control but also places greater responsibility on them to build and manage the application's infrastructure. As such, Flask is best suited for static websites or for experienced developers who are comfortable designing their own infrastructure and interfaces.

1.1.5. Django

Django was developed by a group of web programmers in 2003, using Python to build web applications. It allows developers to create more complex applications with less overhead compared to Flask. Specifically, Django makes it easier to render dynamic content with greater scalability and provides built-in capabilities for interacting with databases through object-relational mapping (ORM).

In addition, Django includes a wide range of modules for various functionalities, such as ecommerce, authentication, and caching. These pre-built packages enable developers to quickly add extended services to their applications. With the inclusion of numerous third-party packages, Django allows developers to focus on the core idea of their project, without needing to handle every detail of the implementation.

1.1.6. Dash

Dash is a web framework developed by Plotly for building enterprise-grade web applications in Python, R, and even Julia. While Plotly is primarily known for its data analytics and visualization tools, Dash is typically used to create interactive dashboards. However, with its extensive customization options, Dash can also be used for general-purpose applications.

Dash natively supports D3.js charts and provides default HTML and CSS templates for developers to use. For more customized interfaces, though, developers need to have proficiency in frontend programming. Additionally, Dash offers an enterprise package that allows experienced developers to deploy their applications on the cloud with production-grade features such as authentication and database integrations.

1.1.7. Web2Py

Web2Py is a full-stack web framework for Python that follows the Model-View-Controller (MVC) architectural pattern, similar to Django. It allows developers to create dynamic content with ease and offers native integration with database systems. One of the unique features of Web2Py is its built-in, web-based integrated development environment (IDE), which includes a ticketing system for error tracking and management, simplifying development and debugging.

However, a key drawback of Web2Py is that it executes objects and controllers in a single global environment, which is reinitialized with each HTTP request. While this setup can be beneficial in some cases, it can also lead to performance issues and incompatibility with certain modules, especially as the application scales.

1.1.8. The Need for a Pure Python Web Framework

Previously, Python developers had to make do with deploying their software locally as desktop applications unless they had proficient knowledge of HTML, CSS, and JavaScript. With Tkinter and PyQt, programmers could create complex, dynamic, and visually appealing interfaces, but the drawback was that they couldn't render these applications on the web. This challenge was faced by many Python enthusiasts, who until recently, had no straightforward way of migrating their work to the cloud using only Python.

It was always frustrating to go through repository after repository of amazing applications, developed by talented people, only to realize that the only way to share their work was by providing the source code and hoping others could replicate it locally. And let us not even consider non-technical users who could not execute the code at all. Many of these efforts went largely unused. In short, there was a clear need for a framework that did not require advanced knowledge of web technologies—something that would allow developers to write their typical Python scripts and deploy them directly to the cloud. Then came Streamlit, which liberated developers from the need for HTML, CSS, and JavaScript. The rest, as they say, is history.

1.1.9. Academic Significance

Being able to create web apps directly from Python easily has made Streamlit a valuable tool for academia [1]. Despite its relatively recent creation, with the first beta release in April 2019, research teams around the world have started adopting the framework to showcase the outcomes of their projects. Today, many publications already mention Streamlit as their visualization framework, covering a wide range of fields. Some of these areas include health [2, 3, 4, 5], computer science [6, 7, 8, 9], economics [10, 11], and civil engineering [12], to name a few.

1.2. Firing It Up

Being the highly versatile and accommodating framework that it is, Streamlit allows developers to utilize it with a variety of computing resources and technical stacks. Even so, there are some recommended best practices to follow for greater ease and usability.

1.2.1. Technical Recommendations

While there is no one-size-fits-all solution when it comes to running Streamlit, the following computing and system requirements, or greater, are recommended for developing and running applications smoothly. Please refer to Tables 1-1, 1-2, 1-3, and 1-4 for a list of recommended specifications.

Table 1-1. *Hardware recommendations*

CPU	RAM	Storage	Internet/Network access
4 x 64-bit 2.8 GHz	8 GB 1600 MHz DDR3	100 GB	10 Mbps

Table 1-2. *System recommendations*

Operating System	Database
Ubuntu 16.04 or higher	PostgreSQL 17 or higher
Windows 7 to 11/Windows Server 2019	
Mac OS X 10.12 or higher	pgAdmin 4 v8.14 or higher
Linux: RHEL 6/7	

Table 1-3. *Software recommendations*

Streamlit	Anaconda
1.41.1 or higher	With Python 3.9 or higher

Table 1-4. *Network recommendations*

Inbound Ports	Outbound Ports
HTTP: TCP 8080, 8443	HTTPS: TCP 443
SSH: TCP 22	SMTP: TCP 25
	LDAP(s): TCP 389/636

1.2.2. Environment Installation with Anaconda

To create a web application running on a local Streamlit server for prototyping and testing, we first need to set up a Python runtime environment with all the necessary dependencies. For this, we will use Anaconda, one of the most widely used and supported Python distributions. Begin by downloading and installing a compatible version of Anaconda. After the installation is complete, create a virtual environment to install the packages required for running your web application.

Programmatic Installation

To create an Anaconda environment through the console, please follow these steps:

1. To create and install your environment programmatically, enter the following commands in Anaconda Prompt sequentially:

    ```
    conda create -n <environment name>
    python=<version number>
    ```

    When conda asks you to proceed, select *y*.

    ```
    proceed ([y]/n)?
    ```

    Next, the new environment will be created in the environments folder within the root directory of Anaconda as *C:/ProgramData/Anaconda3/envs/*.

2. Activate your environment by typing the following:

    ```
    conda activate <environment name>
    ```

3. If you have a list of dependencies, *dependencies. yml*, place it in your newly created environment's directory:

    ```
    C:/ProgramData/Anaconda3/envs/environment name/
    ```

4. Change your root directory to your environment's directory by typing the following:

    ```
    cd C:/ProgramData/Anaconda3/envs/<environment name>/
    ```

5. Ensure that the first line in the *dependencies.yml* is written correctly as the name of your environment, *name: environment name*; otherwise, the environment may not be installed.

6. Update your environment by installing all the dependencies listed in the file *dependencies.yml* by typing the following:

    ```
    conda env update -f dependencies.yml
    ```

7. If prompted by Anaconda, proceed with updating your version of conda by typing the following:

    ```
    conda update -n base -c defaults conda
    ```

8. To check the list of environments, type the following:

    ```
    conda info -envs
    ```

9. To check the list of dependencies in your environment, type the following:

    ```
    conda list
    ```

10. To install additional dependencies that may be required later, please type the following:

    ```
    conda install <dependency name>
    ```

11. Some dependencies may not be available for download via *conda install*; in this case, download pip and then use pip install as shown in the following:

```
conda install pip
pip install <dependency name>
```

12. To deactivate your environment, you may type the following:

```
conda deactivate
```

Graphical Installation

Alternatively, you may use Anaconda Navigator to create and maintain your environments as follows:

1. Launch Anaconda Navigator.

2. Click the *Environments* tab. Please see Figure 1-2.

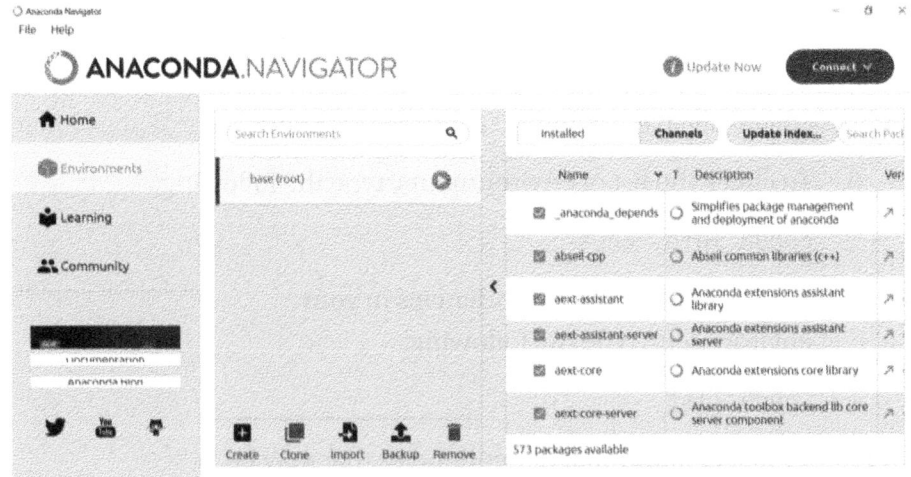

Figure 1-2. *Opening the Environments tab in Anaconda*

3. Click the *Create* button and enter the desired name and Python version for your environment. Please see Figure 1-3.

Figure 1-3. *Creating an environment in Anaconda*

4. Next, follow steps 2–12 in the previous section to install the dependencies. Next, as shown in Figure 1-4, the *test_environment* environment will appear activated with all the required packages installed.

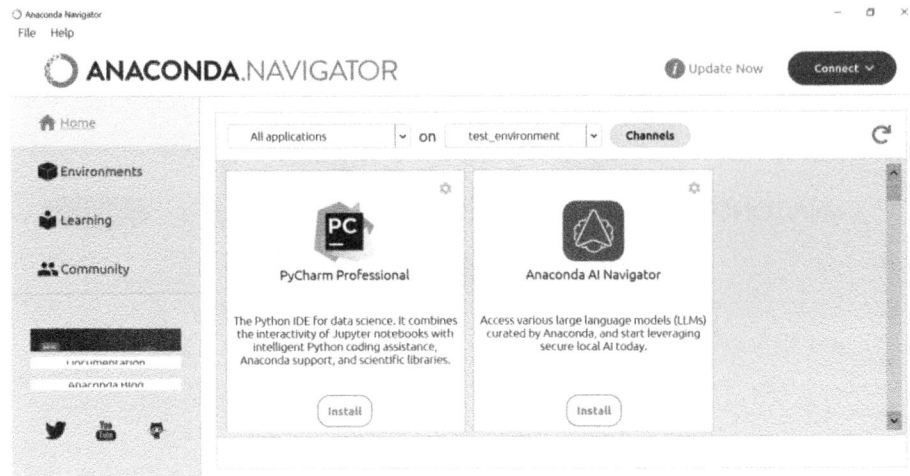

Figure 1-4. *Newly created environment in Anaconda*

5. Finally, you will be able to launch any of the available IDEs in Anaconda in your newly created environment in the *Home* tab. Please see Figure 1-5.

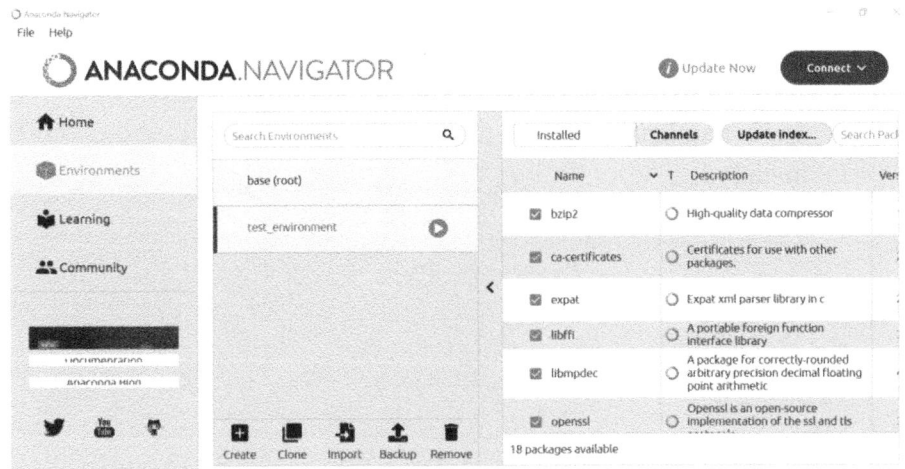

Figure 1-5. *Selection of IDE's in Anaconda*

1.2.3. Downloading and Installing Streamlit

There are multiple ways to download and install the Streamlit library, and in this section, we will cover one of the most commonly used ways of installation.

Direct pip Installation

1. To download and install Streamlit, first ensure that you are in the correct environment by entering the following command in Anaconda Prompt:

   ```
   conda activate <environment name>
   ```

2. Next, you may download and install Streamlit by entering the following command:

   ```
   pip install streamlit
   ```

Manual Wheel File Installation

1. Ensure that you are in the correct environment by entering the following command in Anaconda Prompt:

   ```
   conda activate <environment name>
   ```

2. Manually download the wheel installation file from https://pypi.org/project/streamlit/

3. Change the directory to where the wheel file is located:

   ```
   cd C:/Users/.../
   ```

4. Then install the downloaded wheel file by entering the following command:

```
pip install streamlit-1.41.1-py2.py3-none-any.whl
```

If the installation is successful, you may proceed with creating your script. For good measure, restart Anaconda before you do so.

Importing Streamlit

To import Streamlit into your Python script, ensure that the following line precedes the rest of your code:

```
import streamlit as st
```

Later, any Streamlit method can be invoked by appending *st* to it as follows:

```
st.write('Hello world')
```

1.2.4. Streamlit Console Commands

When Streamlit is installed, the Streamlit command-line (CLI) tool is also installed. The command line can help you run, operate, and diagnose issues related to your Streamlit application.

To get additional help, enter the following command:

```
streamlit --help
```

To run your application, ensure that you have changed the directory to where your script is located:

```
cd C:/Users/.../script directory/
```

Then enter the following to run your script:

```
streamlit run <script.py> [--script args]
```

Then, your application's local URL and network URL will be displayed. Simultaneously, your application will automatically appear on your default web browser. You may use the local URL to connect to your application locally and the network URL to connect on any other device over the local area network. In addition, you will be able to see the console for your Streamlit application as shown in Figure 1-6.

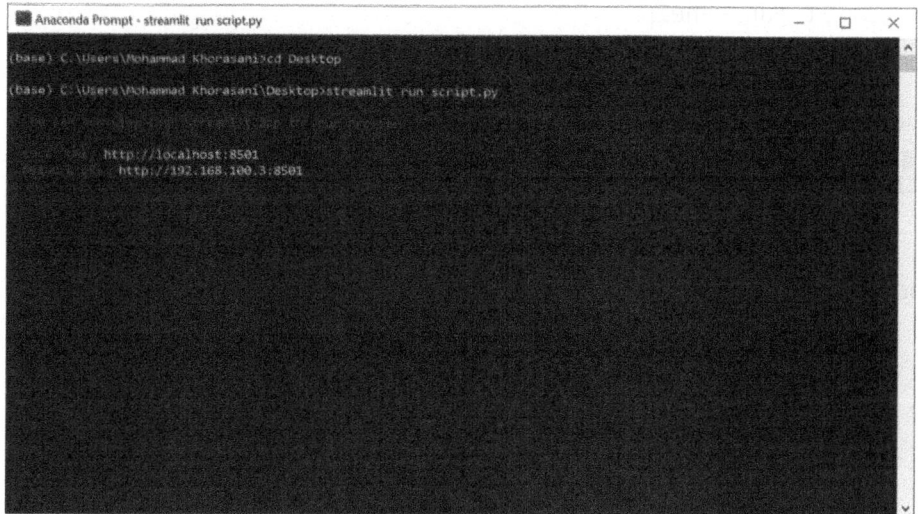

Figure 1-6. *Console while running the Streamlit application*

To clear the cache, enter the following command:

```
streamlit cache clear
```

To open Streamlit's documentation on a web browser, enter the following command:

```
streamlit docs
```

To display Streamlit's version, enter the following command:

```
streamlit --version
```

Configuring Streamlit Through the Console

You may pass config options to *streamlit run* to configure options such as the port the application is being run on, disable run-on-save, and others.

For an exhaustive list of configuration options, enter the following command:

```
streamlit run --help
```

You can view the list of configured options by entering the following command:

```
streamlit config show
```

You may configure these options using one of the four following methods:

1. Using a global config file at *.streamlit/config.toml*:

    ```
    [server]
    port = 80
    ```

2. Using a config file for each project in your project's directory:

    ```
    C:/Users/.../.streamlit/config.toml
    ```

3. Using STREAMLIT_* environment variables as shown in the following:

    ```
    export STREAMLIT_SERVER_PORT=80
    ```

4. Using flags in the command line when running your script as shown in the following:

    ```
    streamlit run <script.py> --server.port 80
    ```

1.2.5. Running Demo Apps

To run Streamlit's demo applications, enter the following command:

```
streamlit hello
```

Then, the following application will be displayed on your default web browser. You may use the menu on the sidebar to visit the four following demo applications, as shown in Figures 1-7, 1-8, 1-9, 1-10, and 1-11.

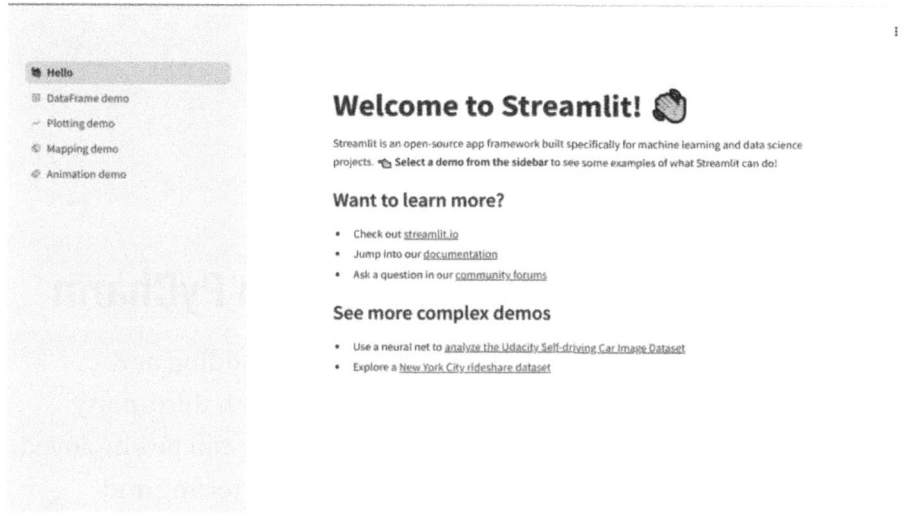

Figure 1-7. *Streamlit demo application home page*

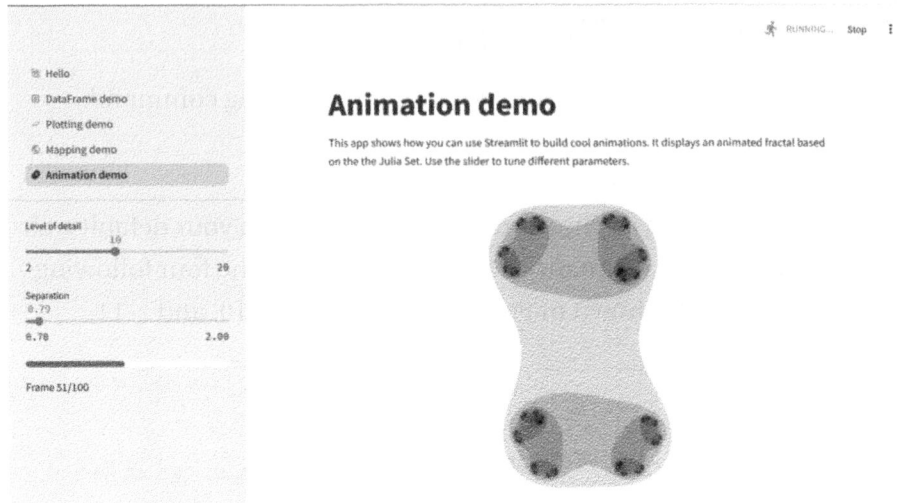

Figure 1-8. *Streamlit animation demo application*

1.2.6. Writing and Testing Code with PyCharm

Generally speaking, code expands over time, either by adding new modules to the original code base or by integrating it with third-party services. To ensure the code performs flawlessly, testing can be employed. Code testing is typically divided into two methods: unit testing and integration testing. Unit testing is used to test individual modules, while integration testing ensures the entire system works as expected. For this example, we will focus on unit testing, but the same concept can be applied to integration testing. In both cases, we need to provide inputs and compare expected outputs with actual ones. For a simple Streamlit application that allows the user to calculate the sum of two numbers, we can test two main aspects: first, if the web application renders as expected, and second, if the summation logic is correct. These represent two separate unit tests, but the first one is common when developing any frontend application. Listing 1-1 shows the sample application we will test, with the output shown in Figure 1-12 when run with Streamlit. Listing 1-2 tests both the rendering and summation logic of the example.

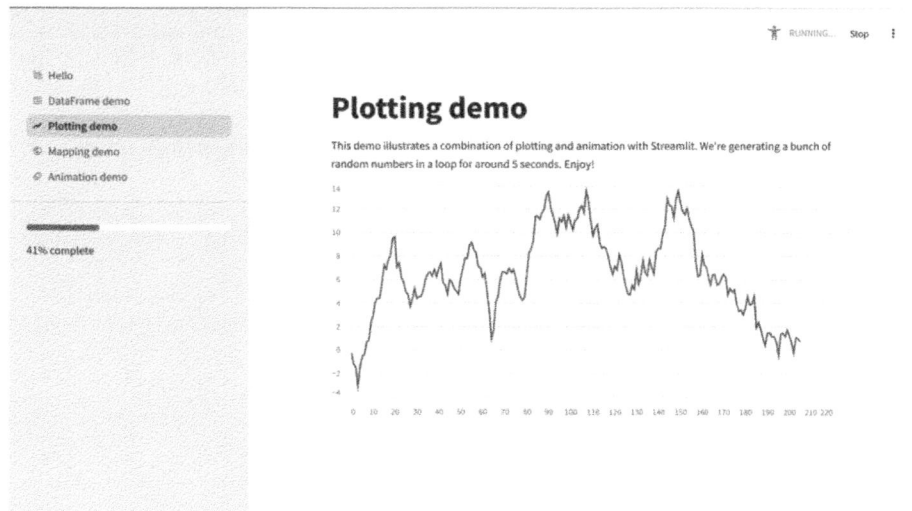

Figure 1-9. *Streamlit plotting demo application*

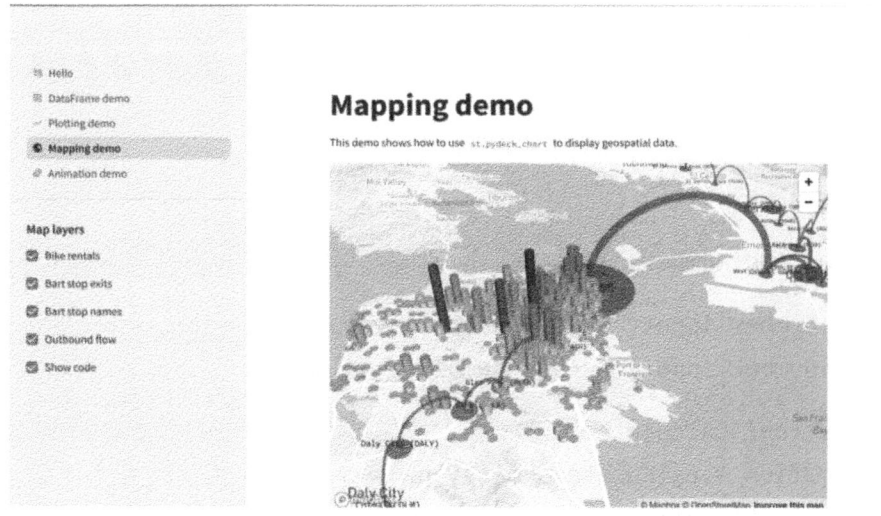

Figure 1-10. *Streamlit mapping demo application*

21

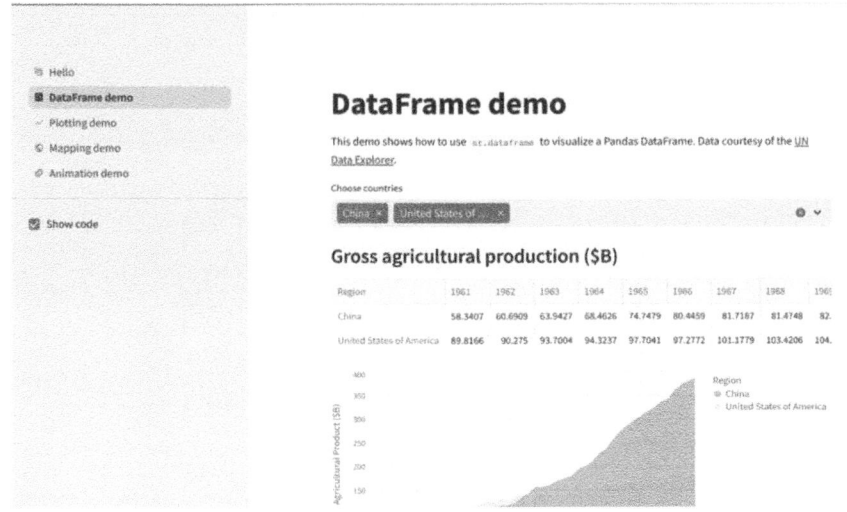

Figure 1-11. *Streamlit dataframe demo application*

Listing 1-1. main.py

```
import streamlit as st

def calculate_sum(n1, n2):
    return n1 + n2

st.title('Add Numbers')

n1 = st.number_input('First Number', value=0)
n2 = st.number_input('Second Number', value=0)

if st.button('Calculate'):
    summation = calculate_sum(n1, n2)
    st.write(f'Summation is: {summation}')
```

Listing 1-2. unit_test.py

```
from main import calculate_sum
from selenium import webdriver
from selenium.webdriver.chrome.options import Options
from selenium.webdriver.common.by import By
from selenium.webdriver.support.ui import WebDriverWait
from selenium.webdriver.support import expected_
conditions as EC
from selenium.webdriver.chrome.service import Service

def test_user_interface():
    # Path to chromedriver. Ensure this is correct for your
    environment
    driver_path = r'----------\chromedriver.exe'

    # Set up options
    options = Options()
    options.add_argument('--headless')  # To not open a real
    chrome window

    # Use Service to specify the driver path
    service = Service(driver_path)

    # Initialize the driver with options and driver path from
    WebDriverManager
    with webdriver.Chrome(service=service, options=options)
    as driver:
        url = 'http://127.0.0.1:8501'
        driver.get(url)

    # Wait for page elements to load
        try:
            WebDriverWait(driver, 10).until(
```

```
            EC.presence_of_element_located((By.TAG_
            NAME, 'h1'))
        )
        html = driver.page_source
    except Exception as e:
        print(f'Error while waiting for page: {e}')
        html = driver.page_source

    # Perform assertions to check page content
    assert 'Add numbers' in html
    assert 'First Number' in html
    assert 'Second Number' in html

def test_logic():
    assert calculate_sum(1, 1) == 2
    assert calculate_sum(1, -1) == 0
    assert calculate_sum(1, 9) == 10

if __name__ == '__main__':
    test_logic()
    test_user_interface()
```

Figure 1-12. *Output of Listing 1-1*

To test rendering, we first need the application to be running so it can be accessed by Selenium's driver, which is Chrome in this example. To automate the process of launching the application before running the tests, we may need an advanced IDE. PyCharm can handle this task for us. First, we need to set up a running configuration to launch Streamlit with a button click, as shown in Figure 1-13. Once we have this configuration for running Streamlit, we can use it as a prerun command in another configuration, which will be used to run the unit tests shown in Figure 1-14.

While browser automation tools like Selenium are powerful for end-to-end testing, it's important to note that Streamlit now offers its own built-in testing framework, AppTest. Designed specifically for Streamlit applications, AppTest allows for faster and more integrated testing without the need to manage a browser. This framework simplifies the testing process and ensures that developers can efficiently verify the functionality of their Streamlit applications. By leveraging AppTest, developers can focus on writing and deploying their applications, knowing that their tests are seamlessly integrated into the Streamlit environment.

1.3. How Streamlit Works

Unlike other web frameworks, which send static files to the browser, Streamlit modifies the real DOM and its state to render the final web document server-side. Under normal user behavior, there should be no security concerns. However, similar to PHP, Streamlit can be susceptible to Remote Code Execution (RCE) if poorly coded, where user input is not sanitized and can be exploited to execute OS-level code. A real-world example of this vulnerability was recently found in the community component, streamlit-geospatial [Ref: (`https://securitylab.github. com/advisories/GHSL-2024-100_GHSL-2024-108_streamlit- geospatial/`)].

Running a Streamlit web application starts by executing the binary—
streamlit.exe on Windows or *streamlit.sh* on macOS or Linux—using the
default Python interpreter. This initializes the application configuration,
including secrets, settings, themes, and, most importantly, the Delta
Generator (DG), which acts as the intermediary between the Python script
and the ReactJS web application served by Streamlit.

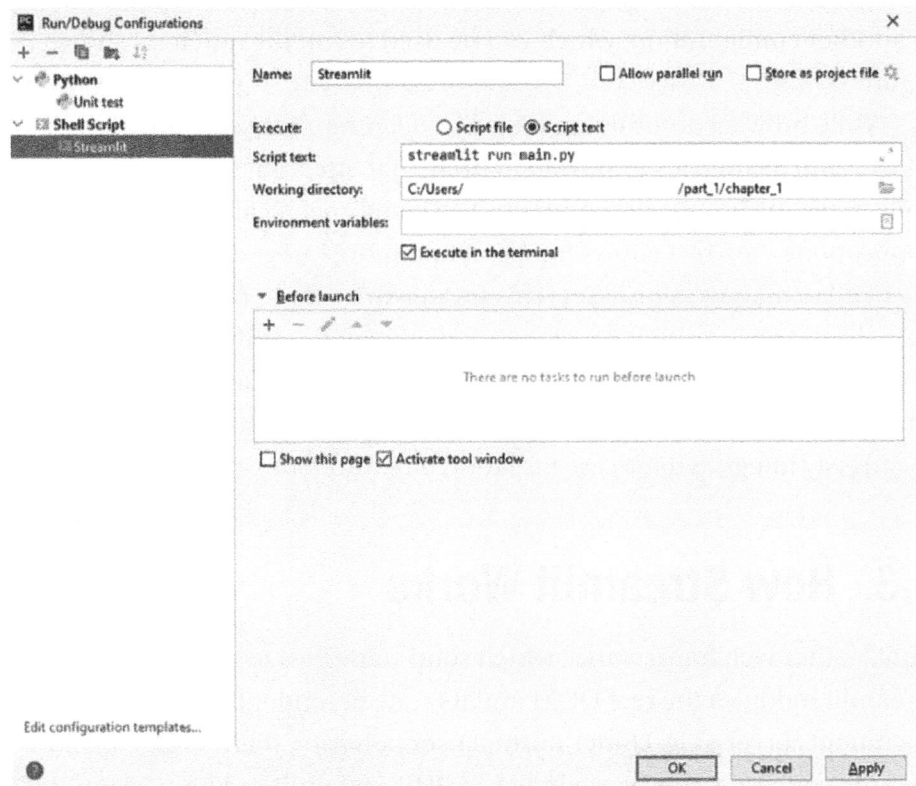

Figure 1-13. *Making a shell command to run once the current
configuration is chosen and ran*

1.3.1. The Streamlit Architecture

The DG is responsible for efficiently transferring HTML components to be rendered on the client side and retrieving their state. The initial render begins at the start of the Python document and continues to the last line. Subsequent renders do not start from the beginning of the file; they begin at the component that was interacted with by the user or had its state changed. This will be covered in more detail in later chapters. Each new render of a component is queued in the DG, where it will either replace an existing HTML snippet or be inserted between other rendered HTML components in the final DOM.

Streamlit components are queued and rendered individually to avoid negatively impacting the user's experience with a blank page if rendering takes too long. Such delays can result from extensive computations, waiting for API responses, or even sleep functions, as demonstrated in Listing 1-3, and shown in Figures 1-15 and 1-16.

Listing 1-3. text_display.py

```
import streamlit as st
import time
# User sees this first
st.title('My Title')
time.sleep(2)

# User sees this second after 2 seconds
st.write('My *markdown* text in **Streamlit**')
```

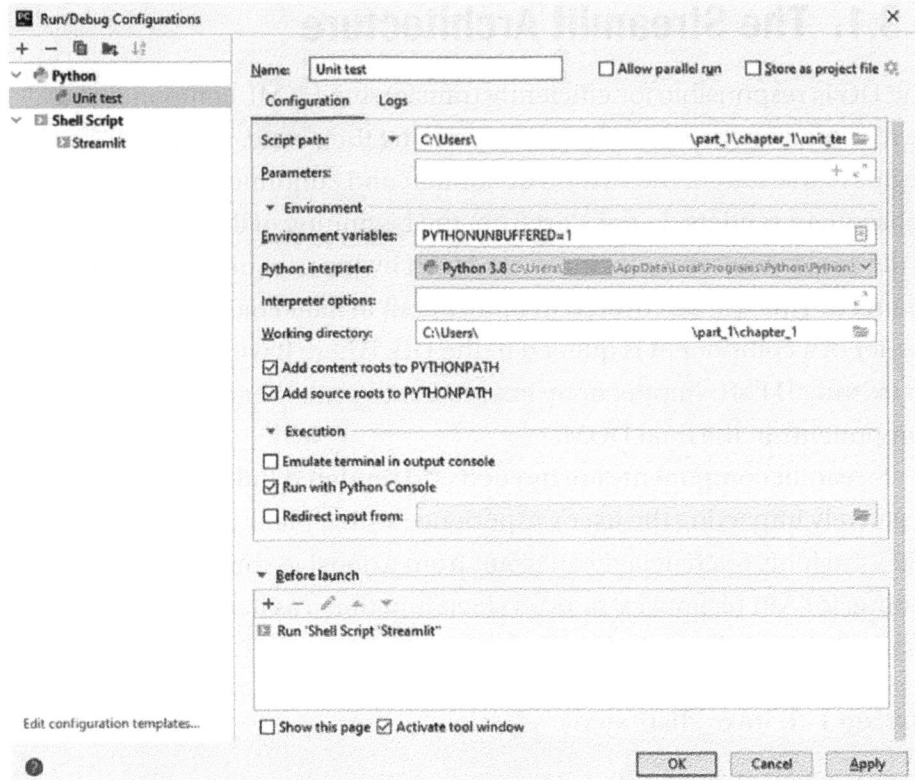

Figure 1-14. *Choosing a Python interpreter to run the unit test file but after running the configuration in Figure 1-13*

The end user will notice the page updates to include the st.write message within two seconds to what seems like a fully loaded page.

1.3.2. ReactJS in Streamlit

For simplicity, we have been referring to Streamlit as inserting HTML into the client's browser. In reality, it uses ReactJS's virtual DOM to insert elements and manage their state. This can be confirmed by using Chrome's *React Developer Tools* extension, as shown in Figure 1-17.

Given this, and understanding Streamlit's source code, we can conclude that Streamlit uses built-in ReactJS components, grouped together to create a fully functional JavaScript web application with Python! Additionally, we can leverage Streamlit's generic handling of components to build custom and complex ones that are not provided out of the box, which we will explore in later chapters.

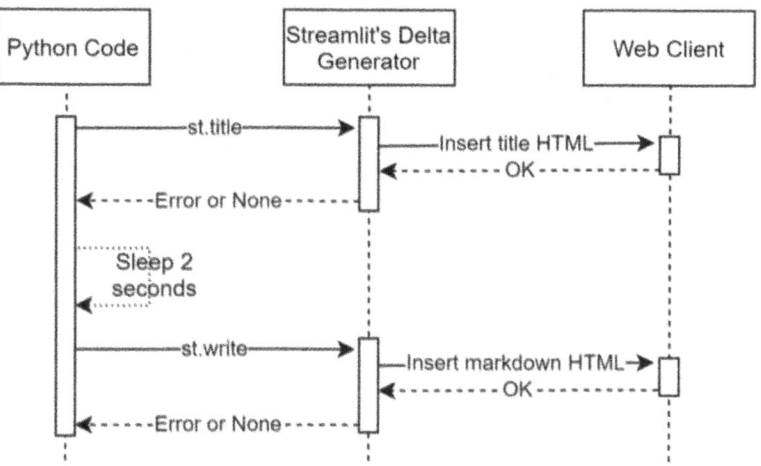

Figure 1-15. *End-to-end execution sequence for Listing 1-3*

My Title

My *markdown* text in **Streamlit**

Figure 1-16. *Streamlit output for Listing 1-3*

My Title

My *markdown* text in **Streamlit**

Figure 1-17. *Streamlit output for Listing 1-3*

1.4. Summary

This chapter highlighted the trend toward cloud computing and the benefits it offers to developers, users, and cloud service providers. We also discussed the four most commonly used Python web frameworks, including one microframework—Flask—and three full-stack frameworks: Django, Dash, and Web2Py. Streamlit was introduced as a pure Python framework, showcasing its competitive advantage in bridging the skills gap and reducing development time from weeks to hours. The reader was then guided through the installation and use of Streamlit to create basic applications on demand. In the next chapter, we will explore the core components of Streamlit, provide a comprehensive overview of its application programming interface, and demonstrate how it can be used to develop customized applications.

CHAPTER 2

Streamlit Basics

Streamlit simplifies the process of creating interfaces, displaying text, visualizing data, rendering widgets, and managing web applications from inception to deployment, thanks to its convenient and highly intuitive API, as highlighted in the Appendix. This chapter covers techniques for creating input forms, implementing conditional flows, handling errors, mutating dataframes, and rendering basic charts. After mastering the basics, developers will be equipped to produce, manage, and deploy a range of simple web applications locally. These applications may include data explorers, machine learning tools, multimedia handlers, data wrangling utilities, and other general-purpose solutions. Once comfortable with these fundamentals, developers can move on to creating more advanced and complex applications, which will be explored in subsequent chapters.

2.1. Creating a Basic Application

By leveraging Streamlit's powerful API, we can create a wide range of applications—from simple microservices to complex systems integrated with distributed architectures. Streamlit allows us to adapt to the diverse needs of our users with ease. In this section, however, we will focus on exploring simpler applications before advancing to more complex ones in the sections that follow.

© Mohammad Khorasani, Mohamed Abdou, Javier Hernández Fernández 2025
M. Khorasani et al., *Streamlit for Web Development*,
https://doi.org/10.1007/979-8-8688-1826-4_2

2.1.1. Generating User Input Forms

Creating forms in Streamlit is as simple as grouping multiple input widgets, such as text and number fields, on a page along with a button to trigger actions like saving entries to a database or storing them in the session state. However, a key consideration with this approach is that Streamlit automatically reruns the entire script from top to bottom whenever the user interacts with any widget. While this ensures a logical and seamless flow for the program, there are situations where it is more practical to group input widgets and rerun the script only when explicitly prompted by the user. This can be achieved using the st.form command.

Listing 2-1. input_form.py

```
import streamlit as st
from datetime import date  # Import to use the current date

# Create a feedback form
with st.form('feedback_form'):
    st.header('Feedback Form')

    # Organize form inputs into columns
    col1, col2 = st.columns(2)
    with col1:
        name = st.text_input('Please enter your name',
        placeholder='Your full name')
        rating = st.slider('Rate this app (0 = Worst, 10 =
        Best)', 0, 10, 5)
    with col2:
        dob = st.date_input('Enter your date of birth')
        recommend = st.radio('Would you recommend this app to
        others?', ('Yes', 'No'))

    # Submit button
    submit_button = st.form_submit_button('Submit')
```

```
# Handle form submission
if submit_button:
    # Check for empty name
    if not name.strip():
        st.error('Name cannot be empty. Please provide
        your name.')
    # Check for valid date of birth
    elif dob > date.today():
        st.error('Date of birth cannot be in the future.')
    else:
        st.success('Thank you for your feedback!')
        st.write('**Name:**', name)
        st.write('**Date of Birth:**', dob)
        st.write('**Rating:**', rating)
        st.write('**Would Recommend?:**', recommend)
```

A Streamlit form can be created using a with statement in combination with the st.form command. In Listing 2-1, we first organize the widgets within the form into two equal-width columns using the st.columns command. In the first column, we include a text input and a slider widget, implemented with the st.text_input and st.slider commands, respectively. In the second column, we add a date input and a radio button widget using the st.date_input and st.radio commands.

Within the same with statement, we include a form submit button using the st.form_submit_button command. This button allows all the form's widget entries to be submitted collectively with a single click, regardless of how many items are included. It is important to note that st.form_submit_button differs from st.button, and without it, Streamlit will raise an error for forms created using st.form.

As demonstrated in Figure 2-1, all widgets are grouped into a single form using the st.form command. Once the form submit button is clicked, the widget entries are processed together, and the output is displayed as shown in Figure 2-2.

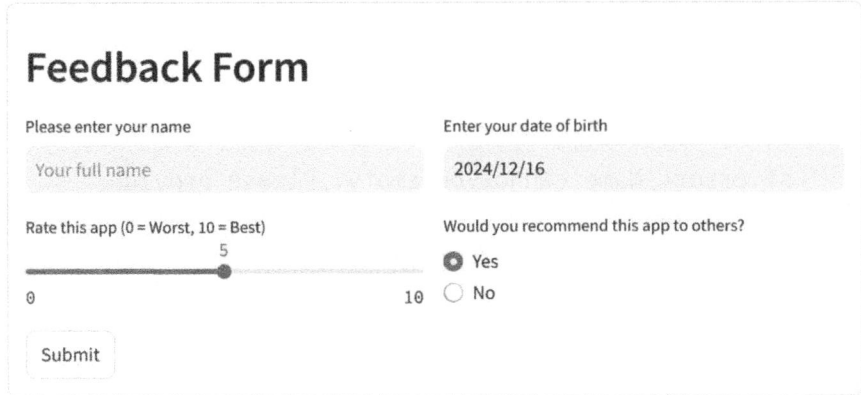

Figure 2-1. *Streamlit input form (output of Listing 2-1)*

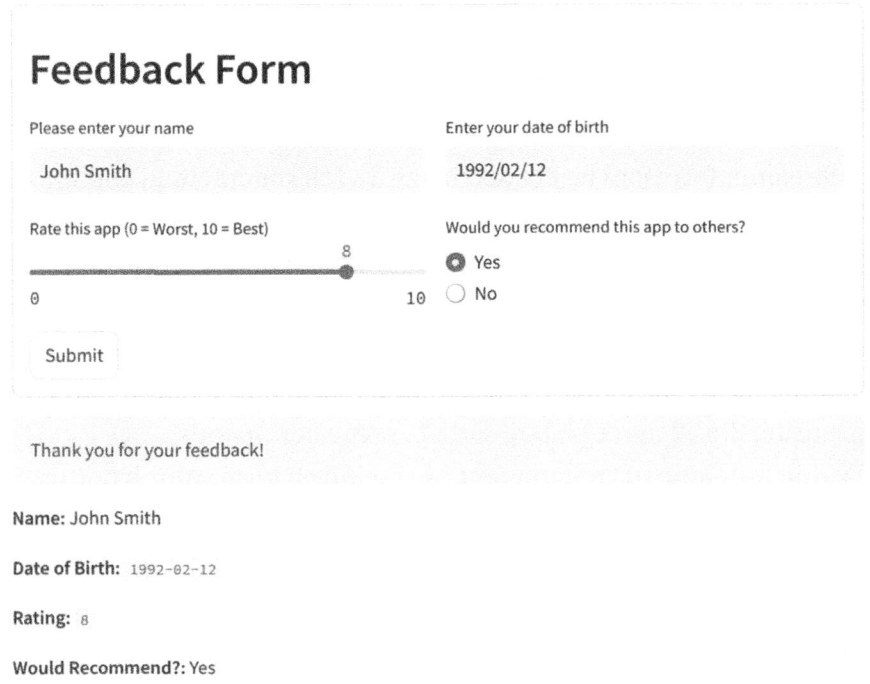

Figure 2-2. *Instantiated Streamlit input form (output of Listing 2-1)*

2.1.2. Introducing Conditional Flow

Introducing conditional flow in your Streamlit applications may be necessary, where certain actions depend on prior actions or the state of widgets. This is particularly useful for guiding users to correctly fill out forms and use the application as intended. Without conditional flow, your application may encounter errors if users interact with it incorrectly.

Example 1

Listing 2-2. conditional_flow_1.py

```python
import streamlit as st

# Function to display the name
def display_name(name):
    st.info(f'**Name:** {name}')

# Input for name
name = st.text_input('Please enter your name')

# Validation: If name is entered, show info; else, show an
error message
if name:
    display_name(name)
else:
    st.error('No name entered')
```

In Listing 2-2, we use an if statement to check whether the name field has been filled out. If the field is empty, the user will be shown an error message (Figure 2-3). If the field is not empty, a function is called to display the user's entry (Figure 2-4).

Example 2

Listing 2-3. conditional_flow_2.py

```python
import streamlit as st

# Function to display the name
def display_name(name):
    st.info(f'**Name:** {name}')

# Input for name
name = st.text_input('Please enter your name')

# Check if name is entered
if not name:
    st.error('No name entered')
else:
    display_name(name)
```

In Listing 2-3, we again use an `if` statement to check whether the name field is not empty. The difference here is that we use the `st.stop` command to halt the execution of the script if the field is empty. If the field is not empty, the script continues, displaying the entered name. The advantage of this approach is that it removes the need for an additional `if` statement, simplifying the script. In terms of functionality, both methods are essentially the same.

Figure 2-3. *Implementing conditional flow (output of Listing 2-2)*

Conditional flow programming can be applied to both simple and complex applications. This technique can be scaled up and implemented with nested if statements, while loops, and other methods when needed.

Please enter your name

John Smith

Name: John Smith

Figure 2-4. *Implementing conditional flow continued (output of Listing 2-2)*

2.1.3. Managing and Debugging Errors

If you are running Streamlit in development mode and have configured showErrorDetails = True as shown in Table 3-1 in Section 3.1, Streamlit will display runtime exceptions on the web page, similar to how an IDE would show such messages in the console. This is not ideal, as users may find it difficult to understand the error and could become confused. More importantly, leaving exceptions unhandled can trigger a series of fatal errors in later parts of your code, potentially affecting other systems. Additionally, Streamlit will reveal the specific segment of your code that caused the exception, which could pose a risk to intellectual property if your source code is subject to such protections.

Listing 2-4. without_try_and_except.py

```
import streamlit as st

# Create columns for inputs
col1, col2 = st.columns(2)

with col1:
```

```
    number_1 = st.number_input('Please enter the first
    number',value=0,step=1)

with col2:
    number_2 = st.number_input('Please enter the second
    number',value=0,step=1)

st.info(f'**{number_1}/{number_2}=** {number_1/number_2}')
```

Running Listing 2-4, we can create a simple application where one number is divided by another. If the user divides by any number other than zero, the application will function correctly and display an output similar to Figure 2-5. However, if the user tries to divide by zero, Python will raise a zero division error, which will be displayed by Streamlit as shown in Figure 2-6.

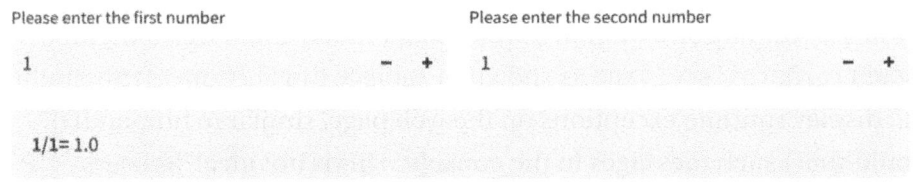

Figure 2-5. *Running Streamlit without a try and except block without an error (output of Listing 2-4)*

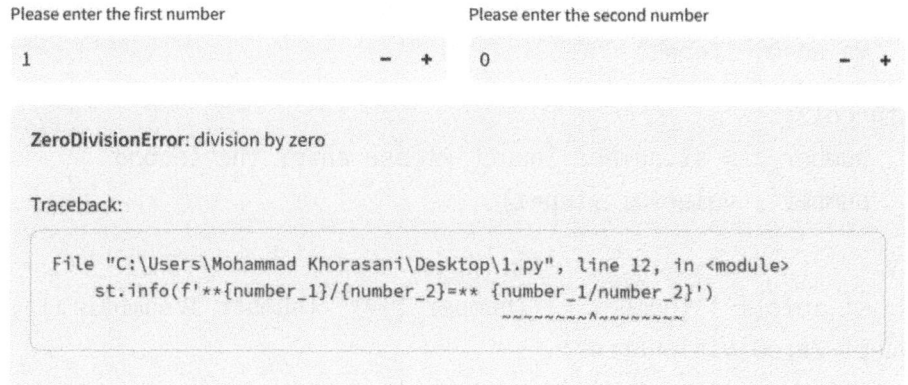

Figure 2-6. *Running Streamlit without a try and except block with an error (output of Listing 2-4)*

Example 1

You can limit the range of input values for the st.number_input widget, but let us assume for a moment that you could not. In such a case, the solution would be to use try and except blocks in your code, as shown in Listing 2-5, wherever there is a potential for an unforeseen issue. In this example, we attempt to execute the potentially problematic part of the script with the try statement. If it fails due to a ZeroDivisionError, it is handled with an except ZeroDivisionError statement, which displays a customized error message to the user, as shown in Figure 2-7. If the error is caused by any other issue, a general except statement can be used to bypass this part of the code without executing it.

Listing 2-5. try_and_except_1.py

```
import streamlit as st

# Create columns for inputs
col1, col2 = st.columns(2)

with col1:
```

```
number_1 = st.number_input('Please enter the first number',
value=0, step=1)
```

```
with col2:
    number_2 = st.number_input('Please enter the second
    number', value=0, step=1)
```

```
try:
    st.info(f'**{number_1}/{number_2}=** {number_1/number_2}')
except ZeroDivisionError:
    st.error('Cannot divide by zero')
```

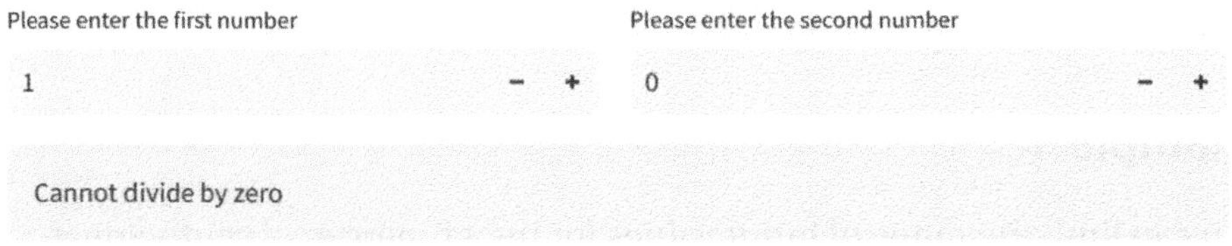

Figure 2-7. *Running Streamlit with a try and except block with an error (output of Listing 2-5)*

Example 2

Another way to manage exceptions is by using a general except statement, which displays a curated message of the actual error, as shown in Figure 2-8. This approach can be especially helpful for debugging the script during development while still maintaining a positive user experience by not revealing too much technical detail to the user.

Listing 2-6. try_and_except_2.py

```
import streamlit as st

# Create columns for inputs
col1, col2 = st.columns(2)
```

```
with col1:
    number_1 = st.number_input('Please enter the first number',
    value=0, step=1)

with col2:
    number_2 = st.number_input('Please enter the second
    number', value=0, step=1)

try:
    st.info(f'**{number_1}/{number_2}=** {number_1/number_2}')
except Exception as e:
    st.error(f'Error: {e}')
```

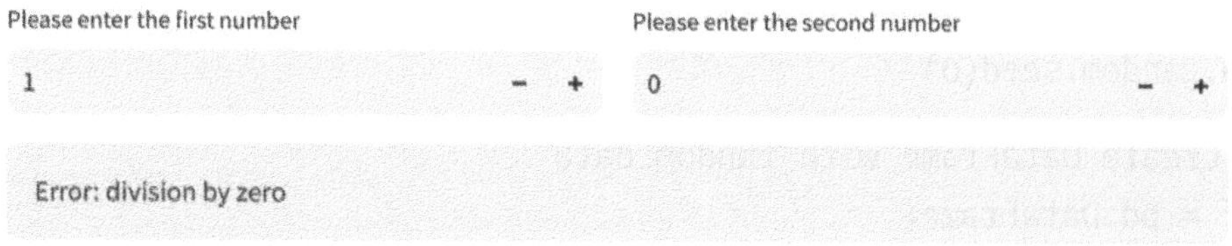

Please enter the first number   Please enter the second number

1   —   +   0   —   +

Error: division by zero

Figure 2-8. *Running Streamlit with a try and except block with an error (output of Listing 2-6)*

2.2. Mutating Dataframes

Given Streamlit's focus on developing machine learning and data science applications, developers often need to mutate dataframes based on user input or requirements. In this section, we will introduce a non-exhaustive list of some of the most commonly used methods for mutating Pandas dataframes.

2.2.1. Filter

Dataframes can be filtered using the method shown in Listing 2-7. By specifying a condition for a column, whether numerical or string, such as df[df['Column 1'] > -1], we can filter the rows based on that condition, as shown in Figure 2-9.

Listing 2-7. mutate_dataframe_filter.py

```python
import streamlit as st
import pandas as pd
import numpy as np

# Set seed for reproducibility
np.random.seed(0)

# Create DataFrame with random data
df = pd.DataFrame(
    np.random.randn(4, 3),
    columns=('Column 1', 'Column 2', 'Column 3')
)

# Display the original DataFrame
st.subheader('Original DataFrame')
st.dataframe(df)

# Filter the DataFrame (mutating it)
df = df[df['Column 1'] > -1]

# Display the mutated DataFrame
st.subheader('Mutated DataFrame')
st.dataframe(df)
```

Original DataFrame

	Column 1	Column 2	Column 3
0	1.7641	0.4002	0.9787
1	2.2409	1.8676	-0.9773
2	0.9501	-0.1514	-0.1032
3	0.4106	0.144	1.4543

Mutated DataFrame

	Column 1	Column 2	Column 3
0	1.7641	0.4002	0.9787
1	2.2409	1.8676	-0.9773
2	0.9501	-0.1514	-0.1032
3	0.4106	0.144	1.4543

Figure 2-9. *Filtering Pandas dataframes (output of Listing 2-7)*

2.2.2. Select

Dataframe columns can be selected using the method shown in Listing 2-8. We can specify which columns to keep by their names, for example, df[['Column 1', 'Column 2']], and remove other columns, as shown in

Figure 2-10. Alternatively, the same result can be achieved using the drop command, like df.drop(columns=['Column 3']).

Listing 2-8. mutate_dataframe_select.py

```python
import streamlit as st
import pandas as pd
import numpy as np

# Set the seed for reproducibility
np.random.seed(0)

# Create a DataFrame with random numbers
df = pd.DataFrame(
    np.random.randn(4, 3),
    columns=('Column 1', 'Column 2', 'Column 3')
)

# Display the original DataFrame
st.subheader('Original DataFrame')
st.dataframe(df)  # Use st.dataframe for interactivity

# Mutate the DataFrame by selecting specific columns
df = df[['Column 1', 'Column 2']]

# Display the mutated DataFrame
st.subheader('Mutated DataFrame')
st.dataframe(df)  # Use st.dataframe for interactivity
```

Original DataFrame

	Column 1	Column 2	Column 3
0	1.7641	0.4002	0.9787
1	2.2409	1.8676	-0.9773
2	0.9501	-0.1514	-0.1032
3	0.4106	0.144	1.4543

Mutated DataFrame

	Column 1	Column 2
0	1.7641	0.4002
1	2.2409	1.8676
2	0.9501	-0.1514
3	0.4106	0.144

Figure 2-10. *Selecting Pandas dataframe columns (output of Listing 2-8)*

2.2.3. Arrange

Dataframe columns can be arranged and sorted in ascending and/or descending order based on the numerical or nominal value of a specified column, as shown in Listing 2-9. We can specify which column to sort and in which order, for example, df.sort_values(by='Column 1', ascending=True), as shown in Figure 2-11. Once the column is sorted, the index will be adjusted to reflect the new order. If needed, you can reset the index using the df.reset_index(drop=True) command to restart the index from zero.

Listing 2-9. mutate_dataframe_arrange.py

```python
import streamlit as st
import pandas as pd
import numpy as np

# Set the seed for reproducibility
np.random.seed(0)

# Create DataFrame with random numbers
df = pd.DataFrame(
    np.random.randn(4, 3),
    columns=('Column 1', 'Column 2', 'Column 3')
)

# Display the original DataFrame
st.subheader('Original DataFrame')
st.dataframe(df)  # Use st.dataframe for interactive display

# Mutate the DataFrame by sorting by 'Column 1'
df = df.sort_values(by='Column 1', ascending=True)

# Display the mutated DataFrame
st.subheader('Mutated DataFrame')
st.dataframe(df)  # Use st.dataframe for interactive display
```

Original DataFrame

	Column 1	Column 2	Column 3
0	1.7641	0.4002	0.9787
1	2.2409	1.8676	-0.9773
2	0.9501	-0.1514	-0.1032
3	0.4106	0.144	1.4543

Mutated DataFrame

	Column 1	Column 2	Column 3
3	0.4106	0.144	1.4543
2	0.9501	-0.1514	-0.1032
0	1.7641	0.4002	0.9787
1	2.2409	1.8676	-0.9773

Figure 2-11. *Sorting Pandas dataframe columns (output of Listing 2-9)*

2.2.4. Mutate

Dataframe columns can be mutated by assigning new columns based on the values of another column, as shown in Listing 2-10. We can specify a simple lambda function to apply to the values of an existing column, for example, `Column_4 = lambda x: df['Column 1']*2`, to compute the output shown in Figure 2-12.

Listing 2-10. mutate_dataframe_lambda.py

```python
import streamlit as st
import pandas as pd
import numpy as np

# Set the seed for reproducibility
np.random.seed(0)

# Create DataFrame with random numbers
df = pd.DataFrame(
    np.random.randn(4, 3),
    columns=('Column 1', 'Column 2', 'Column 3')
)

# Display the original DataFrame
st.subheader('Original DataFrame')
st.dataframe(df)

# Create a new column 'Column 4' based on 'Column 1'
df = df.assign(Column_4 = lambda x: x['Column 1'] * 2)

# Display the mutated DataFrame
st.subheader('Mutated DataFrame')
st.dataframe(df)
```

Original DataFrame

	Column 1	Column 2	Column 3
0	1.7641	0.4002	0.9787
1	2.2409	1.8676	-0.9773
2	0.9501	-0.1514	-0.1032
3	0.4106	0.144	1.4543

Mutated DataFrame

	Column 1	Column 2	Column 3	Column_4
0	1.7641	0.4002	0.9787	3.5281
1	2.2409	1.8676	-0.9773	4.4818
2	0.9501	-0.1514	-0.1032	1.9002
3	0.4106	0.144	1.4543	0.8212

Figure 2-12. *Mutating Pandas dataframes (output of Listing 2-10)*

2.2.5. Group By

Sometimes, it may be necessary to group or aggregate the values in one or more columns of a dataframe. This can be done in Pandas using the method shown in Listing 2-11. We can specify which column or columns to group by using the df.groupby(['Column 1', 'Column 2']) command.

This will reindex the dataframe and group the relevant rows together, as shown in Figure 2-13.

Listing 2-11. mutate_dataframe_groupby.py

```python
import streamlit as st
import pandas as pd
import numpy as np

# Create a DataFrame with random integers between 0 and 100
df = pd.DataFrame(
    np.random.randint(0, 101, size=(6, 3)),
    columns=('Exam 1', 'Exam 2', 'Exam 3')
)

# Assign 'Name' and 'Category' columns directly
df['Name'] = ['John', 'Jessica', 'Jessica', 'John', 'John',
'Jessica']
df['Category'] = ['B', 'A', 'A', 'B', 'A', 'B']

# Display the original DataFrame
st.subheader('Original DataFrame')
st.dataframe(df)

# Group by 'Name' and 'Category' and get the first row of
each group
df_grouped = df.groupby(['Name', 'Category']).first()

# Display the mutated DataFrame after grouping
st.subheader('Mutated DataFrame')
st.dataframe(df_grouped)
```

2.2.6. Merge

Multiple dataframes can be merged together in Pandas using a common column as a reference, as shown in Listing 2-12. We can specify which column to merge on and whether the merge should be a union or intersection of both dataframes using the df1.merge(df2, how='inner', on='Name') command. This will create a combined dataframe, as shown in Figure 2-14.

Listing 2-12. mutate_dataframe_merge.py

```
import streamlit as st
import pandas as pd

# Create the first DataFrame (df1)
df1 = pd.DataFrame(data={'Name': ['Jessica', 'John'],
                         'Exam 1': [77, 56]})

# Create the second DataFrame (df2)
df2 = pd.DataFrame(data={'Name': ['Jessica', 'John'],
                         'Exam 2': [76, 97]})

# Create the third DataFrame (df3)
df3 = pd.DataFrame(data={'Name': ['Jessica', 'John'],
                         'Exam 3': [87, 95]})

# Display the original dataframes
st.subheader('Original DataFrames')
st.dataframe(df1)
st.dataframe(df2)
st.dataframe(df3)

# Merge the dataframes on 'Name' column using inner join
df_merged = df2.merge(df3, how='inner', on='Name')
df_merged = df1.merge(df_merged, how='inner', on='Name')
```

```
# Display the mutated dataframe after merging
st.subheader('Mutated DataFrame')
st.dataframe(df_merged)
```

Original DataFrame

	Exam 1	Exam 2	Exam 3	Name	Category
0	46	81	51	John	B
1	87	15	17	Jessica	A
2	97	27	5	Jessica	A
3	98	18	49	John	B
4	72	87	9	John	A
5	6	84	65	Jessica	B

Mutated DataFrame

Name	Category	Exam 1	Exam 2	Exam 3
Jessica	A	87	15	17
Jessica	B	6	84	65
John	A	72	87	9
John	B	46	81	51

Figure 2-13. *Grouping Pandas dataframes (output of Listing 2-11)*

2.2.7. Data Editor

Streamlit's `st.data_editor` widget offers a powerful and interactive way to edit data within a dataframe directly in the app. This feature is particularly useful for developers working on machine learning and data science applications, where the ability to make real-time adjustments to data on the fly can save some valuable time. Users can update, add, or delete data entries without needing to leave the application or manually edit the source code. The changes made through the `st.data_editor` widget are immediately reflected in the dataframe, making it easier to experiment with different data configurations and see the results in real-time.

In addition to its interactive capabilities, the `st.data_editor` widget also supports various customization options to tailor the editing experience to specific needs. Developers can configure the widget to allow or restrict certain types of edits, ensuring that the data integrity is maintained.

2.3. Rendering Static and Interactive Charts

Data visualization is where Streamlit truly excels. The ease with which a variety of static and interactive charts can be created and displayed is impressive. Streamlit natively supports a wide range of charts, including but not limited to bar, line, and area charts, as well as graphs, maps, and other types of interactive and non-interactive visuals. Additionally, there are numerous third-party plotting libraries that can be integrated with Streamlit. In this section, we will create several examples of static and interactive charts using data from a Pandas dataframe.

2.3.1. Static Bar Chart

A static bar chart can be generated by inputting a Pandas dataframe into a Matplotlib figure using the method shown in Listing 2-13. We can specify the chart type by setting kind='bar'. Other Matplotlib parameters can be found at https://matplotlib.org/stable/api/_as_gen/matplotlib. pyplot.plot.html. The generated chart is shown in Figure 2-15.

Listing 2-13. static_bar_chart.py

```python
import streamlit as st
import pandas as pd
import matplotlib.pyplot as plt

# Create a DataFrame
df = pd.DataFrame(data={'Name': ['Jessica', 'John'],
                        'Exam 1': [77, 56],
                        'Exam 2': [76, 97],
                        'Exam 3': [87, 95]})

# Set the 'Name' column as the index and plot the bar chart
df.set_index('Name').plot(kind='bar', stacked=False,
xlabel='Name', ylabel='Exam')

# Display the plot using Streamlit
st.pyplot(plt)
```

Original DataFrames

	Name	Exam 1
0	Jessica	77
1	John	56

	Name	Exam 2
0	Jessica	76
1	John	97

	Name	Exam 3
0	Jessica	87
1	John	95

Mutated DataFrame

	Name	Exam 1	Exam 2	Exam 3
0	Jessica	77	76	87
1	John	56	97	95

Figure 2-14. *Merging Pandas dataframes (output of Listing 2-12)*

2.3.2. Static Line Chart

Similarly, a static line chart can be generated by inputting a Pandas dataframe into a Matplotlib figure by using the method shown in Listing 2-14. We can specify the chart type and the option of having subplots by setting kind='line', subplots=True.

Other Matplotlib parameters can be found at https://matplotlib. org/stable/api/_as_gen/matplotlib.pyplot.plot.html. The generated chart is shown in Figure 2-16.

Listing 2-14. static_line_chart.py

```python
import streamlit as st
import pandas as pd
import matplotlib.pyplot as plt

# Create a DataFrame
df = pd.DataFrame(data={'Exam': ['Exam 1', 'Exam 2', 'Exam 3'],
                        'Jessica': [77, 76, 87],
                        'John': [56, 97, 95]})

# Set 'Exam' as the index and plot the line chart
df.set_index('Exam').plot(kind='line', xlabel='Exam',
ylabel='Score', subplots=True)

# Display the plot using Streamlit
st.pyplot(plt)
```

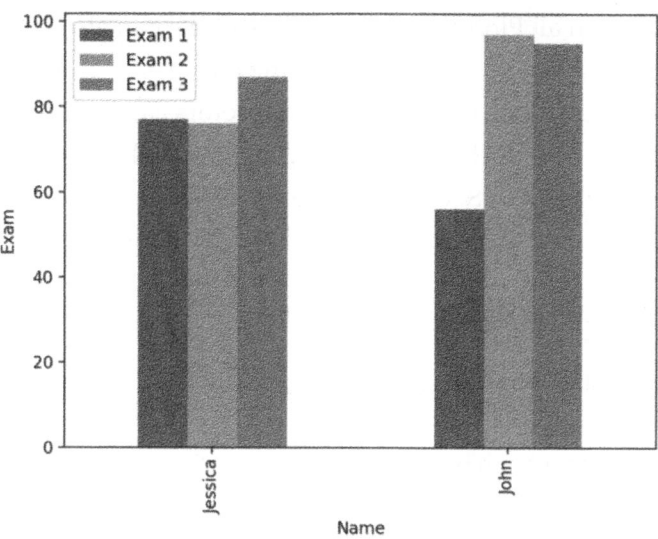

Figure 2-15. *Generating a static bar chart (output of Listing 2-13)*

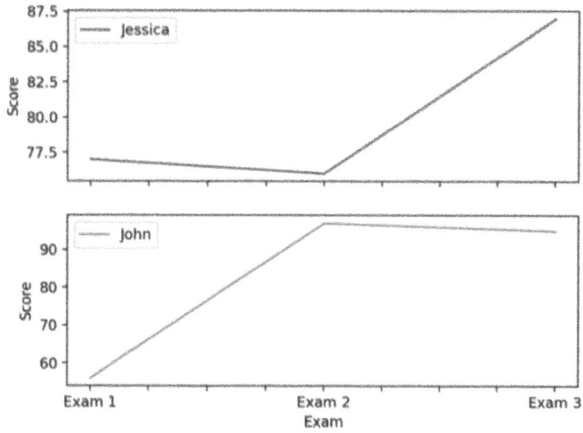

Figure 2-16. *Generating a static line chart (output of Listing 2-14)*

2.3.3. Interactive Line Chart

An interactive line chart can be generated by inputting a Pandas dataframe into a Plotly figure by using the method shown in Listing 2-15. We can declare the chart type and its associated properties by using the JSON

57

notation used with all Plotly charts and figures. We can also interactively return selected points on the chart using the on_select argument for st.plotly_chart widget. Other Plotly parameters can be found at https://plotly.com/python/line-charts/; we will cover Plotly line charts in greater depth in Section 4.2. The generated chart is shown in Figure 2-17.

Listing 2-15. interactive_line_chart.py

```python
import streamlit as st
import pandas as pd
import plotly.graph_objects as go

# Create a DataFrame
df = pd.DataFrame(data={
    'Exam': ['Exam 1', 'Exam 2', 'Exam 3'],
    'Jessica': [77, 76, 87],
    'John': [56, 97, 95]
})

# Create the plotly figure with line plots
fig = go.Figure(data=[
    go.Scatter(name='Jessica', x=df['Exam'], y=df['Jessica'],
    mode='lines+markers'),
    go.Scatter(name='John', x=df['Exam'], y=df['John'],
    mode='lines+markers')
])

# Update the layout
fig.update_layout(
    xaxis_title='Exam',
    yaxis_title='Score',
    legend_title='Name',
)
```

```
# Display the plot using Streamlit with selection enabled
event = st.plotly_chart(fig, on_select='rerun')

# Access selected points
if event and event.selection:
    selected_data = []
    for point in event.selection.points:
        selected_data.append({
            'Exam': point['x'],
            'Student': point['curve_number'],
            'Score': point['y']
        })

    # Map curveNumber to student names
    for item in selected_data:
        item['Student'] = fig.data[item['Student']].name

    st.write('Selected Exam Scores:')
    st.dataframe(selected_data)
```

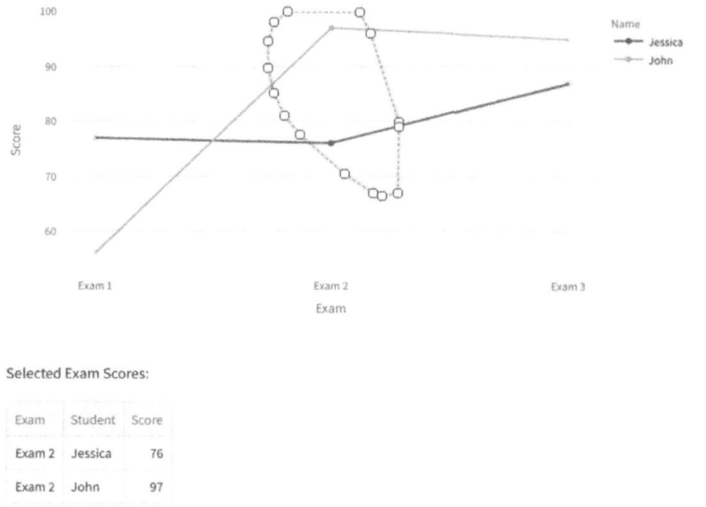

Figure 2-17. *Generating an interactive line chart (output of Listing 2-15)*

2.3.4. Interactive Map

Likewise, an interactive geospatial map can be generated by inputting a Pandas dataframe containing the longitude and latitude of a set of points into a Plotly figure using the method shown in Listing 2-16. Additionally, we can specify the exact geospatial location to zoom into by setting geo_scope='usa'. Other Plotly parameters can be found at https://plotly.com/python/scatter-plots-on-maps/; we will cover Plotly geospatial charts in greater depth in Section 4.2. The generated map is shown in Figure 2-18.

Listing 2-16. interactive_map.py

```python
import streamlit as st
import pandas as pd
import plotly.graph_objects as go

# Data with university locations
df = pd.DataFrame(data={'university': ['Harvard University',
'Yale University', 'Princeton University',
                       'Columbia University', 'Brown
                       University', 'Dartmouth University',
                        'University of Pennsylvania', 'Cornell
                        University'],
             'latitude': [42.3770, 41.3163, 40.3573,
             40.8075, 41.8268, 43.7044, 39.9522, 42.4534],
             'longitude': [-71.1167, -72.9223, -74.6672,
             -73.9626, -71.4025, -72.2887, -75.1932,
             -76.4735]
             })

# Create the scattergeo plot
fig = go.Figure(data=go.Scattergeo(
    lon=df['longitude'],
```

```
    lat=df['latitude'],
    text=df['university'],
    mode='markers',
    marker=dict(size=10, color='red', opacity=0.7)
))

# Update the layout to focus on the USA and set additional map
properties
fig.update_layout(
    geo_scope='usa',
    geo=dict(
        projection_type='albers usa',
        showland=True,
        landcolor='lightgray',
        subunitwidth=1,
    ))

# Display the map using Streamlit
st.plotly_chart(fig)
```

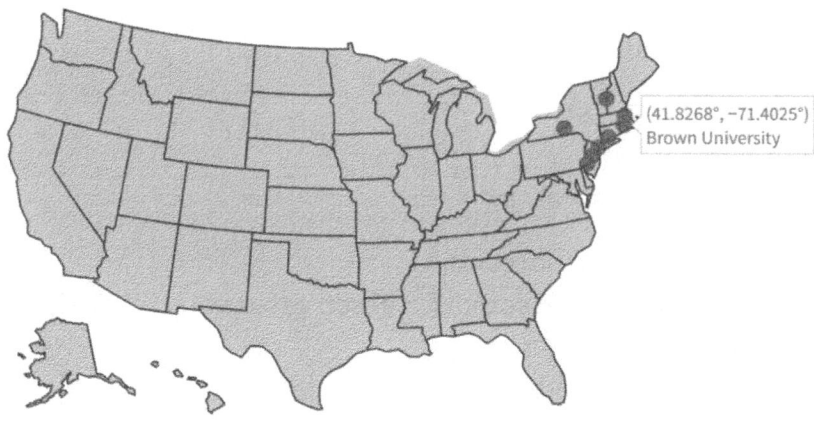

Figure 2-18. *Generating an interactive map (output of Listing 2-16)*

2.4. Developing the User Interface

Typically, developing a user interface for a web application requires a separate skill set related to graphical design and usability studies. A frontend developer starts by conceptualizing their idea with a wireframe diagram that lays out the elements of the page. This is then iteratively refined and tested to create the final user interface. Streamlit has largely simplified this process with its intuitive, responsive, and standardized interface, allowing the developer to render a web page without worrying about intricate design details.

In other words, Streamlit interfaces are plug-and-play, enabling developers to focus on the logic of their program while leaving the visual implementation to Streamlit. However, for those who need something more customized, they can integrate their own HTML and/or JavaScript components. Customizability and external components will be covered in subsequent chapters.

In this section, we will develop an application similar to the dataframe demo application from the previous chapter as an example of how to create a basic user interface.

Listing 2-17. dataframe_demo.py

```python
import streamlit as st
import pandas as pd
import plotly.express as px

# Sidebar for program selection
program = st.sidebar.selectbox('Select program', ['Dataframe
Demo', 'Other Demo'])
code = st.sidebar.checkbox('Display code')

# Program logic
if program == 'Dataframe Demo':
```

```
    df = px.data.stocks()
    st.title('DataFrame Demo')

    # Multiselect for stock selection
    stocks = st.multiselect('Select stocks', df.columns[1:],
    default=df.columns[1:])

    # Displaying stock data as a DataFrame
    st.subheader('Stock value')
    st.write(df[['date'] + stocks].set_index('date'))

    # Plotting a Plotly line chart
    fig = px.line(df, x='date', y=stocks, hover_data={'date':
    '|%Y %b %d'})
    st.write(fig)

    # Displaying the code when checkbox is selected
    if code:
        st.code(
            """
import streamlit as st
import pandas as pd
import plotly.express as px

df = px.data.stocks()
st.title('DataFrame Demo')

program = st.sidebar.selectbox('Select program', ['Dataframe
Demo', 'Other Demo'])
code = st.sidebar.checkbox('Display code')

if program == 'Dataframe Demo':
    df = px.data.stocks()
    st.title('DataFrame Demo')
```

```
    stocks = st.multiselect('Select stocks', df.columns[1:],
    default=df.columns[1:])
    st.subheader('Stock value')
    st.write(df[['date'] + stocks].set_index('date'))
    fig = px.line(df, x='date', y=stocks, hover_data={'date':
    '1%Y %b %d'})
    st.write(fig)
"""
        )
elif program == 'Other Demo':
    st.title('Other Demo')
```

As always, we begin by importing the stack of dependencies that we will use for this application, namely Streamlit, Pandas for dataframe handling, and Plotly Express to plot a simple time-series chart of the value of several blue-chip stocks over time. We then download a dataset from Plotly's list of available open source datasets and initialize our user interface by invoking a title with the `st.title` command.

Next, we add a `st.sidebar.selectbox` command to define a list of programs/pages for this application. We follow this with a checkbox on the sidebar to display our code using the `st.sidebar.checkbox` command. Widgets can be added to the sidebar by appending the `st.sidebar` prefix if applicable. We then use a st.multiselect command to select the list of stocks we want to visualize. The selection will filter the dataframe containing the stock values, and the filtered data will be displayed using the `st.write` command.

Afterward, we will use the filtered dataframe to create a time-series line chart with Plotly, using the reference at `https://plotly.com/python/time-series/`. Once the figure is generated, it can be displayed with `st.write`, known as the *pocket knife* command due to its versatility in rendering virtually anything. Finally, we will use a `st.code` command to present our snippet of code if the checkbox is selected by the user. And there you have it (Figures 2-19 and 2-20), a basic dataframe application in just over 40 lines of code.

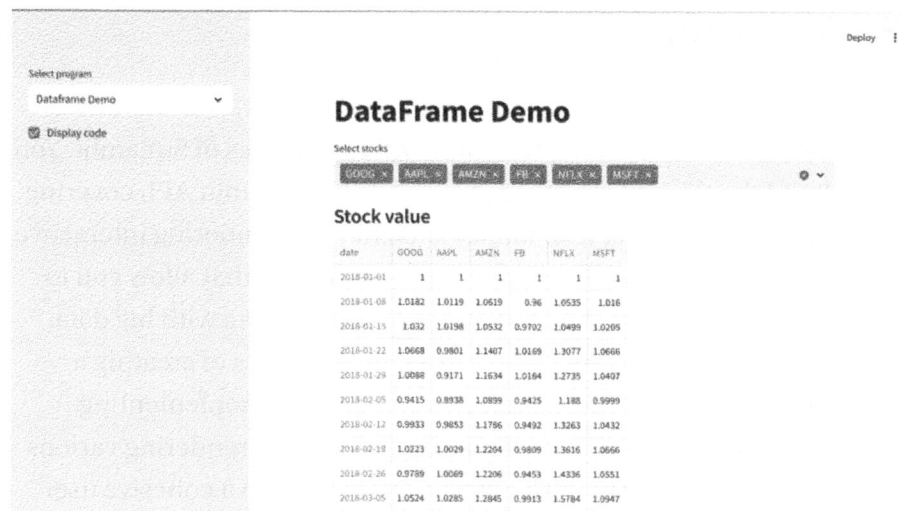

Figure 2-19. *Dataframe demo application (output of Listing 2-17)*

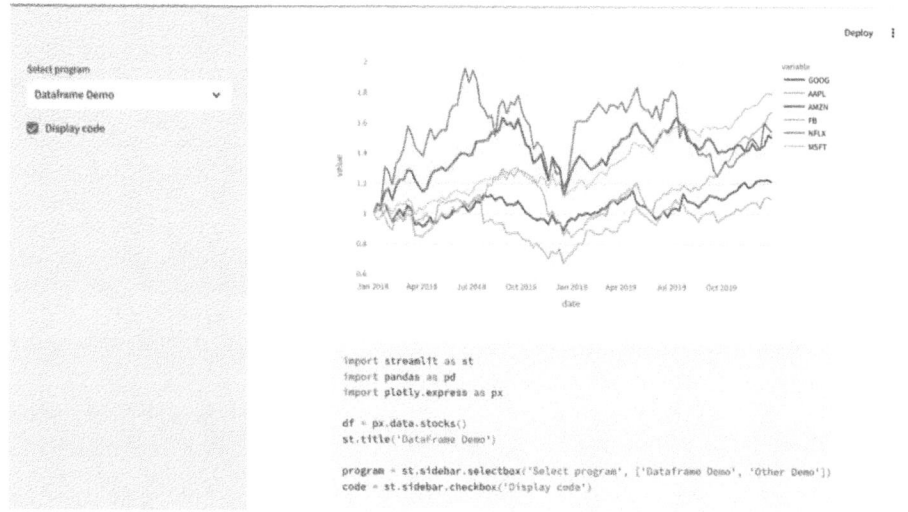

Figure 2-20. *Dataframe demo application continued (output of Listing 2-17)*

2.5. Summary

This chapter has certainly been a thorough one. By now, you should be well-acquainted with the core principles and capabilities of Streamlit. You have explored the diverse set of commands in the Streamlit API, covering everything from displaying text, tables, and charts to rendering interactive widgets and multimedia objects, as well as commands that allow you to organize the page and optimize Streamlit for efficient use with big data. In the latter part of the chapter, we focused on the basics of creating a simple web application. This included creating forms, implementing conditional flow, managing exceptions, mutating data, rendering various visualizations, and integrating all of these elements into a cohesive user interface. In short, after reviewing this chapter, you should feel confident in your ability to start developing your own basic web applications using Streamlit.

CHAPTER 3

Developing the User Interface

With Streamlit, developers can focus on implementing backend logic while relying on the framework to handle most of the frontend tasks. Additionally, Streamlit allows you to create responsive interfaces for PC, tablet, and mobile platforms effortlessly, with no extra overhead. However, if more bespoke and tailored applications are required, Streamlit offers a significant degree of frontend customization without requiring any knowledge of HTML, CSS, or JavaScript. Developers can configure their applications with various color schemes, fonts, and appearances, both graphically and programmatically.

Streamlit also enables you to structure and organize web pages effectively using a combination of a sidebar, columns, expanders, and containers. These elements work together to enhance the user experience while optimizing the use of page space. Additionally, placeholders and progress bars allow you to render dynamic content on demand or in response to events. Most importantly, Streamlit supports the creation of multiple pages and nested subpages, enabling a highly modular and scalable approach to application development.

© Mohammad Khorasani, Mohamed Abdou, Javier Hernández Fernández 2025
M. Khorasani et al., *Streamlit for Web Development*,
https://doi.org/10.1007/979-8-8688-1826-4_3

3.1. Designing the Application

When designing a Streamlit application, we can utilize its wide array of native methods to customize the page exactly as desired. From color schemes and themes to columns, expanders, sidebars, and placeholders, the design possibilities are virtually limitless.

3.1.1. Configuring the Page

With Streamlit, you can configure various attributes of a web page, such as the page layout, initial sidebar state, page title (as displayed in the browser), icon, hamburger menu state, footer, and more. While some of these settings can be configured directly within your script, others must be set in the global configuration file, `/.streamlit/config.toml`, as discussed in Section 1.2.

Basic Page Configuration

Listing 3-1 can be used to configure the page title, icon, layout, initial sidebar state, and menu items, as shown in Figure 3-1. Note that the page icon supports `.ico` files, and you can use the *Pillow* package to import and handle images. The page layout can be set to either `centered` or `wide`, while the initial sidebar state can be configured as *auto*, *expanded*, or *collapsed*. Additionally, you can customize one or more of the following pages in the hamburger menu: *Get help*, *Report a bug*, or *About*. The Get help and Report a bug pages can only be instantiated with a URL to redirect users to another web page. The *About* page, however, can be displayed as a modal window, as shown in Figure 3-2.

Listing 3-1. page_config.py

```python
import streamlit as st
from PIL import Image

icon = Image.open('favicon.ico')

# Page configuration
st.set_page_config(
    page_title='Hello World',
    page_icon=icon,
    layout='centered',
    initial_sidebar_state='auto',
    menu_items={
        'Get Help': 'https://streamlit.io/',
        'Report a bug': 'https://github.com',
        'About': 'About your application: **Hello World**'
    }
)

# Set up titles
title = 'Hello World'
st.sidebar.title(title)
st.title(title)
```

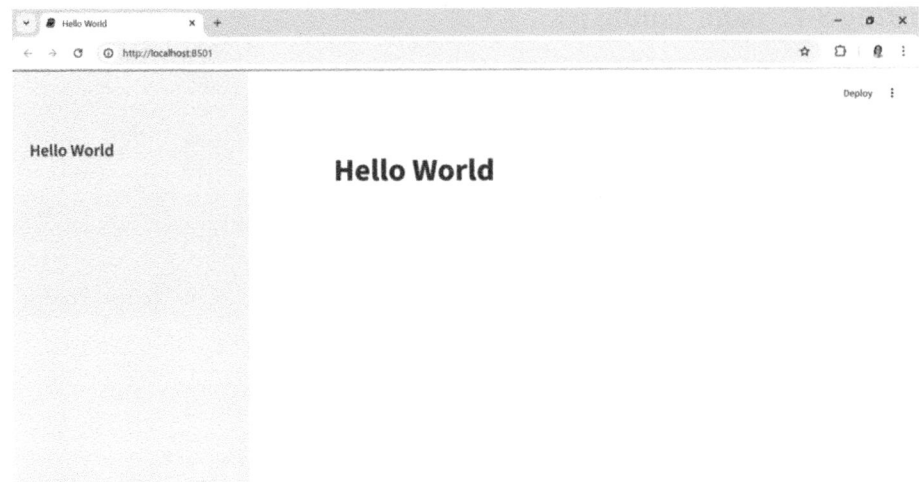

Figure 3-1. *Streamlit page configured with Listing 3-1*

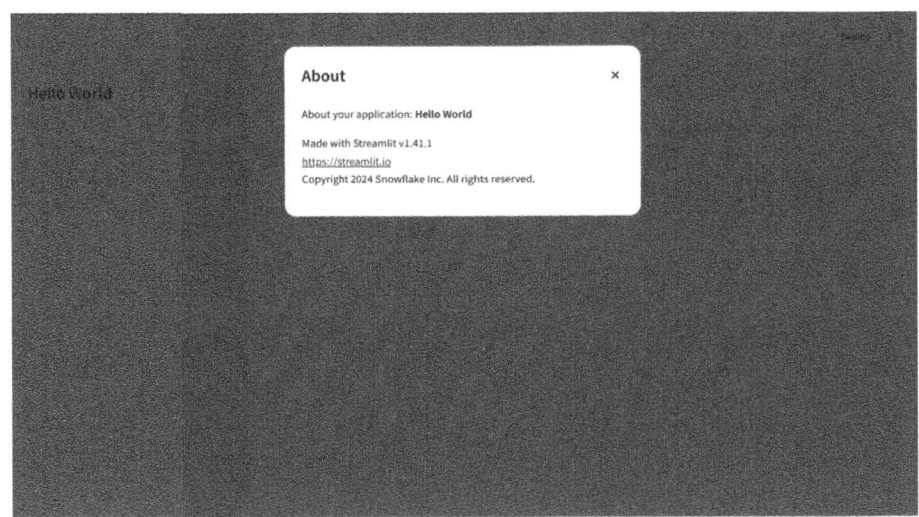

Figure 3-2. *Displaying the About modal window*

Removing Footer and Hamburger Menu

You can remove the default footer provided by Streamlit, as well as the entire hamburger menu, by using the commands shown in Listing 3-2. The resulting output is illustrated in Figure 3-3. However, please note that while modifying the CSS may work in the current version of Streamlit, this method is not guaranteed to function in future versions if the internal implementation changes.

Listing 3-2. remove_footer_menu.py

```
# Custom CSS to hide header and footer
hide_streamlit_style = """
    <style>
    /* Hide Streamlit header */
    header {
        visibility: hidden;
    }
    /* Hide Streamlit footer */
    footer {
        visibility: hidden;
    }
    </style>
"""
st.markdown(hide_streamlit_style, unsafe_allow_html=True)
```

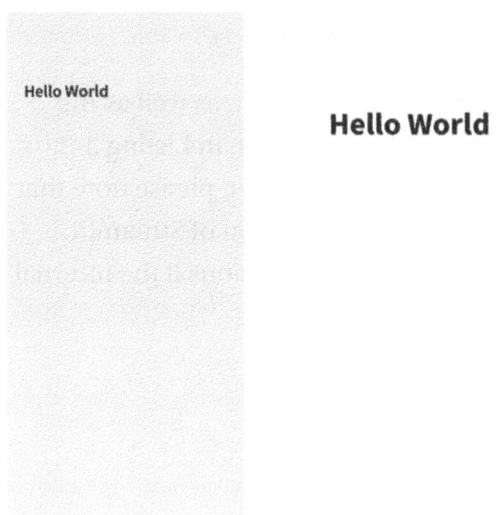

Figure 3-3. *Removed footer and hamburger menu from the page*

Adding a Customized Footer

Additionally, you can add a customized footer by using the markdown command shown in Listing 3-3. The resulting output is displayed in Figure 3-4.

Listing 3-3. footer.py

```
# Add custom footer to the sidebar
custom_footer_style = """
    <div class="markdown-text-container stText" style="width:
    698px;">
        <footer>
            <p></p>
        </footer>
        <div style="font-size: 12px;">Hello world v 0.1</div>
        <div style="font-size: 12px;">Hello world LLC.</div>
    </div>
```

```
"""
st.sidebar.markdown(custom_footer_style, unsafe_allow_
html=True)
```

Advanced Page Configuration

In addition to the basic configurable settings of a Streamlit web page, numerous other parameters can be adjusted by modifying the global configuration file */.streamlit/config.toml*, as discussed earlier in Section 1.2. These parameters include settings for global, logger, client, runner, server, browser, mapbox, deprecation, AWS S3, and theme configurations, as outlined in Tables 3-1, 3-2, and 3-3. For more details, refer to https:// docs.streamlit.io/library/advanced-features/configuration. An example of configuring the web page theme is provided in Listing 3-4.

Table 3-1. *config.toml file parameters*

Configuration Options
[global]
• *disableWidgetStateDuplicationWarning = False*
Streamlit watchdog will check for duplicate values being set to a widget through session state and the widget key. If this parameter is disabled, Streamlit will not display a warning message if duplicate values are found.
• *showWarningOnDirectExecution = True*
Streamlit will display a warning when you try to run a script using python script.py when this parameter is set to true.

(continued)

Table 3-1. (*continued*)

Configuration Options

[logger]

- *level = 'info'*

Level of logging specified for Streamlit's internal logger. Available options include '*error*', '*warning*', '*info*', and '*debug*'.

- *messageFormat = '%(asctime)s %(message)s'.*

This parameter will specify the string format for logging messages.

[client]

- *showErrorDetails = 'full'*

Controls whether an uncaught exception and/or deprecation warning will be displayed in the browser. Available options include '*full*', '*stacktrace*', '*type*', '*none*', *True*, and *False*.

- *toolbarMode = 'auto'*

Controls the visibility of items located in the toolbar, options, and settings menu of the application. Available options include '*auto*', '*developer*', '*viewer*', and '*minimal*'.

- *showSidebarNavigation = True*

Controls whether the sidebar page navigation will be displayed in a multipage application.

[runner]

- *magicEnabled = True*

Setting this parameter to true will allow you to write strings and variables outside of a *st.write* command.

- *fastReruns = True*

(*continued*)

Table 3-1. (*continued*)

Configuration Options

Setting this parameter to true will handle script rerun requests immediately, making applications far more responsive.

- *enforceSerializableSessionState = False*

Setting this parameter to true will raise exceptions if unserializable data is added to the session state.

- *enumCoercion = 'nameOnly'*

Controls how certain widgets such as the *radio*, *selectbox*, and *multiselect* widgets coerce Enum numbers. Available options include *'off'*, *'nameOnly'*, and *'nameAndValue'*.

Table 3-2. *config.toml file parameters (continued—1)*

Configuration Options

[server]

- *folderWatchBlacklist = [ ]*

This parameter specifies the list of folders that should not be inspected by Streamlit for any changes.

- *fileWatcherType = 'auto'*

Setting this parameter to auto will ensure Streamlit uses the watchdog module if it is available, the watchdog will force Streamlit to use the watchdog module, the poll forces Streamlit to use polling, and none will stop Streamlit from inspecting files.

- *cookieSecret = 'key'*

This parameter specifies the key to use to produce cookies; if not set, Streamlit will randomly assign a value.

- *headless = False*

(*continued*)

Table 3-2. (*continued*)

Configuration Options

Setting this parameter to false will force Streamlit to start the application on a browser window.

- *runOnSave = False*

Setting this parameter to true will force Streamlit to automatically run the script upon resaving the script.

- *address =*

This parameter will specify the address where the server will listen for client and/or browser connections.

- *port = 8501*

This parameter will specify the port where the server will listen to for browser connections.

- *baseUrlPath = 'URL'*

This parameter will specify the base path for the URL from where the Streamlit application will be served.

- *enableCORS = True*

Setting this parameter to true will enable cross-origin request sharing protection.

- *enableXsrfProtection = True*

Setting this parameter to true will enable cross-site request forgery protection.

- *maxUploadSize = 200*

This parameter specifies the maximum uploadable file size in megabytes.

- *maxMessageSize = 200*

(*continued*)

Table 3-2. (*continued*)

Configuration Options

This parameter specifies the maximum size of messages that can be sent through the WebSocket connection.

- *enableWebsocketCompression = False*

Setting this parameter to true will enable support for WebSocket compression.

- *enableStaticServing = False*

Setting this parameter to true will enable serving files from a static directory in the application's directory.

- *disconnectionSessionTTL = 120*

Specifies the time for sessions with disconnected WebSockets, after which the server may clean the session state and uploaded files.

- *sslCertFile =*

Specifies the certificate file for connecting through HTTPS.

- *sslKeyFile =*

Specifies the cryptographic key file for connecting through HTTPS.

[browser]

- *serverAddress = 'localhost'*

This parameter specifies the URL which users should enter into their browsers to connect to the Streamlit application; can be an IP address or DNS with path.

- *gatherUsageStats = True*

Setting this parameter to true will enable sending usage statistics to Streamlit.

- *serverPort = 8501*

This parameter sets the port at which users should point their browsers to, in order to connect to the Streamlit application.

Table 3-3.   *config.toml file parameters (continued—2)*

Configuration Options

[mapbox]

- *token = ' '*

This parameter specifies the token for custom Mapbox elements; for further information, please refer to www.mapbox.com/.

[theme]

- *base =*

This parameter specifies the Streamlit theme to use with your custom theme; can be one of 'light' or 'dark'.

- *primaryColor =*

This parameter specifies the color HEX to use for the interactive Streamlit elements.

- *backgroundColor =*

This parameter specifies the color HEX to use for the main content of the Streamlit page.

- *secondaryBackgroundColor =*

This parameter specifies the color HEX to use for the sidebar.

- *textColor =*

This parameter specifies the color HEX to use for the text.

- *font =*

This parameter specifies the font to use for the text; can be 'sans serif', 'serif', or 'monospace'.

[secrets]

- *files =*

Specifies the list of locations where secrets will be searched for. Can be a path to a TOML file or a Kubernetes styles secret.

Figure 3-4. *Adding a customized footer*

3.1.2. Developing Themes and Color Schemes

Streamlit allows both developers and users to customize the application's theme and color scheme, either graphically or programmatically.

Customizing the Theme Graphically

You can choose one of the available theme appearances, Light or Dark, from the settings menu within the hamburger menu, as shown in Figure 3-5. Additionally, you can select colors for the following areas: Primary color, Background color, Text color, and Secondary background color, and choose one of the available fonts—Sans serif, Serif, or *Monospace*—as shown in Figure 3-6.

Table 3-4 provides more details about each color setting and the Streamlit elements they affect. Please note that interactive widgets, such as st.slider, will use the Secondary background color when placed in the main body of the application. However, when the widget is placed in the sidebar, it will use the Background color instead, as shown in Figure 3-7.

Table 3-4. *Theme color settings*

Color Parameter	Altered Elements
Primary color	Interactive widgets such as *st.slider*.
Background color	Main body of application.
Text color	All text elements.
Secondary background color	Sidebar background color.

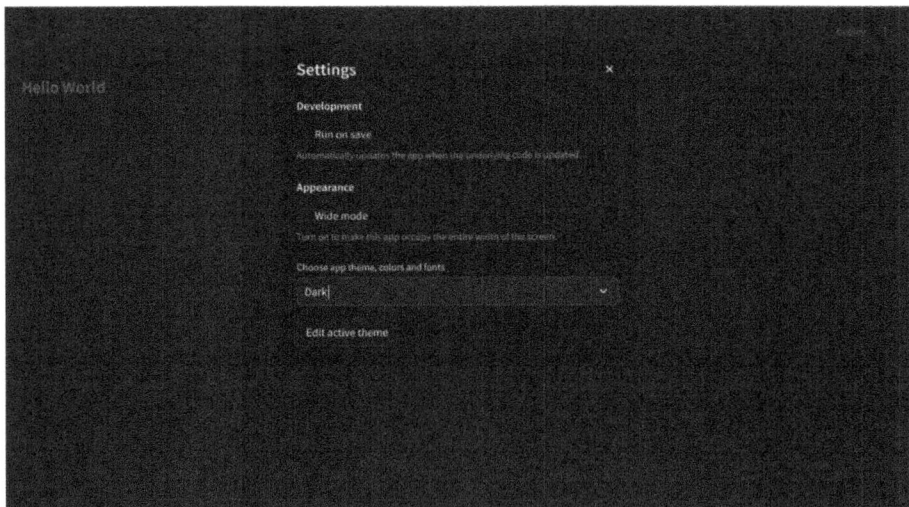

Figure 3-5. *Customizing the theme's appearance from the settings menu*

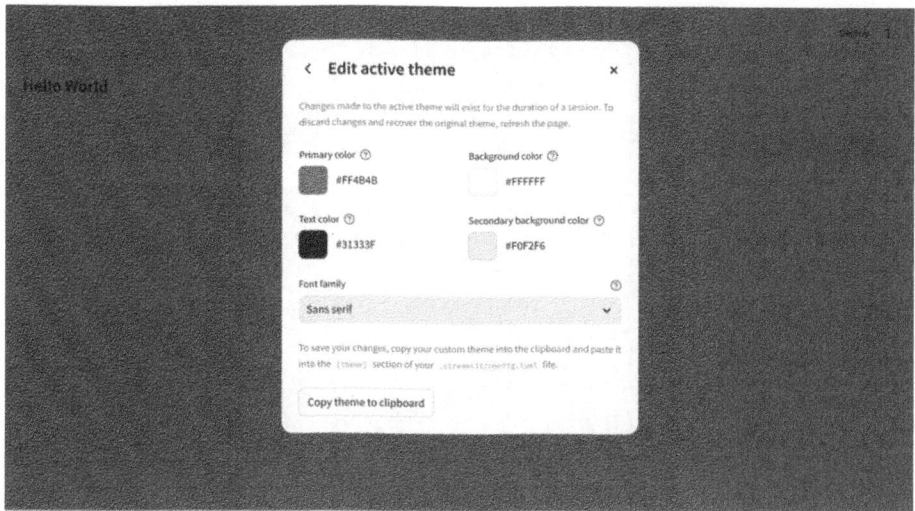

Figure 3-6. *Customizing the theme's colors from the settings menu*

Customizing the Theme Programmatically

Alternatively, you can customize the theme's appearance and colors programmatically by modifying the global config file /.streamlit/ config.toml, as discussed earlier in Section 1.2. To specify the theme settings, modify the [theme] parameters, as shown in Listing 3-4. Please note that the color convention used is color HEX. For more information on this convention, please refer to www.w3schools.com/colors/colors_ hexadecimal.asp HEXadecimal.asp.

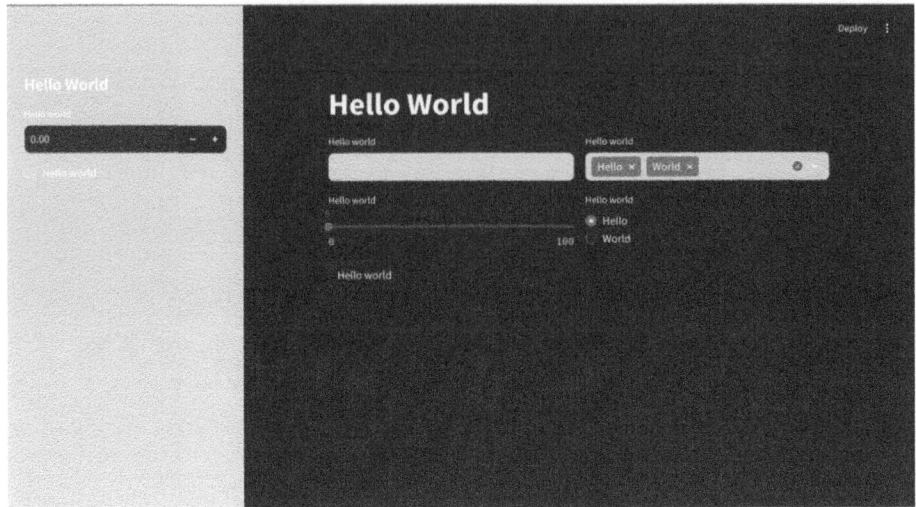

Figure 3-7. *Customized theme's colors*

Listing 3-4. config.toml

```
[theme]
base = "light"
primaryColor = "#7792E3"
backgroundColor = "#273346"
secondaryBackgroundColor = "#B9F1C0"
textColor = "#FFFFFF"
font = "sans serif"
```

Using Themes with Custom Components

If you are developing custom Streamlit components, you may need to pass the application's theme settings to your component. Make sure you have installed the latest version of streamlit-component-lib by running the following command:

```
npm install streamlit-component-lib
```

This package will automatically update the colors of your custom component to match the theme settings of your Streamlit application. Additionally, it will enable you to read the theme settings in your JavaScript and/or CSS scripts, as shown below.

The object settings can be exposed as CSS variables as follows:

```
--primary-color
--background-color
--secondary-background-color
--text-color
--font
```

Accordingly, these settings can be accessed as follows:

```
.mySelector {
  color: var(--primary-color);
}
```

Alternatively, you can expose the object settings as a ReactJS prop, which can be accessed as follows:

```
{
  "primaryColor": ""
  "backgroundColor": "",
  "secondaryBackgroundColor": "",
  "textColor": "",
  "font": "",
}
```

3.1.3. Organizing the Page

Streamlit offers several methods to organize and customize the frontend design of an application. As a developer, you can enable a sidebar, divide the web page into columns, display expander boxes to hide content, and create containers to group multiple widgets together. When used in combination, these features allow you to achieve a high level of customization and provide a tailored experience for your users.

Sidebar

With Streamlit, you can elegantly subdivide your page using a sidebar that can be expanded and contracted on demand with the st.sidebar command. Additionally, as shown in Section 3.1, you can configure Streamlit to keep the sidebar expanded, contracted, or automatically adjusted at the start based on the screen size. Practically, every Streamlit element and widget, except for st.echo and st.spinner, can be used within the sidebar. You can even render other page organization features, such as st.columns, st.expander, and st.container, within the sidebar, as shown in Listing 3-5 and Figure 3-8.

Expanders

With Streamlit, you can collapse content into expanders to make more efficient use of space in the main body or sidebar of your application. Expanders can be expanded and contracted on demand, or set to either state by default. Additionally, expanders can contain any element, including columns and containers, but not nested expanders. An example of using expanders is shown in Listing 3-5 and Figure 3-8.

Columns

Similarly, you can divide the main body and sidebar using Streamlit's columns feature, which can be called with the st.columns command. You can specify the number of columns you need by writing st.columns(2), or alternatively, use a list to set both the number and width of each column arbitrarily, like st.columns([2, 1]). Columns can be invoked within a with statement and used concurrently with expanders and containers, but they cannot be nested within one another. An example of using columns is shown in Listing 3-5 and Figure 3-8.

Containers

If you need to bundle several widgets or elements together, you can do so with Streamlit's container feature, which can be called with the st.container command in the main body or sidebar. Containers can be invoked within a with statement and can be used with columns, expanders, and even nested containers. They can also be altered out of order; for instance, if you display some text outside the container and then display more text within the container, the latter will be shown first. An example of using containers is shown in Listing 3-5 and Figure 3-8.

Popovers

If you need to introduce a popover window in your application to render another widget, this can be easily done so with the use of a st.popover command in the main body or sidebar. Popovers can be invoked within a with statement and can be rendered within columns, expanders, and containers. The only limitation is that popovers cannot be nested within one another. An example of using popovers is shown in Listing 3-5 and Figure 3-9.

Dialog Boxes

Similarly, if you need to display some information or render another widget on demand in response to a user action, you may use the @ st.dialog() decorator. This decorator must precede the function that will be used to define the dialog box and can be rendered upon invoking that function. Please note that if you are using dialog boxes to collect user input, such as rendering an st.selectbox widget, then you should also include an st.button that upon press saves any entry to user made to st.session_state and subsequently rerun the page using an st. rerun command. For further information please refer to Listing 3-5 and Figure 3-10.

Listing 3-5. page_organization.py

```
import streamlit as st
from datetime import datetime

tab1, tab2 = st.tabs(['Tab 1', 'Tab 2'])

with tab1:
    st.subheader('_Tab 1_')

    # Expander in sidebar
    st.sidebar.subheader('Expander')
    with st.sidebar.expander('Time'):
        time = datetime.now().strftime('%H:%M:%S')
        st.write(f'**{time}**')

    # Columns in sidebar
    st.sidebar.subheader('Columns')
    col1, col2 = st.sidebar.columns(2)
    with col1:
        option_1 = st.selectbox('Please select option 1',
        ['A', 'B'])
    with col2:
        option_2 = st.radio('Please select option 2',
        ['A', 'B'])

    # Container in sidebar
    container = st.sidebar.container()
    container.subheader('Container')
    option_3 = container.slider('Please select option 3')
```

```python
st.sidebar.warning('Elements outside of container will be
displayed externally')
container.info(f'**Option 3:** {option_3}')

# Expander in main body
st.subheader('Expander')
with st.expander('Time'):
    time = datetime.now().strftime('%H:%M:%S')
    st.write(f'**{time}**')

# Columns in main body
st.subheader('Columns')
col1, col2 = st.columns(2)
with col1:
    option_4 = st.selectbox('Please select option 4',
    ['A', 'B'])
with col2:
    option_5 = st.radio('Please select option 5',
    ['A', 'B'])

# Container in main body
container = st.container()
container.subheader('Container')
option_6 = container.slider('Please select option 6')
st.warning('Elements outside of container will be displayed
externally')
container.info(f'**Option 6:** {option_6}')
with tab2:
    # Popover in main body
    st.subheader('Popover')
    with st.popover('Popover'):
        option_7 = st.radio('Please select option 7',
['A', 'B'])
```

```python
st.write(f'**Option 7:** {option_7}')

# Dialog box in main body
st.subheader('Dialog box')
@st.dialog('Option 8')
def dialog_box():
    option_8 = st.selectbox('Please select option 8',
    ['A', 'B'])
    if st.button('Submit'):
        st.session_state['option_8'] = option_8
        st.rerun()
if 'option_8' not in st.session_state:
    if st.button('Dialog box'):
        dialog_box()
else:
    st.write(f'**Option 8:** {st.session_
    state['option_8']}')
```

Placeholders

A placeholder is one of the most versatile and powerful features offered by Streamlit. By using the st.empty or st.sidebar.empty command, you can reserve space at any location on the main body or sidebar of your application. This is particularly useful for displaying content out of order or on demand after a specific event or trigger. A placeholder can be created by writing placeholder = st.empty(), and any widget or element can be attached to it as needed. For example, you can attach text by writing placeholder.info('Hello world'), and later replace the placeholder by assigning it a different element. Finally, when no longer needed, the placeholder can be cleared using the placeholder.empty() command.

Tabs

A tab, as the name suggests, allows you to organize your application into separate containers within the same page using the st.tab command. You can create as many tabs as needed by specifying their names, such as tab1, tab2 = st.tabs(['Tab 1', 'Tab 2']). The tab names will appear at the top of the page, and users can navigate freely between them. The content for each tab can be defined using a *with* statement. It's important to note that, unlike pages, Streamlit will by default invoke the logic in each tab, but only render the tab which is selected. This means that navigating to a page with tabs may be unexpectedly slow while Streamlit executes the logic of each tab before the page loads. An example of using expanders is shown in Listing 3-5 and Figure 3-8.

3.2. Displaying Dynamic Content

To display dynamic content such as a constantly updating map, chart, or clock, you can place an element within a placeholder and invoke it within a for loop or while loop to iterate over multiple instances of that element. As a result, the element will appear dynamic, with its state constantly changing with each iteration of the loop. An example of dynamic content is the clock application built using a placeholder, as shown in Listing 3-6 and Figures 3-11 and 3-12. In this case, a while loop is used to continuously update the st.info element to display the current time until a predefined point is reached, at which point the placeholder is cleared and the while loop ends.

Listing 3-6. placeholder.py

```
import streamlit as st
from datetime import datetime

st.title('Clock')
```

```
# Create an empty placeholder for time display
clock = st.empty()

# Infinite loop to continuously update the time
while True:
    time = datetime.now().strftime('%H:%M:%S')

    # Display the current time in the placeholder
    clock.info(f'**Current time:** {time}')

    if time > '21:19:15':
        # Clear the time display when the alarm condition is
        met and display the alarm
        clock.empty()
        st.warning('Alarm!!')
        break
```

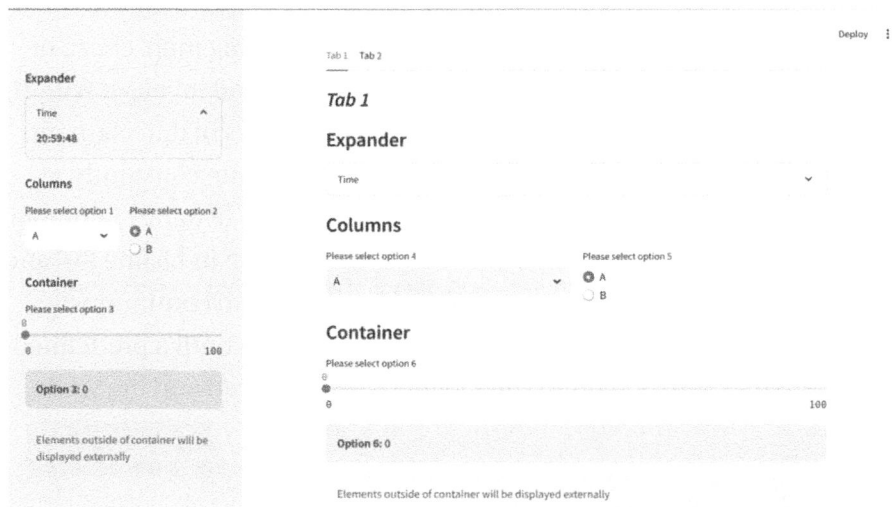

Figure 3-8. *Organizing the page using Listing 3-5*

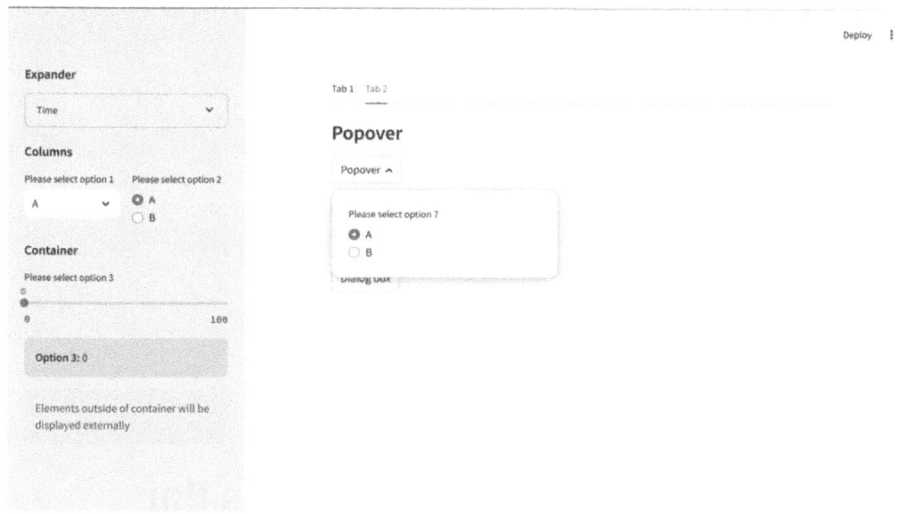

Figure 3-9. *Displaying a popover widget using Listing 3-5*

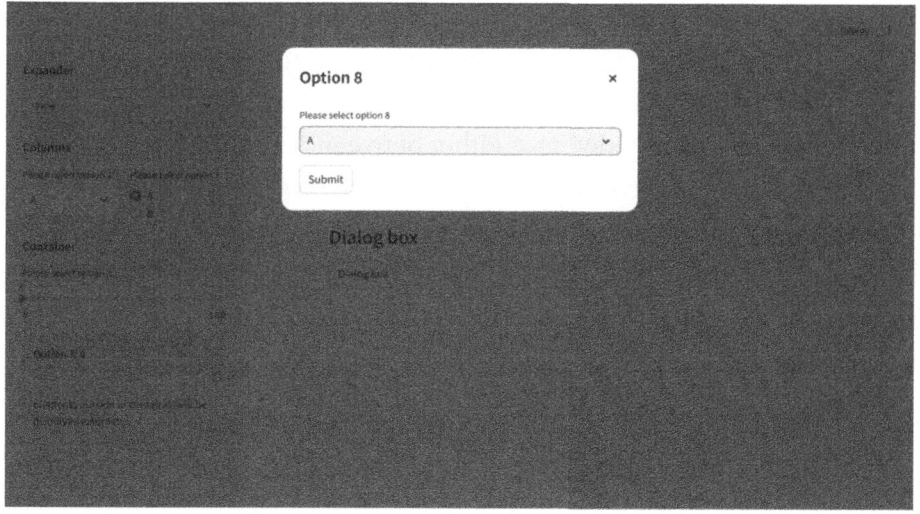

Figure 3-10. *Displaying a dialog box widget using Listing 3-5*

Clock

Current time: 21:18:30

Figure 3-11. *Output of Listing 3-6*

Clock

Alarm!!

Figure 3-12. *Output of Listing 3-6 (continued)*

3.2.1. Creating a Real-Time Progress Bar

When working with big data, it can be helpful to visualize the progress of downloading, uploading, or performing computations that take a long time. Users need to clearly see how much progress has been made and how much longer they can expect to wait for the process to complete. For this purpose, we can use Streamlit's st.progress widget, which renders a progress bar that shows the value provided to it, either between 1 and 100 as an integer, or 0.0 and 1.0 as a float. For example, in Listing 3-7, we visualize the progress of downloading a file from a URL using the requests package. If you haven't already, install it using pip install wget. From requests, we can read the total file size in bytes and the current amount downloaded in bytes, which we then feed to our progress bar for visualization, as shown in Figure 3-13.

Listing 3-7. progress_bar.py

```
import streamlit as st
import requests

# Create an empty placeholder for progress text
progress_text = st.empty()
```

```python
# Create a progress bar widget, initially at 0%
progress_bar = st.progress(0)

def download_file(url, filename):
    response = requests.get(url, stream=True)
    total_size = int(response.headers.get('content-length', 0))

    with open(filename, "wb") as f:
        downloaded = 0
        for chunk in response.iter_content(chunk_size=8192):
            if chunk:
                f.write(chunk)
                downloaded += len(chunk)
                percent = int(downloaded * 100 / total_size) if
                total_size else 0

                # Update the progress text and progress bar
                progress_text.subheader(f'Progress: {percent}%')
                progress_bar.progress(percent)

    return filename

# Download a file using requests, with the custom progress bar
download_file('file url', 'output.file')
```

Progress: 49%

Figure 3-13. *Output of Listing 3-7*

3.3. Implementing Multipage Applications

Pagination and scalability are essential for any web application, and
Streamlit offers both native and non-native ways to address the need to
scale. In simple terms, the only limit to the breadth of an application in
Streamlit is the limit of one's imagination.

3.3.1. Creating Pages

The need to create pages within any web application is inherent, and with Streamlit, you can natively create additional pages to organize your content accordingly. To start, you will need one main script that defines the pages in your application, as shown in Listing 3-8. Next, you can add as many other pages as you need as shown in Listings 3-9 and 3-10, each as an independent script located in the same directory or a sub-directory. You may also add an icon to the page title to display when rendered as shown in Listing 3-8. When you run your application, each page will be accessible as a button that will automatically appear in the sidebar in order, as shown in Figure 3-14.

Listing 3-8. navigation.py

```
import streamlit as st

pg = st.navigation([st.Page('home.py', title='🏠 Home'),
                    st.Page('contact_us.py', title='📞
                    Contact us')])
pg.run()
```

Listing 3-9. pages/1_🏠_Home.py

```
import streamlit as st
st.title('Home')
```

Listing 3-10. pages/2_📞_Contact_us.py

```
import streamlit as st
st.title('Contact us')
```

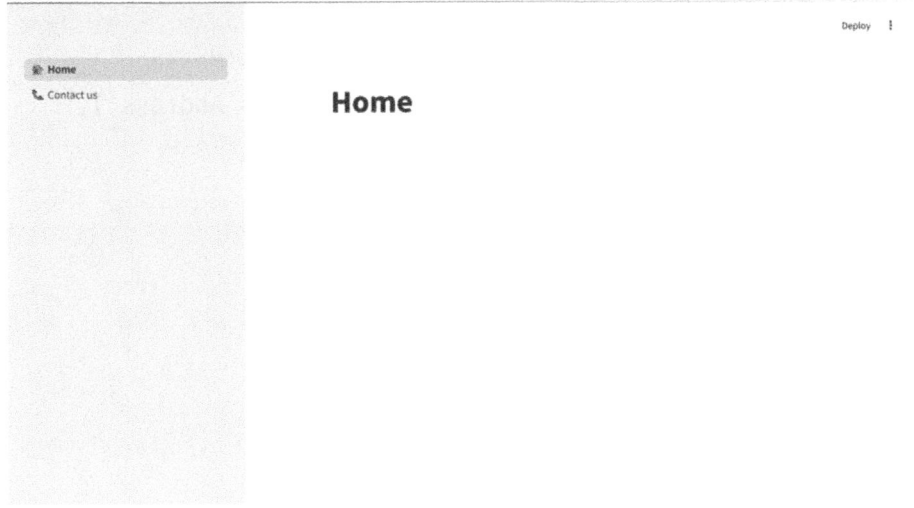

Figure 3-14. *Multipage Streamlit application*

3.3.2. Grouping Subpages

With Streamlit, you can also group pages together in one drop down menu. For example, we will group two pages *Message* and *Address* within the Contact us menu. For clarity, create a folder named *contact_us* inside the rootfolder and place a script for each page in it. Then, call these scripts into your main script as a dictionary where each key is the menu name, and the values are the associated pages. Please refer to Figure 3-15 and Listings 3-11 to 3-13 for more details.

Listing 3-11. navigation_2.py

```
import streamlit as st

pages = {
    '🏠 Home': [
        st.Page('home.py', title='Home')
    ],
```

```python
'📞 Contact us': [
    st.Page('contact_us/message.py', title='Message'),
    st.Page('contact_us/address.py', title='Address'),
],
}

pg = st.navigation(pages)
pg.run()
```

Listing 3-12. contact_us/message.py

```python
import streamlit as st

st.title('Message')
```

Listing 3-13. contact_us/address.py

```python
import streamlit as st

st.title('Address')
```

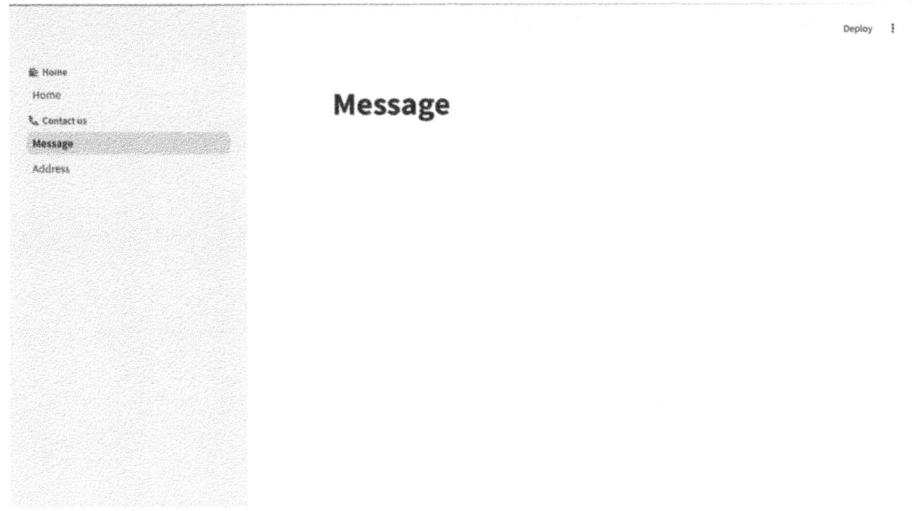

Figure 3-15. *Multipage Streamlit application with subpages*

3.3.3. Enabling Sub URL Paths

While Streamlit does not directly support sub URL paths, you can implement the appearance of unique URL paths in your single or multipage Streamlit application by using the st.query_params command. An example of implementing sub URL paths is shown in Listing 3-14 and Figure 3-16.

Listing 3-14. sub_url_paths.py

```
import streamlit as st

# Determine the current page
current_page = st.query_params.get('page', ['home'])

# Display the correct content based on the page
if current_page == 'home':
    st.title('Home Page')
```

```
elif current_page == 'contact':
    st.title('Contact Page')

# Add links to navigate between sub URLs
st.sidebar.title('Pages')
if st.sidebar.button('Home'):
    st.query_params['page'] = 'home'
    st.rerun()
if st.sidebar.button('Contact'):
    st.query_params['page'] = 'contact'
    st.rerun()
```

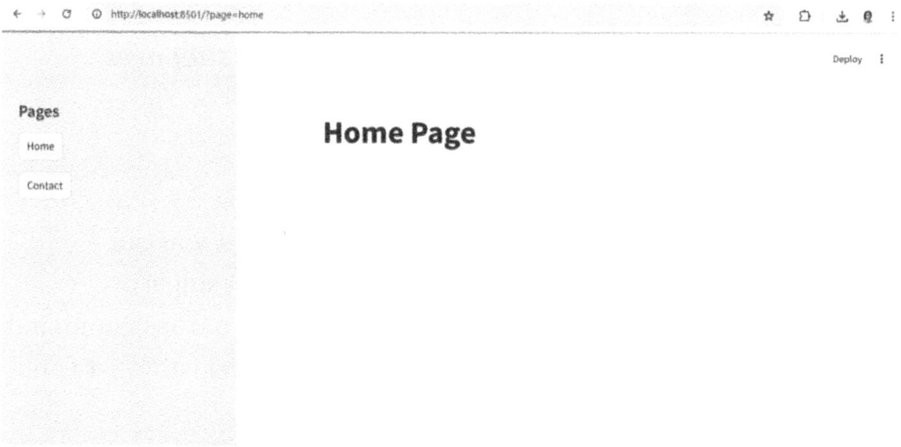

Figure 3-16. *Enabling sub URL paths for applications*

3.4. Modularizing Application Development

In almost every web project, there is a need for visual components and code that manage the overall experience, which is not directly seen by the end user but is still experienced. This is often referred to as the business logic of the application, responsible for controlling and managing intermodule communication, particularly when a reaction is required in response to user actions or to initiate an action, such as prompting the user to sign in.

3.4.1. Example: Developing a Social Network Application

For instance, a simple social network application, like the one shown in Figure 3-17, will need components to create posts and read fields. These two seemingly simple requirements can be broken down into three main parts: views, action handling services, and a database connection or API (Application Programming Interface) client for another backend service. In this example, everything is post-centric, meaning it should be a reusable, shared resource. A basic application like this would have an architecture similar to the one shown in Figure 3-18.

Displayed name?

Mohammad

What is in your mind?

It can be both!

Post

Post added!

Adam: Python is a snake | 2021-05-01 00:00:00

Sara: Python is a programming language | 2021-05-03 00:00:00

Figure 3-17. *Demo social network app*

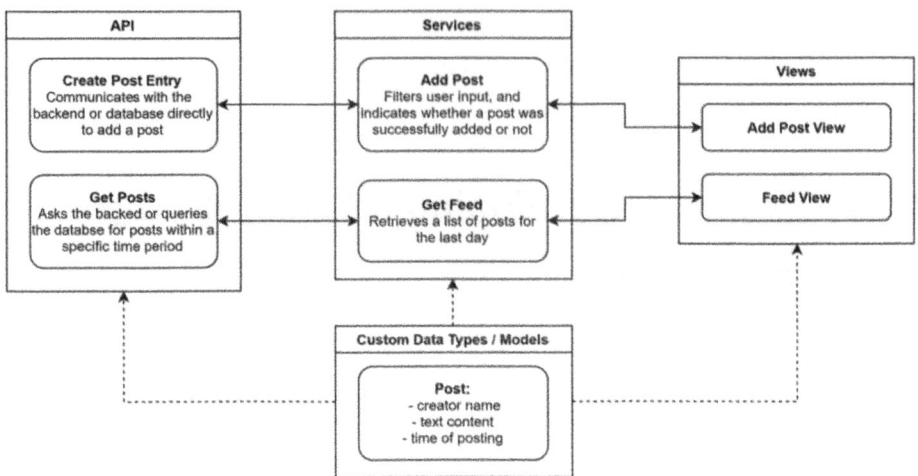

Figure 3-18. *Basic social network Streamlit architecture*

To build the mentioned project, a bottom-up approach should be followed, starting with the most dependent object in the design, which is the Post class, and building upward to the user-visible views. The post should be a class, as shown in Listings 3-15 and 3-16, because it encapsulates related data in one structure. In Python, we can use the dataclasses decorator to indicate that this is a class intended to hold data. We can also provide a default initialization function to assign values to the declared variables. This can be seen as the Pythonic alternative to C#'s DTOs (Data Transfer Objects).

Listing 3-15. Models/Post.py

```
from dataclasses import dataclass
import datetime
@dataclass(init=True)
class Post:
    creator_name: str
    content: str
    posting_date: datetime.datetime
```

Listing 3-16. Models/__init__.py

```
from .Post import Post
```

Next, there needs to be a data source access mechanism, whose sole responsibility is to store and write new posts, whether directly in a database or through an external service that can be accessed via HTTP methods or a messaging service like Kafka, RabbitMQ, or AWS's SQS. For this example, we will assume that a backend service is already built, exposing two methods: one to add posts and another to retrieve posts between two timestamps, as shown in Listing 3-17.

Listing 3-17. API.py

```
from Models import Post
import datetime
class API:
    def __init__(self, config=None):
        self.config = config
    def add_post(self, post: Post):
        # POST HTTP request to backend to add the post
        # Returns true as if post has been added
        return True
    def get_posts(self, start_date: datetime.datetime, end_
    data: datetime.datetime):
        # GET HTTP request to backend to posts within a
        time period
        # Returns a list of posts
        return [
            Post(
                'Adam', 'Python is a snake',
                datetime.datetime(year=2021, month=5, day=1)
            ),
```

```
Post(
    'Sara', 'Python is a programming language',
    datetime.datetime(year=2021, month=5, day=3)
)]
```

Once our API is ready, we can begin building an internal service to act as the middleware between the visual components and the API. This is typically referred to as a *Service* by experienced developers.

Listing 3-18. Services/AddPost.py

```
from API import api_instance
from Models import Post
def add_post(post: Post):
    # Check if the post is None or if any required fields
    are empty
    # Returns the result of addition operation
    if post is None or len(post.creator_name) == 0 or len(post.
    content) == 0:
        return None
    # Adding the post using the API instance
    did_add = api_instance.add_post(post)
    return did_add
```

Listing 3-19. Services/GetFeed.py

```
from API import api_instance
import datetime
def get_feed():
    # Returns the posts fed to the API instance

    to_date = datetime.datetime.now()
    from_date = to_date - datetime.timedelta(days=1)
```

```
posts = api_instance.get_posts(from_date, to_date)
return posts
```

Listing 3-20. Services/__init__.py

```
from .AddPost import add_post
from .GetFeed import get_feed
```

Although the application is not yet complete due to the absence of the key components that will make it interactive for users, it can still function as a stand-alone service for any software, as it is structured end-to-end to serve a clear purpose of adding and retrieving posts with filtering applied to the data. To wrap things up, we will place our Streamlit visual components within a class-like structure for consistency with the rest of the code base.

Additionally, instead of directly using the service function by importing it, we can introduce the concept of *dependency injection*. This pattern, widely used in strongly typed languages like C# and Java, allows different implementations of the same function to be provided to the class if needed, such as when creating test cases where an actual post should be avoided. In addition to improving testability, this pattern is preferred in many frameworks due to its readability.

Listing 3-21. FeedView.py

```
import streamlit as st
from Models import Post
from typing import Callable
class FeedView:
    def __init__(self, get_feed_func: Callable[[], list]):
        posts = get_feed_func()
        for post in posts:
            _PostView(post)
```

```
class _PostView:
    def __init__(self, post: Post):
    # Renders the feed from the posts
        st.write(f'**{post.creator_name}**: {post.content} |
        _{post.posting_date}_')
```

Listing 3-22. AddPostView.py

```
import datetime
import streamlit as st
from Models import Post
from typing import Callable
class AddPostView:
    def __init__(self, add_post_func: Callable[[Post], bool]):
    # Adds the required fields to the post

        user_name_text = st.text_input('Displayed name? ')
        post_text = st.text_input('What is in your mind? ')
        clicked = st.button('Post')
        if clicked:
            post = Post(
                creator_name=user_name_text,
                content=post_text,
                posting_date=datetime.datetime.now()
            )
            did_add = add_post_func(post)
            if did_add:
                st.success('Post added! ')
            else:
                st.error('Error adding post')
```

Listing 3-23. main.py

```
import streamlit as st
from Views import FeedView, AddPostView
from Services import get_feed, add_post
AddPostView(add_post)
st.write('___')
FeedView(get_feed)
```

3.4.2. Fragmenting Parts of the Application

Another useful practice that comes in handy when organizing your
Streamlit application is to fragment widgets into modular parts of code
using the @st.fragment decorator. Basically, instead of re-running the
entire script every time something changes, you can wrap parts of your
application inside a fragment. This creates an isolated container with
its own state that only re-executes when needed, making it especially
useful for applications with heavy computations or multiple independent
sections. As an example, please refer to Listing 3-24.

Listing 3-24. fragmenting.py

```
import streamlit as st

# Define a fragment
@st.fragment
def my_fragment():
    name = st.text_input('Enter your name')
    if name:
        st.write(f'Hello, {name}!')

st.write('This runs every time. ')
my_fragment()  # Only this part re-runs when the input changes
st.write('This also stays the same.')
```

3.4.3. Best Practices for Folder Structuring

The example discussed in Section 3.4 can have all the files placed in the project's root folder. While this setup might result in a bug-free application initially, it can lead to confusion for anyone reading or maintaining the code as the application grows. To address this, we should structure the files into folders and expose them as modules, making them easier to integrate into other Python scripts in a clean and professional manner. A folder structure like the one shown in Figure 3-19 groups similar files together. The _init_.py script is included in every subfolder to export the files within it as modules, as demonstrated in Listing 5. In the API/_init_. py script, as shown in Listing 6, we expose an instance of the class rather than the class itself. The underscore before the class instance name is a naming convention to indicate that this property is intended to be private to this script. This serves as a warning to developers when trying to access it directly, particularly in IDEs that highlight such naming patterns.

Listing 3-25. Views/_init_.py

```
from .AddPostView import AddPostView
from .FeedView import FeedView
```

Listing 3-26. API/_init_.py

```
from .API import API as _API
api_instance = _API()
```

It is important to note that in Listing 3-25 and 3-26, the imports are from a relative path to a file, not an absolute one. This is evident from the presence of the "dot" in front of *.AddPostView* and *.FeedView*. The dot indicates that the file being imported is located in the same folder as the importing file, rather than searching for it in the project's root folder.

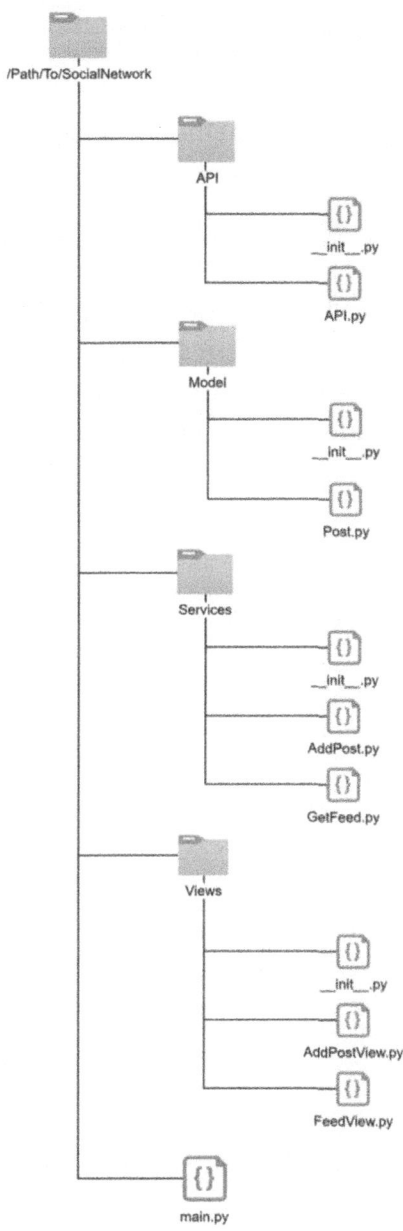

Figure 3-19. *Organized folder structure for Figure 3-18*

3.5. Summary

In this chapter, we explored the various ways to design the frontend of a Streamlit application. We covered methods for configuring color schemes and themes, as well as organizing the page with features like columns, expanders, sidebars, and containers, giving developers the tools to create tailored user interfaces. Additionally, we discussed how to build multipage and subpage applications with a modular and scalable system architecture. Finally, we looked at ways to display dynamic content and visualizations using Streamlit's powerful placeholder feature. In the next chapter, we will dive into the fundamentals of caching large datasets, data mutation, and rendering both static and interactive data visualizations.

CHAPTER 4

Managing and Visualizing Data

As with any web application, data management is an integral part of the process. With the rise of big data, there is a growing need to develop techniques that can handle the sheer volume of data in an efficient and robust manner. In this chapter, we will explore some of the key methods used to manage big data. Specifically, we will cover how to encode large multimedia files and dataframes into bytes, allowing for more robust storage in database systems or memory. Next, we will demonstrate the utility of Streamlit's built-in caching capabilities, which can be used to cache data, function executions, and objects to significantly reduce execution time on subsequent runs of the application. Finally, we will look at techniques for mutating dataframes and tables within our application on demand.

In the second part of this chapter, we will delve into the depths of data visualization, with a special focus on the Plotly visualization library for Python. We will provide boilerplate scripts that can be used to render basic, statistical, time-series, geospatial, and animated data visualizations in Streamlit.

© Mohammad Khorasani, Mohamed Abdou, Javier Hernández Fernández 2025
M. Khorasani et al., *Streamlit for Web Development*,
https://doi.org/10.1007/979-8-8688-1826-4_4

4.1. Data Management

The need to wrangle data is inherent in most, if not all, web applications. While we will not dive into the depths of pre- and post-processing data in this section, we will explore some of the most effective methods for managing data, with a particular focus on big data.

4.1.1. Processing Bytes Data

Depending on your application, you may need to work with binary/bytes data. For example, you might need to stream multimedia content or store files in a database system. Fortunately, Streamlit handles much of the overhead involved in dealing with such data. By using the `st.image`, `st.video`, and `st.audio` commands, we can natively process not only saved files on disk but also Numpy arrays, URLs, and, most importantly, bytes data.

    While structured databases will be covered in more detail in Section 5.1, it is worth noting here that almost any bytes data can be saved and retrieved in a PostgreSQL table, provided the column data type is set to `bytea`. This is especially useful when working with large objects, such as image, video, and audio files, which need to be stored as blobs (binary large objects). For these purposes, you will need to encode your data as follows.

Text

String and text can simply be encoded as follows for storage:

```
bytes_data = b'Hello world'
# Or alternatively
text = 'Hello world'
bytes_data = text.encode()
```

110

Subsequently, encoded string or text may be decoded as follows:

```
bytes_data.decode()
```

The default encoding used in the preceding method will be *UTF-8* unless otherwise specified.

Multimedia

To convert any uploaded image, video, or audio file to bytes data, simply use the following:

```
uploaded_file = st.file_uploader('Please upload a
multimedia file')
if uploaded_file is not None:
    bytes_data = uploaded_file.read()
```

Then, you may render the bytes data as an image, video, or audio by using the following commands:

```
# Image
st.image(bytes_data)
st.video(bytes_data)
# Audio
st.audio(bytes_data)
```

Dataframes

To read and display dataframes, you may use the following method:

```
import pandas as pd
uploaded_file = st.file_uploader('Please upload a CSV file',
type='csv')
if uploaded_file is not None:
    df = pd.read_csv(uploaded_file)
    st.write(df)
```

Alternatively, to encode dataframes (for storage as BLOB data in databases, for example), you can use the Python module *StringIO*, which stores content, such as CSV files, in memory as a file-like object, also known as string-based I/O. These objects can then be accessed by other functions and libraries, such as Pandas, as shown in the following:

```
from io import StringIO
import pandas as pd
uploaded_file = st.file_uploader('Please upload a CSV file',
type='csv')
if uploaded_file is not None:
    stringio = StringIO(uploaded_file.getvalue().decode())
    st.write(pd.read_csv(stringio))
```

Please note that while you can use the preceding method to store Pandas dataframes as string-based I/O, you cannot store the StringIO object directly in a database. To store a Pandas dataframe, it is better to save it as a table using the Pandas command `dataframe.to_sql`, which will be covered in detail in later sections.

4.1.2. Caching Big Data

Given the sheer magnitude of data available to us, it may sometimes be necessary to cache data in volatile storage for quicker access later. Streamlit offers native methods to cache both data you can store in a database and data you cannot, using the `@st.cache_data` and `@st.cache_resource` decorators, respectively. You simply write a function that returns data or an object and precede it with the appropriate decorator to leverage this feature. The first time you invoke the function, the returned data or object is cached in memory. For every subsequent invocation, the return will come from the cache, not the function itself, unless you change the function's arguments.

You can use Streamlit's caching feature with Listing 4-1 to benchmark the percentage of runtime saved by retrieving your dataframe from the cache. As shown in Figure 4-1, there is a significant positive effect on runtime, especially as the dataframe grows to over 100,000 rows. The effect starts to level off at around 100,000,000 rows, with roughly 70% of runtime saved.

Listing 4-1. cache.py

```python
import streamlit as st
import pandas as pd
import numpy as np
import time
@st.cache_data
def dataframe(rows):
    df = pd.DataFrame(
        np.random.randn(rows, 5),
        columns=('col %d' % i for i in range(5)))
    return df
runtime = pd.DataFrame(data={'Number of rows':[10, 100,
1000, 10000, 100000, 1000000, 10000000, 100000000], 'First
runtime (s)':None, 'Second runtime (s)':None, 'Runtime saved
(%)':None})
for i in range(0,len(runtime)):
    start = time.time()
    dataframe(runtime.loc[i]['Number of rows'])
    stop = time.time()
    runtime.loc[i, 'First runtime (s)'] = stop - start
    start = time.time()
    dataframe(runtime.loc[i]['Number of rows'])
    stop = time.time()
    runtime.loc[i, 'Second runtime (s)'] = stop - start
```

113

```
runtime.loc[i, 'Runtime saved (%)'] = 100 -
int(100*(runtime.loc[i, 'Second runtime (s)']/runtime.loc[i,
'First runtime (s)']))
st.write(runtime)
```

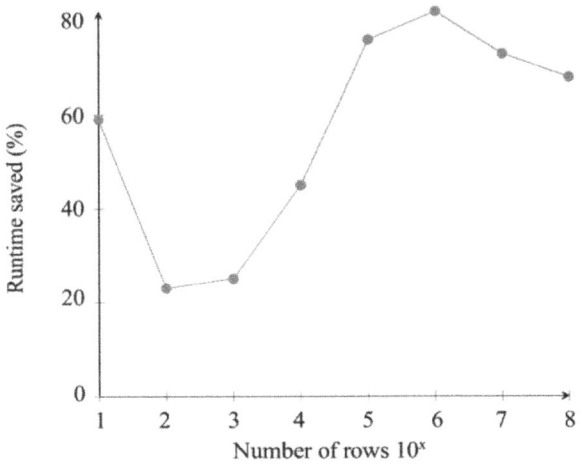

Figure 4-1. *Average percent runtime saved for six trials vs. number of rows while using st.cache_data*

4.1.3. Mutating Data in Real Time

You may need to mutate data, specifically dataframes, on demand within your application. Whether it is filtering a time-series dataset based on a given date-time range or appending data to an existing column, mutating data is often necessary. To that end, Streamlit provides the option to mutate data natively or by using third-party toolkits, as demonstrated in the following sections.

Native Data Mutation

Streamlit offers an intuitive and native method to add data to existing tables using the st.add_rows command. With this method, you can easily append a dataframe to a previously created table and instantly regenerate and view any associated charts in real time, as shown in Listing 4-2 and Figures 4-2 and 4-3.

Listing 4-2. mutate_data_real_time.py

```
import streamlit as st
import pandas as pd
import random

def random_data(n):
    y = [random.randint(1, n) for value in range(n)]
    return y

if __name__ == '__main__':
    df1 = pd.DataFrame(data={'y': [1, 2]})
    # Create columns for table and chart
    col1, col2 = st.columns([1, 3])
    with col1:
        # Use st.dataframe for dynamic updates
        table = st.dataframe(df1)

    with col2:
        # Display the initial chart
        chart = st.line_chart(df1)
        # User input for number of rows to add
        n = st.number_input('Number of rows to add', 0, 10, 1)
        # Update button
        if st.button('Update'):
            y = random_data(n)
            df2 = pd.DataFrame(data={'y': y})
```

```
# Append the new data to the existing dataframe
table.add_rows(df2)
chart.add_rows(df2)
```

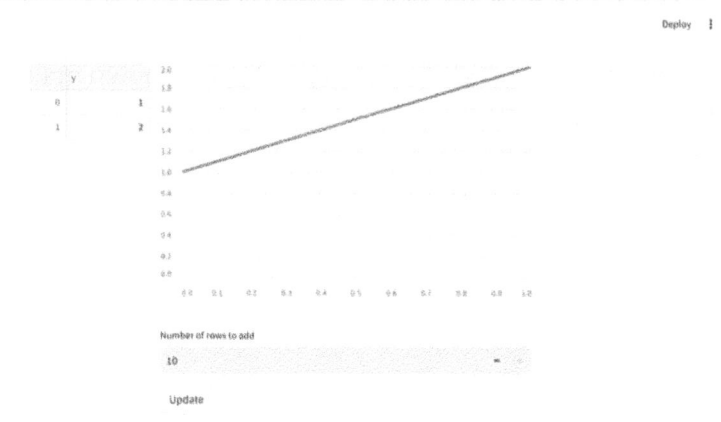

Figure 4-2. *Mutating data in real time using Listing 4-2*

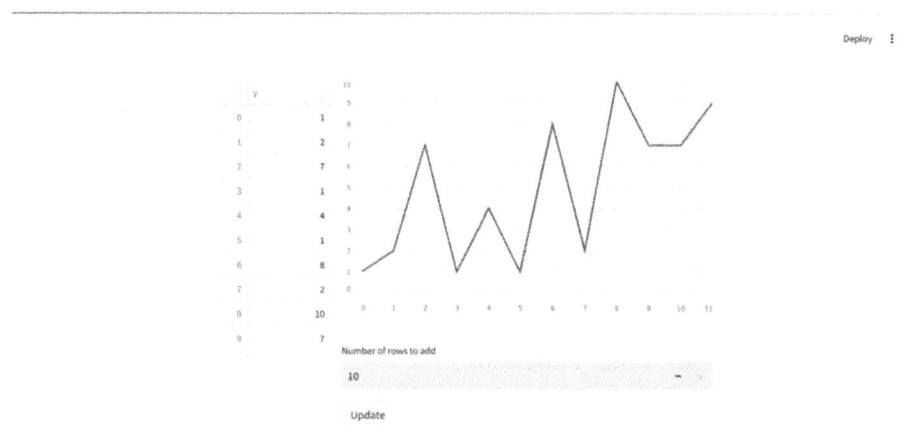

Figure 4-3. *Mutating data in real time using Listing 4-2 (continued)*

4.1.4. Advanced and Interactive Data Mutation

While Streamlit's native method of mutating data allows you to append rows to existing dataframes and charts, it does not provide other advanced data manipulation methods, such as modifying individual cells, removing data, or filtering. Fortunately, a highly versatile third-party component called *streamlit-aggrid* fills this gap. Built on top of the AG Grid library for JavaScript frameworks, streamlit-aggrid displays data in an interactive grid widget, allowing users to manipulate data with filtering, sorting, selecting, updating, pivoting, aggregating, querying, and many other methods. For more information on additional features, visit www.ag-grid.com.

To use streamlit-aggrid in your Streamlit application, you first need to initiate the widget and configure the features you require. Then, you can insert your Pandas dataframe using the AgGrid() command. The widget will be rendered, and the return value, when invoked, will be provided as a dictionary. To access the data within the widget, retrieve the data key from the dictionary. Similarly, to access the selected rows, you must retrieve the selected_rows key. The data will be returned as a table, while the selected rows will be returned as a list of dictionaries.

Specifically, Listing 4-3 will enable you to perform create, read, update, and delete operations on any provided dataset, as shown below:

- Create: To create a new record in the widget, you can simply append an empty row to the end of the dataframe as follows:

```
index = len(df)
df_new['data'].loc[index,:] = 'None'
df_new['data'].to_csv(path, index=False)
st.rerun()
```

- Read: You can read the data by rendering the dataframe as a grid widget. Note that this step must be performed before any other operation in your script, and the widget should be invoked with a new name, different from the original dataframe:

```
df = pd.read_csv(path)
df = df.fillna('None')
index = len(df)
gb = GridOptionsBuilder.from_dataframe(df)
gb.configure_side_bar()
gb.configure_default_column(groupable=True, value=True,
enableRowGroup=True, aggFunc='sum',editable=True)
gb.configure_selection(selection_mode='multiple', use_
checkbox=True)
gridOptions = gb.build()
df_new = AgGrid(df,gridOptions=gridOptions,enable_
enterprise_modules=True, update_mode=GridUpdateMode.
MODEL_CHANGED)
```

- Update: You can interactively update the value of each individual cell in the widget and immediately save the modified value to disk, as follows:

```
if not df.equals(df_new['data']):
    df_new['data'].to_csv(path, index=False)
    st.rerun()
```

- Delete: You can also delete any row whose checkbox has been selected in the widget, as follows:

```
if len(df_new['selected_rows']) > 0:
    exclude = pd.DataFrame(df_new['selected_rows'])
```

```
pd.merge(df_new['data'], exclude, how='outer',
indicator=True).query('_merge == "left_only"').
drop('_merge', 1).to_csv(path, index=False)
st.rerun()
```

In addition, you can choose to delete duplicate rows by using the following method:

```
df_new['data'] = df_new['data'].drop_duplicates()
df_new['data'].to_csv(path, index=False)
st.rerun()
```

Please note that for our create, update, and delete operations, we are using the st. rerun() command to automatically rerun the script after a modification is made. This is necessary to use it to render the modified widget without requiring further input from the user. Alternatively, you can add a dummy button to rerun the script and update the widget when clicked by the user, as shown below:

```
if st.button('Update'):
    pass
```

The final rendered widget can be seen in Figure 4-4.

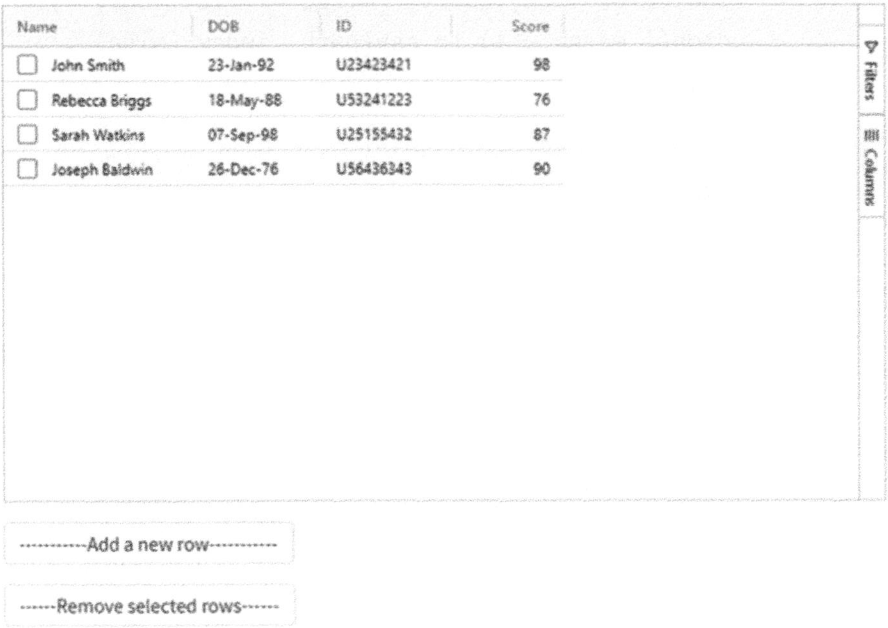

Name	DOB	ID	Score	
☐ John Smith	23-Jan-92	U23423421	98	
☐ Rebecca Briggs	18-May-88	U53241223	76	
☐ Sarah Watkins	07-Sep-98	U25155432	87	
☐ Joseph Baldwin	26-Dec-76	U56436343	90	

▽ Filters   ▥ Columns

-----------Add a new row-----------

------Remove selected rows------

Figure 4-4. *Mutating data in real time using Listing 4-3*

In addition to data mutation capabilities, the *streamlit-aggrid* widget offers a range of filtering and aggregation options. On the right pane of the widget, you can use the Filters tab to filter ordinal columns based on entries and numerical columns using simple mathematical conditions, as shown in Figure 4-5. Similarly, the *Columns* tab allows you to aggregate numerical columns, as seen in Figure 4-6. Please note that both filtering and aggregation are non-mutable features and are intended solely for visual purposes.

Listing 4-3. crud.py

```python
import streamlit as st
import pandas as pd
from st_aggrid import AgGrid
from st_aggrid.shared import GridUpdateMode
from st_aggrid.grid_options_builder import GridOptionsBuilder
def crud(path):
    df = pd.read_csv(path)
    df = df.fillna('None')
    index = len(df)
    # Initiate the streamlit-aggrid widget
    gb = GridOptionsBuilder.from_dataframe(df)
    gb.configure_side_bar()
    gb.configure_default_column(groupable=True, value=True,
    enableRowGroup=True, aggFunc='sum',editable=True)
    gb.configure_selection(selection_mode='multiple', use_
    checkbox=True)
    gridOptions = gb.build()
    # Insert the dataframe into the widget
    df_new = AgGrid(df,gridOptions=gridOptions,enable_
    enterprise_modules=True, update_mode=GridUpdateMode.MODEL_
    CHANGED)
    # Add a new row to the widget
    if st.button('-----------Add a new row-----------'):
        df_new['data'].loc[index,:] = 'None'
        df_new['data'].to_csv(path, index=False)
        st.rerun()
    # Save the dataframe to disk if the widget has been
    modified
    if df.equals(df_new['data']) is False:
        df_new['data'].to_csv(path, index=False)
```

```
        st.rerun()
    # Remove selected rows from the widget
    if st.button('-----------Remove selected rows-----------'):
        if len(df_new['selected_rows']) > 0:
            exclude = pd.DataFrame(df_new['selected_rows'])
            pd.merge(df_new['data'], exclude, how='outer',
            indicator=True).query('_merge == "left_only"').
            drop('_merge', 1).to_csv(path, index=False)
            st.rerun()
        else:
            st.warning('Please select at least one row')
    # Check for duplicate rows
    if df_new['data'].duplicated().sum() > 0:
        st.warning(f'**Number of duplicate rows:** { df_
        new['data'].duplicated().sum()}')
        if st.button('-----------Delete duplicates-----------'):
            df_new['data'] = df_new['data'].drop_duplicates()
            df_new['data'].to_csv(path, index=False)
            st.rerun()
if __name__ == '__main__':
    st.title('Data')
    crud('data.csv')
```

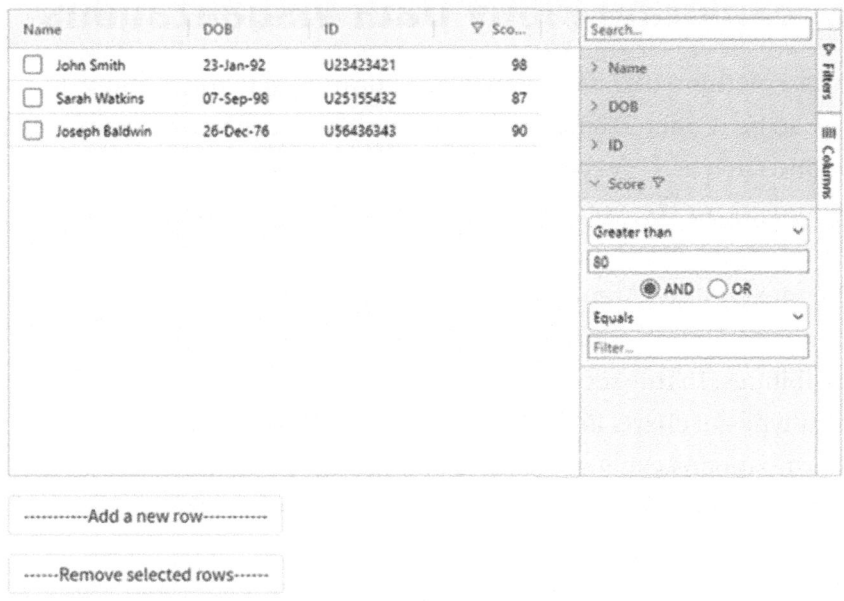

Figure 4-5. *Filtering data with the streamlit-aggrid widget*

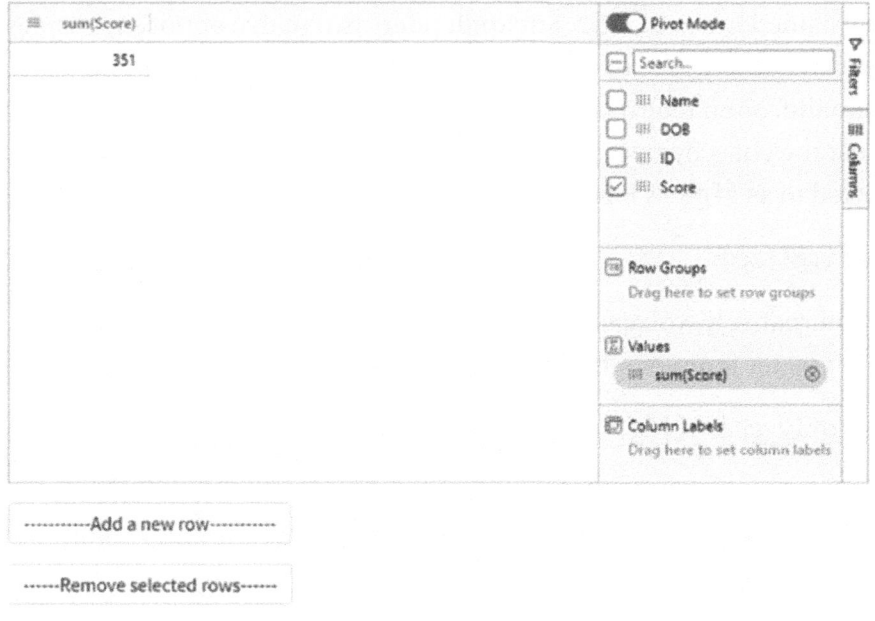

Figure 4-6. *Aggregating data with the streamlit-aggrid widget*

4.2. Exploring Plotly Data Visualizations

There is a plethora of data visualization libraries in Python, many of which can be rendered easily in Streamlit. Whether you use a more native command such as `st.vega_lite_chart` or resort to the Swiss Army knife command, `st.write`, you have at your disposal the ability to visualize data extensively. Among the many visualization libraries, one stands out the most: Plotly. Arguably one of the most versatile, interactive, and visually appealing visualization stacks available, Plotly offers a wealth of possibilities. In this section, we will showcase some of the most relevant types of charts for web development. However, the following list is by no means exhaustive. For a complete list of charts, please refer to Plotly's official documentation at `https://plotly.com/python/` for a complete list.

4.2.1. Rendering Plotly in Streamlit

As explained in Section 4.2, Streamlit offers two native options to display Plotly and other types of charts. Specifically, you can use the `st.write` command, often referred to as the Swiss Army knife of commands, to render the chart by simply writing the Plotly chart object (hereafter referred to as `fig`), as follows:

```
st.write(fig)
```

Alternatively, you can use the `st.plotly_chart` command, which offers greater functionality when rendering Plotly charts:

```
st.plotly_chart(fig, use_container_width=True)
```

You can use the *st.plotly_chart* command with the additional `use_container_width` argument to specify whether the chart width should be restricted to the encapsulating column width.

4.2.2. Basic Charts

In this section, we will cover Plotly line, scatter, bar, and pie charts. Before proceeding, we will first import all the necessary libraries for this section, as listed below:

```
import streamlit as st
import numpy as np
import pandas as pd
import plotly.express as px
import plotly.graph_objects as go
```

For consistency, we will use the same randomly generated Pandas dataframe (shown below) as our dataset to generate each of the charts:

```
data = np.random.randint(0, 10, size=(40,2))
df = pd.DataFrame(data, columns=['Column 1', 'Column 2'])
```

Line Chart

```
fig = go.Figure()
fig.add_trace(go.Scatter(x=df.index, y=df['Column 1'],
                    mode='lines',
                    name='Column 1'))
fig.add_trace(go.Scatter(x=df.index, y=df['Column 2'],
                    mode='lines',
                    name='Column 2'))
```

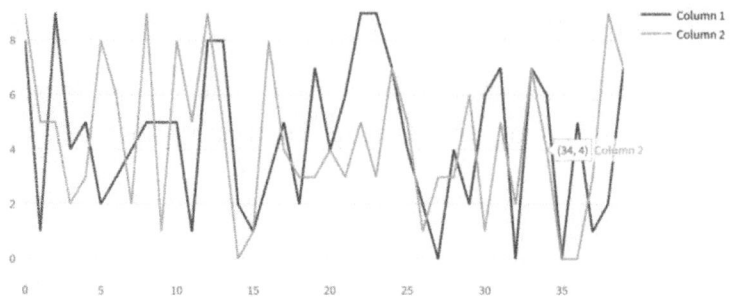

Scatter Chart

```
fig = go.Figure(data=go.Scatter(
    y = df['Column 1'],
    mode='markers',
    marker=dict(
        size=10,
        color=df['Column 2'], # Set color equal to a variable
        colorscale='Viridis', # Select colorscale
        showscale=True
    )
))
```

Bar Chart

```
fig = go.Figure(data=[
    go.Bar(name='Column 1', x=df.index, y=df['Column 1']),
    go.Bar(name='Column 2', x=df.index, y=df['Column 2'])
])
```

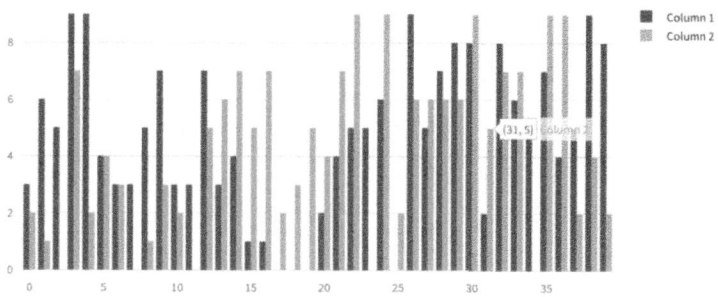

Pie Chart

```
fig = px.pie(df, values=df.sum(), names=df.columns)
```

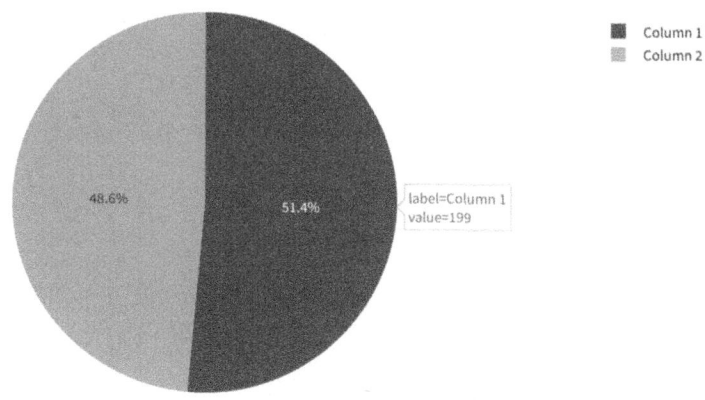

Chart Layout

To update the properties and layout of the chart, you can use the update_
layout method, as shown below:

```
fig = go.Figure(data=[
    go.Bar(name='Column 1', x=df.index, y=df['Column 1']),
    go.Bar(name='Column 2', x=df.index, y=df['Column 2'])
])
fig.update_layout(
    title='Column 1 vs. Index',
    xaxis_title='Index',
    yaxis_title='Value',
    legend_title='Columns',
    font=dict(
        family='Arial',
        size=10,
        color='black'
    )
)
```

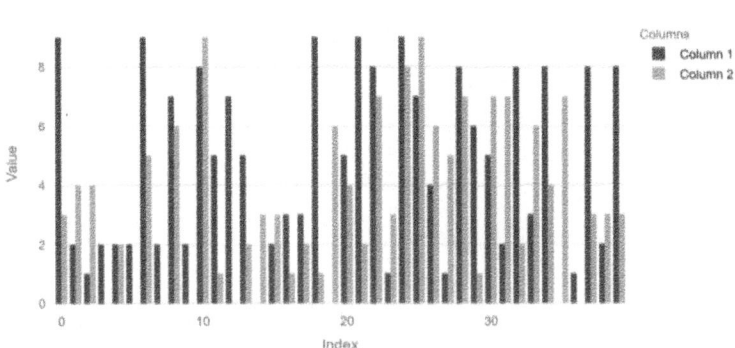

4.2.3. Statistical Charts

In this section, we will generate a Plotly histogram and box plot. The following randomly generated dataframe will be used for both charts:

```
data = np.random.randn(40, 2)
df = pd.DataFrame(data, columns=['Column 1', 'Column 2'])
```

Histogram

```
fig = go.Figure()
fig.add_trace(go.Histogram(name='Column 1', x=df['Column 1']))
fig.add_trace(go.Histogram(name='Column 2', x=df['Column 2']))
fig.update_layout(barmode='overlay')
fig.update_traces(opacity=0.75)
```

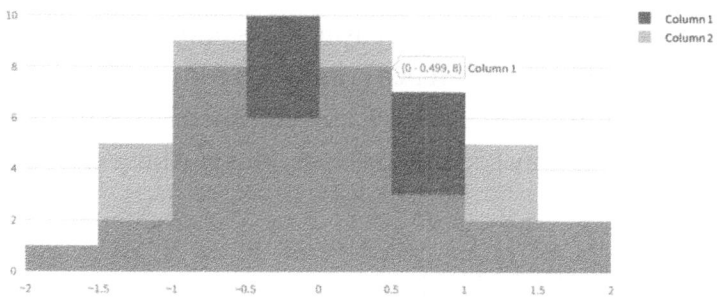

Box Plot

```
fig = go.Figure()
fig.add_trace(go.Box(
    y=df['Column 1'],
    name='Column 1',
    boxmean='sd' # Display mean, median and standard deviation
))
fig.add_trace(go.Box(
```

```
    y=df['Column 2'],
    name='Column 2',
    boxmean='sd' # Display mean, median and standard deviation
))
```

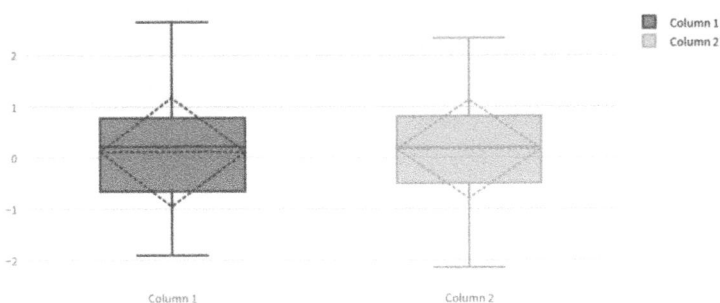

4.2.4. Time-Series Charts

Time-series charts can be generated using the same line chart function
from Section 4.2; the only difference is that the index provided must be in
a date-time format. You can use the following function to create a Pandas
dataframe with randomly generated values, indexed between a specified
range of dates:

```
data = np.random.randn(40, 2)
df = pd.DataFrame(data, columns=['Column 1', 'Column 2'])
df.index = pd.date_range(start='1/1/2018', end='2/9/2018',
freq='D')
```

Then, the line chart function can be invoked as follows:

```
fig = px.line(df, x=df.index, y=df.columns)
```

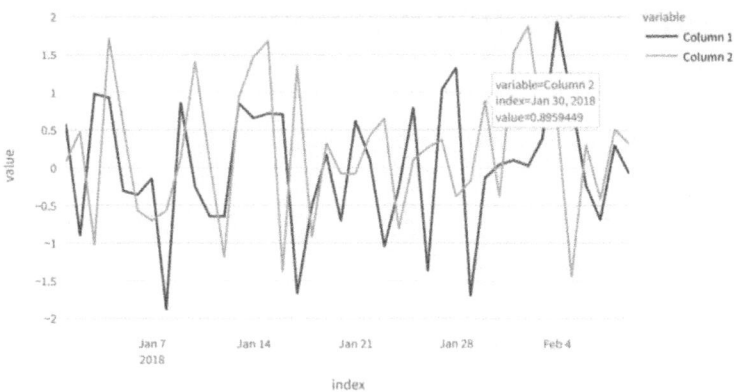

4.2.5. Geospatial Charts

Depending on your application, you may need to render interactive maps with geospatial data. Fortunately, Plotly offers geospatial charts with a wide range of features and attributes. In this section, we will focus on one such chart, the choropleth map, using a dataset of world GDP per capita from 1990 to 2023 [22]:

```
df = pd.read_csv('gdp-per-capita-worldbank.csv').sort_
values(by='Year', ascending=False)
fig = px.choropleth(df, locations=df['Code'],
    color=df['GDP per capita, PPP (constant 2021
    international $)'],
    hover_name=df['Entity'])
```

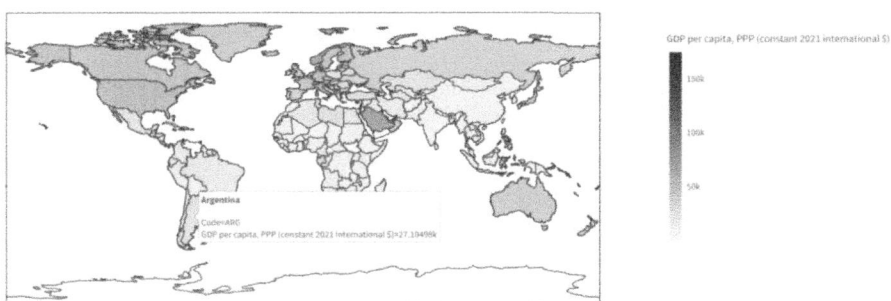

4.2.6. Animated Visualizations

With Plotly, you can incorporate simple animations into your charts. This is especially useful when displaying time-varying values in a time-series dataset. However, you are not limited to time-series data and can animate other types of numeric data as well. In this section, we will animate the same dataset of world GDP per capita from 1990 to 2023 [22], using both an animated bubble map and a bar chart, as shown below.

Animated Bubble Map

```
df = pd.read_csv('gdp-per-capita-worldbank.csv').sort_
values(by=['Year', 'Entity'])
fig = px.scatter_geo(df, locations=df['Code'],
    color=df['GDP per capita, PPP (constant 2017
    international $)'],
    hover_name=df['Entity'],
    size=df['GDP per capita, PPP (constant 2017
    international $)'],
    animation_frame=df['Year'])
```

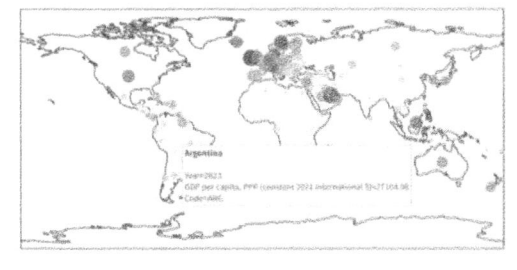
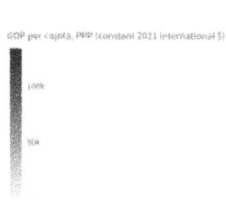

Animated Bar Chart

```
df = pd.read_csv('gdp-per-capita-worldbank.csv').sort_
values(by=['Year', 'Entity'])
df = df[df['GDP per capita, PPP (constant 2021 international
$)'] > 50000]
fig = px.bar(df, x=df['Entity'],
    y=df['GDP per capita, PPP (constant 2021
    international $)'],
    animation_frame=df['Year'])
```

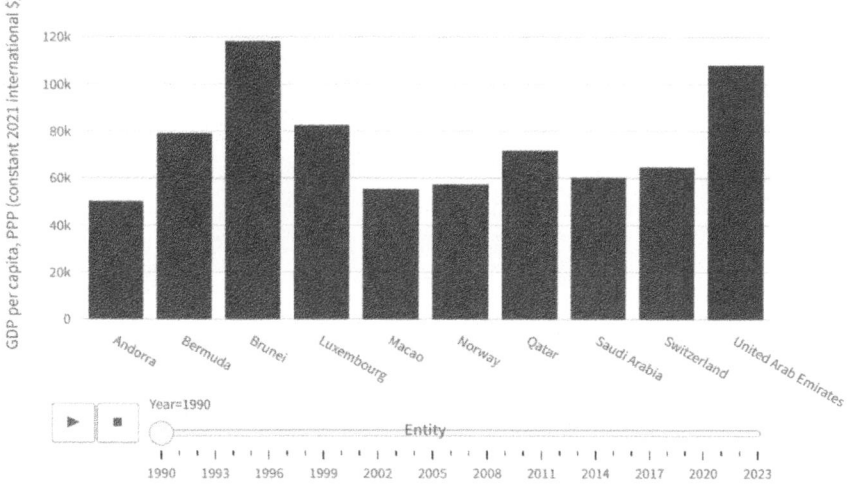

4.3. Summary

In this chapter, we explored several techniques for managing big data. Specifically, we learned how to encode multimedia files and dataframes into byte data, enabling the robust storage of large quantities of data in databases or memory. We also saw how Streamlit's caching functions can significantly reduce execution time when our application is rerun. Additionally, we covered both a native technique and a third-party toolkit for mutating dataframes and tables within our application. In the latter part of this chapter, we gained the knowledge to generate various types of charts, including basic, statistical, time-series, geospatial, and animated charts in Streamlit, using the Plotly data visualization library. By the end of this chapter, we should have developed the ability to manage and visualize data at varying scales efficiently and robustly within our web application.

CHAPTER 5

Integrating Databases

Before we begin utilizing application data and user interaction insights, we must first understand how to store and manage data of varying schemas persistently using robust and distributed database systems in an organized manner. This chapter will focus on two types of database systems: relational and nonrelational. We will demonstrate use cases for each by interfacing with PostgreSQL and MongoDB. Additionally, advanced features such as fuzzy matching and full-text indexing will be introduced, with boilerplate code provided as building blocks for your own applications. Finally, you will learn how to seamlessly integrate these databases with Streamlit to visualize data and perform create, read, update, and delete (CRUD) operations. For full comprehension of this chapter, the installation of PostgreSQL and pgAdmin is required.

5.1. Relational Databases

Since most apps built with Streamlit manipulate data in one way or another, that data often needs to be stored on disk for later use. In many cases, the data follows a specific format—i.e., it is structured. We can leverage this characteristic by using a SQL database to store it. PostgreSQL will be the tool of choice for demonstrating this use case, as it is both free and open source.

© Mohammad Khorasani, Mohamed Abdou, Javier Hernández Fernández 2025
M. Khorasani et al., *Streamlit for Web Development*,
https://doi.org/10.1007/979-8-8688-1826-4_5

5.1.1. Introduction to SQL

Structured Query Language (SQL) is used to perform CRUD operations on data with a similar structure. *Same structure* data refers to different entries (rows) that share the same features (columns). An example of a relational SQL database is a company directory containing employee data, split into two separate tables: one for employees' personal information and another for their pay grades. Both types of data can be represented as tables in the database, as shown in Tables 5-1 and 5-2, where a one-to-one linkage between the tables indicates that every employee has a corresponding pay grade.

A one-to-one relationship exists when every row in one table corresponds to a unique ID in another table, extending the information of the first table with data from the second.

There are additional types of relationships between tables, such as one-to-many and many-to-many, but we will not cover them here, as they do not add further value to the purpose of this book. However, for the sake of real-world scenario demonstration, we will proceed with one-to-one relationships in some of the examples.

CRUD, which stands for Create, Read, Update, and Delete, refers to the main operations that can be performed within a database using SQL commands, as follows:

- Create: To make a new person entry with pay grade 3

  ```
  INSERT INTO Persons VALUES ("Charlie",
  "01/01/1995", 3);
  ```

- Read: To retrieve all pay grade data with a base salary level equal to L3

  ```
  SELECT * FROM INTO PayGradeLevels WHERE
  BaseSalary = "L3";
  ```

- Update: To update the pay grade of Bob to pay grade 2

  ```
  UPDATE Persons SET PayGradeId = 2 WHERE ID = 3;
  ```

- Delete: To remove pay grade 4 from existence

  ```
  DELETE FROM PayGradeLevels WHERE id = 4;
  ```

Table 5-1. *Persons table*

ID	Name	DOB	Pay Grade ID
1	Adam	01/01/1990	2
2	Sara	01/01/1980	1
3	Bob	01/01/1970	1
4	Alice	01/01/2000	3

Table 5-2. *Pay grade levels table*

ID	Base Salary	Reimbursements	Bonuses
1	L3	L2	L0
2	L1	L1	L1
3	L3	L3	L3
4	L1	L3	L1

One of the most important concepts to understand when building a database is the primary key. This refers to the ID in both Tables 5-1 and 5-2. A *primary key* is a unique, always valid (i.e., not null) identifier used to refer to a single row in a table. It is also indexed, meaning it is internally managed by the database in a way that significantly speeds up query performance when filtering by this ID.

It is worth noting that indexing is a feature that can be applied to any column—not just primary keys—but it is generally used with care. Indexing a column can increase its storage footprint to as much as twice its original size. However, indexing is highly beneficial when used on columns that are frequently searched, especially those representing IDs, as it enables faster data retrieval.

Another key term that backend developers often encounter is the *foreign key*. A foreign key is an ID that refers to a row in a different table. For example, the Pay Grade ID column in Table 5-1 acts as a foreign key pointing to the ID column in Table 5-2.

5.1.2. Connecting a PostgreSQL Database to Streamlit

First, we need to create the database and the tables described in Section 5.1 using *pgAdmin 4*, a graphical user interface (GUI) tool for managing PostgreSQL databases. Assuming pgAdmin 4 is already installed and configured on your system, we can proceed to create a new database by following the steps illustrated in Figures 5-1 and 5-2 sequentially.

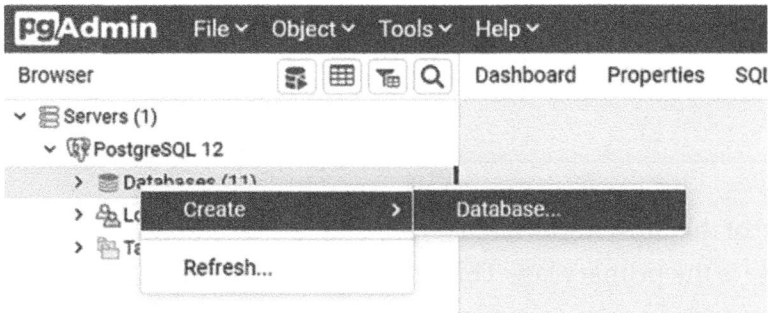

Figure 5-1. *Creating a new PostgreSQL database*

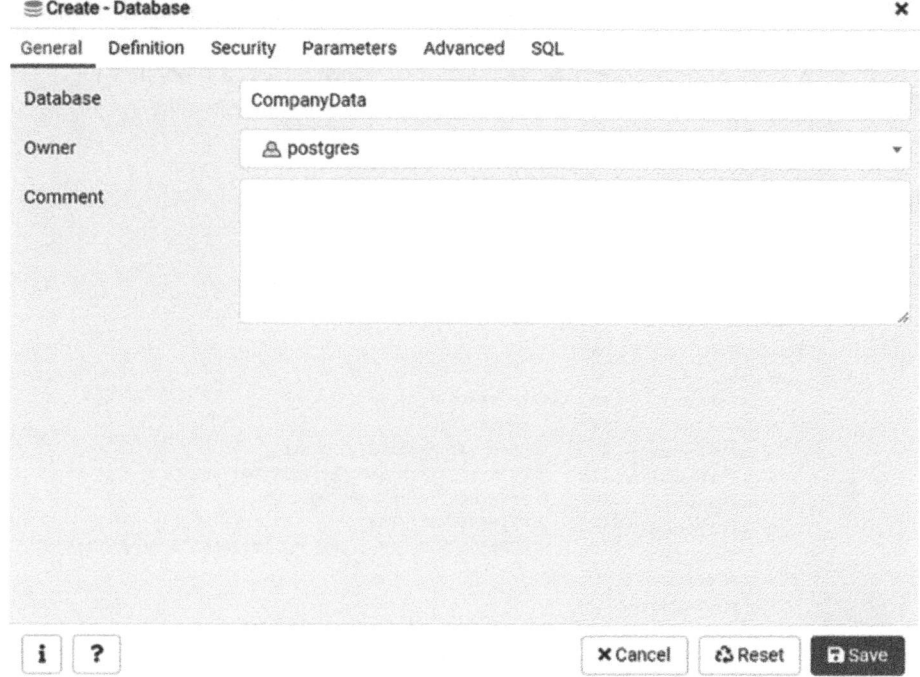

Figure 5-2. *Creating a new PostgreSQL database (continued)*

Once the database is ready, click the *Query Tool* in the top-left corner to run raw SQL commands. As shown in Figure 5-3, we will create two tables—each with a primary key, and one containing a foreign key. Some additional features of the columns—commonly referred to as constraints in database terminology—include setting columns as NOT NULL and enabling auto-incrementation.

Setting a column as NOT NULL instructs the database to reject any INSERT or UPDATE operation where that column is either missing or explicitly set to NULL. PostgreSQL provides a special data type called SERIAL, which automatically ensures the column is not null and enables auto-incrementation of its integer value for each new row inserted.

139

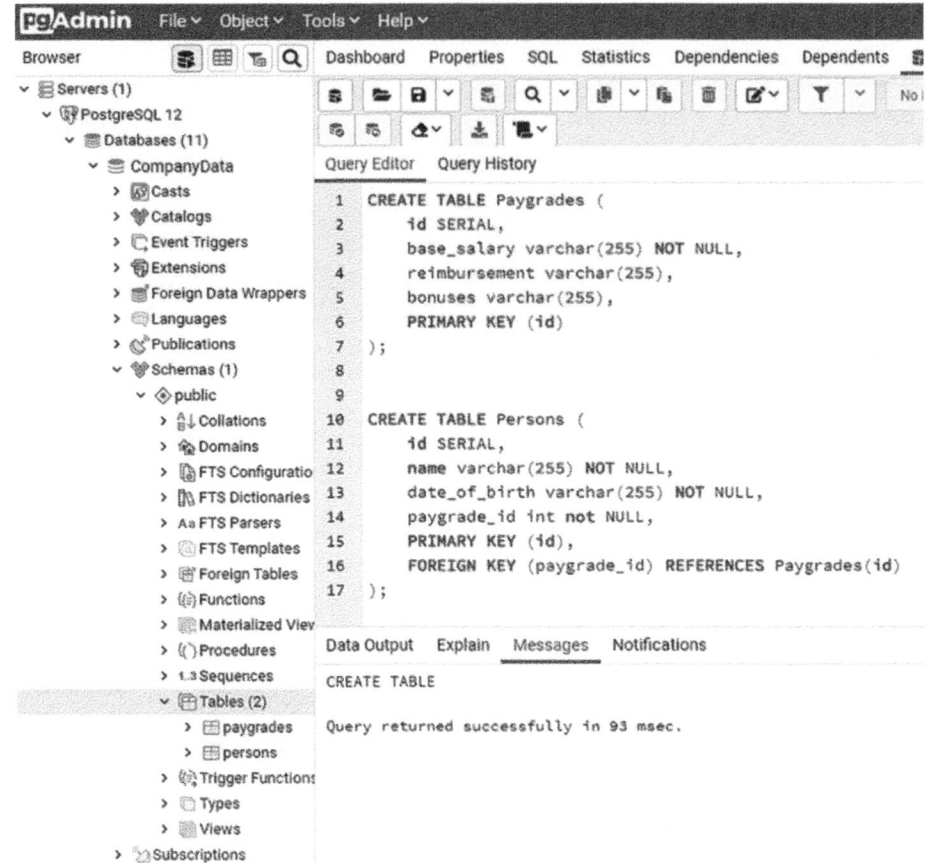

Figure 5-3. *Running SQL commands from create_tables.sql to create the database tables*

Before proceeding with the Streamlit integration, we will first insert some data into the database using raw SQL, as demonstrated in Figure 5-4. Notice that we did not need to manually set the ID values for either table—these are automatically generated by the database thanks to the SERIAL data type.

Next, we need to configure our database access credentials for use within Streamlit. These credentials—including the username and password—can be stored securely in various ways:

- As environment variables in a *.env* file

- In a *secrets.yaml* file (read and parsed by the app)

- Recommended: In a *secrets.toml* file located inside a *.streamlit* folder, as shown in Listing 5-1.

This *secrets.toml* file is automatically parsed by Streamlit, making the variables inside easily accessible to your application. For consistency and proper parsing, the database connection details should be grouped under a label like [db_postgres], which can then be referenced in your code.

⚠**Security Tip**   Always use strong passwords, especially if your database is publicly accessible. Weak passwords are susceptible to brute-force attacks, potentially exposing sensitive data.

Listing 5-1. .streamlit/secrets.toml

```
[db_postgres]
host = "127.0.0.1"
port = "5432"
user = "postgres"
password = "82qeD\t_K7n~`7A&"
dbname = "CompanyData"
```

Query Editor   Query History

```
1   INSERT INTO paygrades(base_salary, reimbursement, bonuses) VALUES ('L3', 'L2', 'L0');
2   INSERT INTO paygrades(base_salary, reimbursement, bonuses) VALUES ('L1', 'L1', 'L1');
3   INSERT INTO paygrades(base_salary, reimbursement, bonuses) VALUES ('L3', 'L3', 'L3');
4   INSERT INTO paygrades(base_salary, reimbursement, bonuses) VALUES ('L1', 'L3', 'L1');
5
6   INSERT INTO persons(name, date_of_birth, paygrade_id) VALUES ('Adam', '01/01/1990', 2);
7   INSERT INTO persons(name, date_of_birth, paygrade_id) VALUES ('Sara', '01/01/1980', 1);
8   INSERT INTO persons(name, date_of_birth, paygrade_id) VALUES ('Bob', '01/01/1970', 1);
9   INSERT INTO persons(name, date_of_birth, paygrade_id) VALUES ('Alice', '01/01/2000', 3);
```

Data Output   Explain   Messages   Notifications

INSERT 0 1

Query returned successfully in 55 msec.

Figure 5-4. *Inserting data using inserting_data.sql into the database*

To interface Python with PostgreSQL, we need to use a capable library, such as *psycopg3*. While psycopg3 is a great choice for this example, other libraries like *SQLAlchemy* can also accomplish the same task, and we will cover that in later chapters.

As mentioned in previous chapters, Streamlit automatically reruns the Python script whenever the user interacts with the app. This is not usually a concern, but in this case, it could lead to inefficiencies. For example, every time the app reruns, a new database connection will be established. To prevent this unnecessary overhead, we can cache the first established connection. Streamlit provides an easy way to do this using its native @ st.cache_resource decorator. This decorator can accept additional parameters, such as an expiration date for the cache. If the cache expires, the function will re-execute when called again. In Listing 5-2, line 5 demonstrates how to save the established connection in the cache.

Once a connection is established, we will need a cursor to execute SQL queries. It is important to properly dispose of the cursor after the query is executed to avoid memory issues. If the cursor is not closed, it will remain in memory, and as more queries are executed, this can lead to memory leaks—a nightmare for any developer. There are two ways to manage the cursor: manually closing it or using a context manager. The context manager will automatically close the cursor once its scope is exited. In Listing 5-2, lines 14 and 22 show examples of both methods, with their outputs illustrated in Figure 5-5.

Listing 5-2. main.py

```
import streamlit as st
import psycopg2
@st.cache_resource
def init_connection():
    return psycopg2.connect(**st.secrets['db_postrgres'])
conn = init_connection()
def run_query(query_str):
    cur = conn.cursor()
    cur.execute(query_str)
    data = cur.fetchall()
    cur.close()
    return data
def run_query_with_context_manager(query_str):
    with conn.cursor() as cur:
        cur.execute(query_str)
        return cur.fetchall()
query = st.text_input('Query')
c1, c2 = st.columns(2)
output = None
with c1:
    if st.button('Run with context manager'):
        output = run_query_with_context_manager(query)
```

```
with c2:
    if st.button('Run without context manager'):
        output = run_query(query)
st.write(output)
```

5.1.3. Displaying Tables in Streamlit

After querying data from the database, we can display it in plain text or use more visually engaging tools from Streamlit, which may require modifying how the data is represented.

In the data science and development communities, it is common to parse structured data, whether it is sensor readings, identification information, or any repeating data organized into a structured format, such as a Pandas dataframe. Dataframes are essentially Numpy arrays with additional functionality, including column names and SQL-like querying capabilities. Furthermore, they share the same efficient vectorization features as Numpy arrays, enabling parallelized mathematical computations on entire arrays rather than on individual elements.

Streamlit offers two ways to display dataframes. The first is with `st.table`, which provides a non-interactive representation of the dataframe, as shown in Figure 5-6. The second option is `st.dataframe`, which renders an interactive version of the dataframe. In this interactive format, users can sort any column by simply clicking its header, as demonstrated in Figure 5-7. However, there is a trade-off: this interactive functionality requires additional CPU and memory resources, which can slow down the application. The sorting operation, for instance, has a time complexity of $O(n*log(n))$, meaning that as the dataset grows, the application may experience performance degradation.

Listing 5-3. df_demo.py

```
import streamlit as st
import pandas as pd
df = pd.DataFrame([['Adam', '01/01/1990', 2],
                   ['Sara', '01/01/1980', 1],
                   ['Bob', '01/01/1970', 1],
                   ['Alice', '01/01/2000', 3]
                   ], columns=['Name', 'DOB', 'Paygrade ID'])
st.table(df)
st.dataframe(df)
```

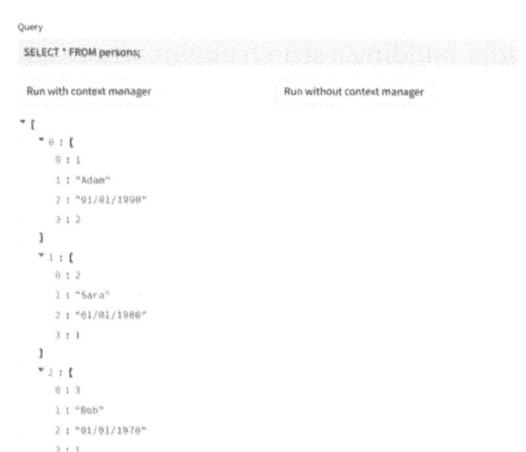

Figure 5-5. *Running user SQL commands from Streamlit*

	Name	DOB	Paygrade ID
0	Adam	01/01/1990	2
1	Sara	01/01/1980	1
2	Bob	01/01/1970	1
3	Alice	01/01/2000	3

Figure 5-6. *st.table from Listing 5-3*

	Name	DOB	Paygrade ID
0	Adam	01/01/1990	2
1	Sara	01/01/1980	1
2	Bob	01/01/1970	1
3	Alice	01/01/2000	3

Figure 5-7. st.dataframe from Listing 5-3

5.2. Nonrelational Databases

While in most use cases you will be working with a structured dataset, where the schema, attributes, data types, and metadata are known beforehand, there are instances where this information is not available. For example, consider building a search engine where users can upload documents of varying lengths, with different numbers of headers, images, and types of media. In such cases, it is nearly impossible to define a fixed schema or table structure to accommodate the data. This is where the utility of a NoSQL database, like MongoDB, becomes crucial. NoSQL databases are designed to handle and store unstructured or semi-structured data, offering flexibility in how the data is stored and queried.

5.2.1. Introduction to MongoDB

MongoDB allows you to store data as JSON documents, which can have varying attributes and data types, all within a *collection* that can have a dynamic schema. In this context, a document is similar to a row in a relational database, and a collection is analogous to a table. Even if your dataset starts off structured, using a NoSQL database like MongoDB can be beneficial as your application scales, especially when you begin to deal with unstructured data. Moreover, if you need advanced features such as full-text indexing (which indexes every word in every document within a collection) or fuzzy matching (which helps mitigate typos in queries), MongoDB is an ideal choice.

In this section, we will explore MongoDB's capabilities and demonstrate how it can be integrated with Streamlit by building a search engine for restaurants using a publicly available unstructured dataset of restaurant ratings. The goal of the application is to allow users to search for restaurants based on the type of cuisine and address. For the cuisine, we will use a simple one-to-one match with a predefined list of cuisine types to filter the data. For the address, full-text indexing will be necessary to match n-grams (continuous sequences of words or tokens) in borough and street address fields, which may be stored in different objects or arrays within the document, as shown in Figure 5-8. Additionally, fuzzy matching will be implemented to ensure that search queries with minor typos (at most two characters different) are still matched correctly with the relevant records.

5.2.2. Provisioning a Cloud Database

MongoDB can be set up both locally and in the cloud. However, to take advantage of the full-text indexing feature provided by MongoDB's *Atlas Search* service, you must host your database on the cloud. Below are the steps to do so:

1. Begin by setting up an account and project at `www.mongodb.com/atlas/database`.

2. Provision the free *M0 Sandbox* cluster, as shown in Figures 5-9 and 5-10. If needed, modify the hosted region to minimize latency between your database and server.

3. After provisioning the cluster, whitelist the IP
    addresses that will access the database in the
    Network Access menu. While not recommended, you
    can whitelist all addresses (as shown in Figure 5-11)
    to allow access from anywhere.

4. Next, create user credentials for database access
    from the *Overview* tab in the *Databases* menu, as
    shown in Figure 5-12.

```
_id: ObjectId("5eb3d668b31de5d588f4292a")
v address: Object
    building: "2780"
    v coord: Array
        0: -73.98241999999999
        1: 40.579505
    street: "Stillwell Avenue"
    zipcode: "11224"
  borough: "Brooklyn"
  cuisine: "American"
v grades: Array
    v 0: Object
        date: 2014-06-10T00:00:00.000+00:00
        grade: "A"
        score: 5
    v 1: Object
        date: 2013-06-05T00:00:00.000+00:00
        grade: "A"
        score: 7
    v 2: Object
        date: 2012-04-13T00:00:00.000+00:00
        grade: "A"
        score: 12
    v 3: Object
        date: 2011-10-12T00:00:00.000+00:00
        grade: "A"
        score: 12
  name: "Riviera Caterer"
  restaurant_id: "40356018"
```

Figure 5-8. *A sample document from the restaurants dataset*

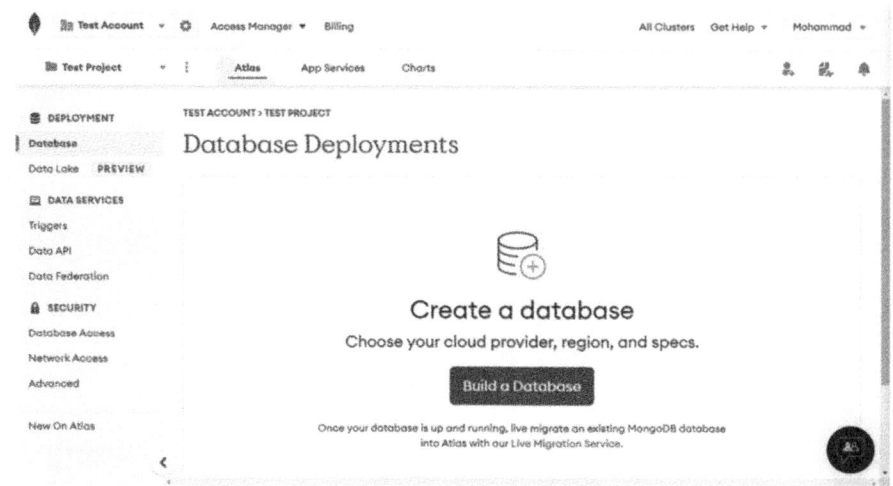

Figure 5-9.   *Setting up a MongoDB database*

5. Next, create a connection string by selecting the
    Connect your application option in the *Choose a
    connection method* tab. Then, choose the Python
    driver that best suits your application, as shown in
    Figures 5-13 and 5-14.

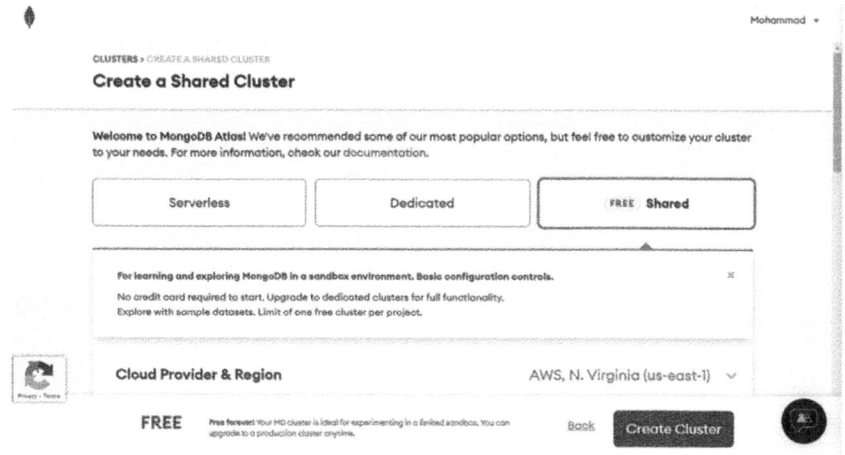

Figure 5-10.   *Provisioning a free M0 Sandbox cluster*

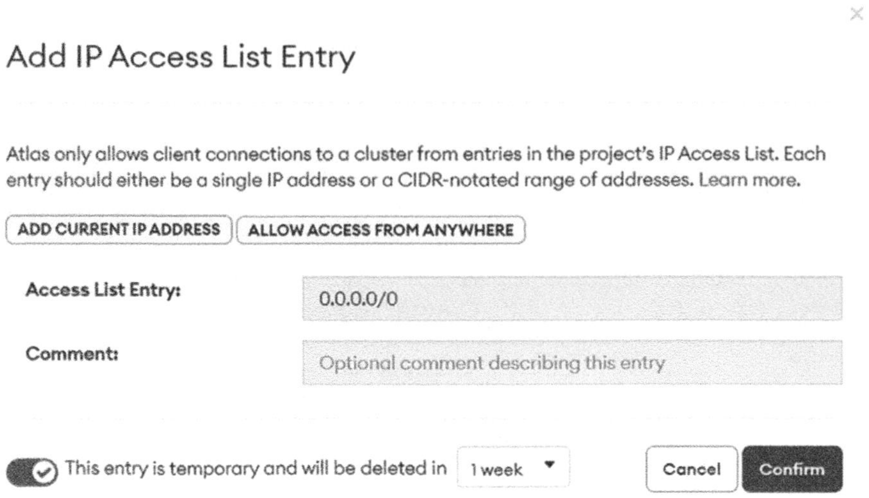

Add IP Access List Entry

Atlas only allows client connections to a cluster from entries in the project's IP Access List. Each entry should either be a single IP address or a CIDR-notated range of addresses. Learn more.

[ADD CURRENT IP ADDRESS] [ALLOW ACCESS FROM ANYWHERE]

Access List Entry: 0.0.0.0/0

Comment: Optional comment describing this entry

(✓) This entry is temporary and will be deleted in   [1 week ▾]   [Cancel]   [Confirm]

Figure 5-11. *Configuring network access to the database*

6. Finally, you can either upload your own dataset or load a sample dataset provided by MongoDB in the *Collections* tab under the *Databases* menu, as shown in Figure 5-15. For this example, we will use the sample *restaurants* collection from MongoDB's own datasets.

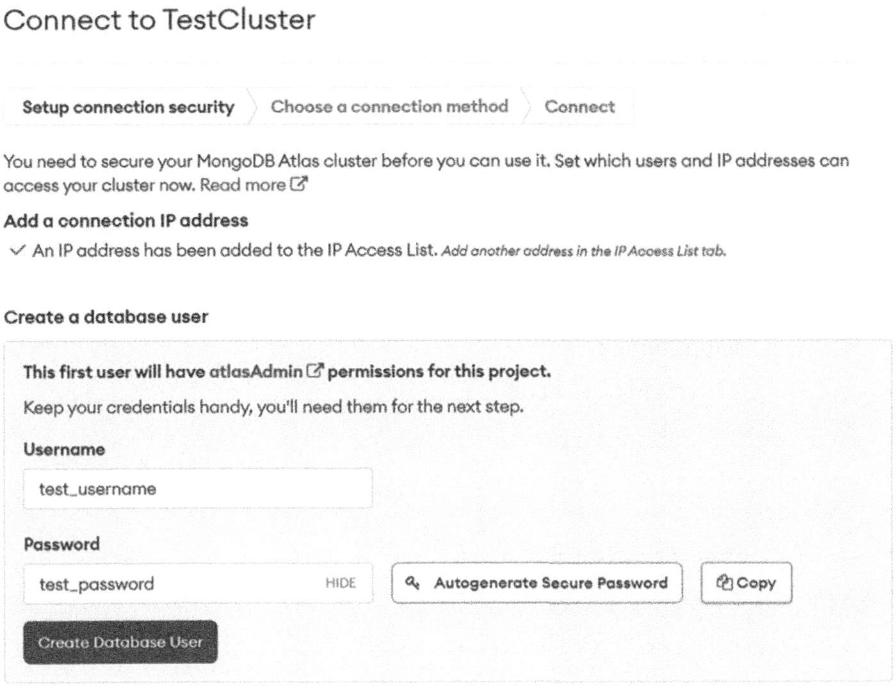

Connect to TestCluster

Setup connection security 〉 Choose a connection method 〉 Connect

You need to secure your MongoDB Atlas cluster before you can use it. Set which users and IP addresses can access your cluster now. Read more ☑

1. **Add a connection IP address**

   ✓ An IP address has been added to the IP Access List. *Add another address in the IP Access List tab.*

2. **Create a database user**

   This first user will have atlasAdmin ☑ permissions for this project.

   Keep your credentials handy, you'll need them for the next step.

   Username

   | test_username |

   Password

   | test_password | HIDE | 🔍 Autogenerate Secure Password | 📋 Copy |

   Create Database User

Figure 5-12. *Creating user credentials for the database*

5.2.3. Full-Text Indexing

Full-text indexing indexes every token in all objects across all documents in a database. It is a highly powerful form of indexing that enables accurate queries and the retrieval of all matching documents, much like how search engines function. In MongoDB, you can create a full-text index on a cloud database with the following steps:

1. Open the Search tab located in the *Databases* menu and click *Create Search Index,* as shown in Figure 5-16.

2. Next, select *JSON Editor* from the *Configuration Method* tab.

3. Choose the database and collection you want to create the index for, name the index, and enter the following index configuration, as shown in Figure 5-17:

```
{
  "mappings": {
    "dynamic": true
  }
}
```

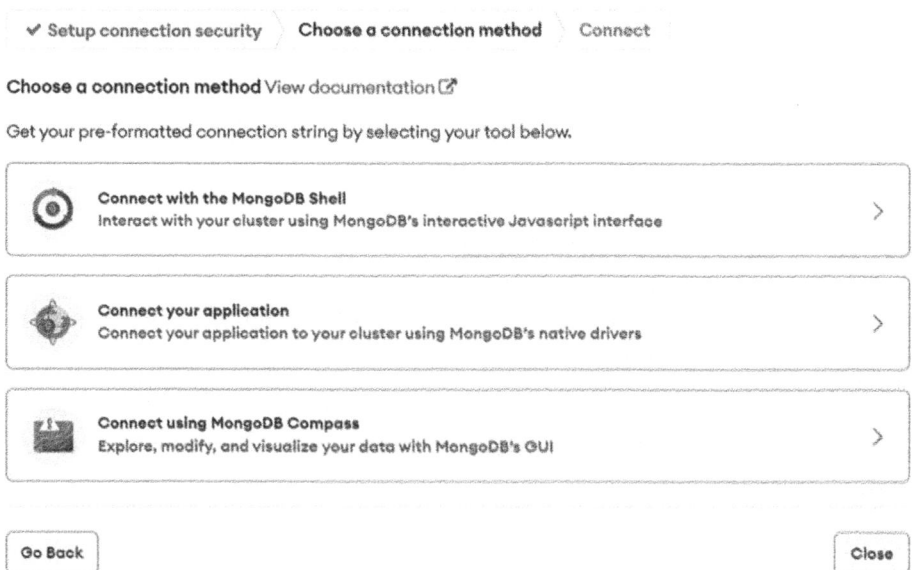

Connect to TestCluster

✔ Setup connection security   **Choose a connection method**   Connect

Choose a connection method View documentation ☑️

Get your pre-formatted connection string by selecting your tool below.

◎ **Connect with the MongoDB Shell**
Interact with your cluster using MongoDB's interactive Javascript interface   >

◆ **Connect your application**
Connect your application to your cluster using MongoDB's native drivers   >

🔧 **Connect using MongoDB Compass**
Explore, modify, and visualize your data with MongoDB's GUI   >

Go Back   Close

Figure 5-13. *Creating a connection string for the database*

5.2.4. Querying the Database

To query your indexed database in MongoDB, you should first connect to your database using the connection string obtained in Figure 5-13. This string will help you establish a client connection. To optimize performance, it is recommended to invoke the client as a function and cache it using the `@st.cache_resource` decorator. By doing so, Streamlit will reuse the cached client on subsequent queries instead of establishing a new client each time, which helps save runtime and resources. The following example demonstrates this approach:

```
from pymongo import MongoClient
@st.cache_resource
def create_client():
    return MongoClient('<connection_string>')
```

Next, you will need to create an *Aggregation*, which is essentially a multi-stage filtering pipeline written in JSON format. This pipeline allows you to apply various filters and transformations to your data before querying it. The structure of the aggregation will depend on the filters and operations you want to perform, and it can be used to shape your query results accordingly, as shown in the following example:

1. **Search using fuzzy matching**

   At this stage, we need to specify the name of the index that we created previously for searching the documents. Additionally, we need to input the user's query with string concatenation. We must also specify the path, or in other words, the objects to search through in the documents, such as borough and street address (nested elements and/or objects can be accessed with a period, i.e., address.street). Most importantly, we need to enable fuzzy matching

and specify the number of single-character edits
needed to match the query with the token using
maxEdits, and we also need to determine the
number of characters at the start of each query that
must match the token using prefixLength.

```
"$search": {
    "index": "default",
    "text": {
        "query": f"{address}",
        "path": ["borough", "address.street"],
        "fuzzy": {
            "maxEdits": 2,
            "prefixLength": 2
        }
    }
}
```

Connect to TestCluster

✔ Setup connection security ✔ Choose a connection method **Connect**

1 **Select your driver and version**

DRIVER   VERSION

| Python   ▼ | | 3.6 or later   ▼ |

2 **Add your connection string into your application code**

☑ Include full driver code example

```
client = pymongo.MongoClient("mongodb+srv://test_username:
<password>@testcluster.cpits8o.mongodb.net/?retryWrites=true&w=majority")
db = client.test
```

Replace **<password>** with the password for the **test_username** user. Ensure any option params are URL encoded.

Having trouble connecting? View our troubleshooting documentation

| Go Back | | Close |

Figure 5-14. *Creating a connection string for the database (continued)*

2. **Project documents with search score**

   At this stage, we will pass only the objects we want from the documents and compute the relevance score using the searchScore tag:

```
"$project": {
    "Name": "$name",
    "Cuisine": "$cuisine",
```

155

```
"Address": "$address.street",
"Borough": "$borough",
"Grade": "$grades.grade",
"Score": {
    "$meta": "searchScore"
}
}
}
```

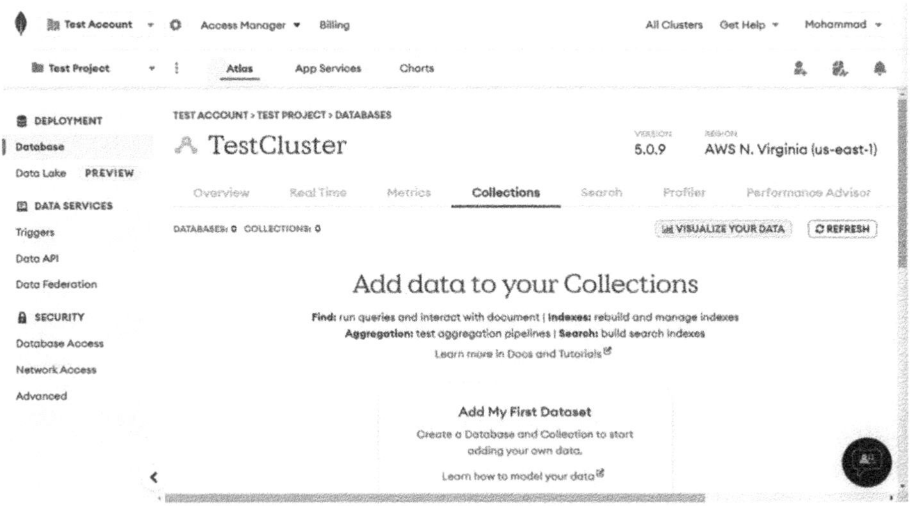

Figure 5-15. *Loading a dataset into the database*

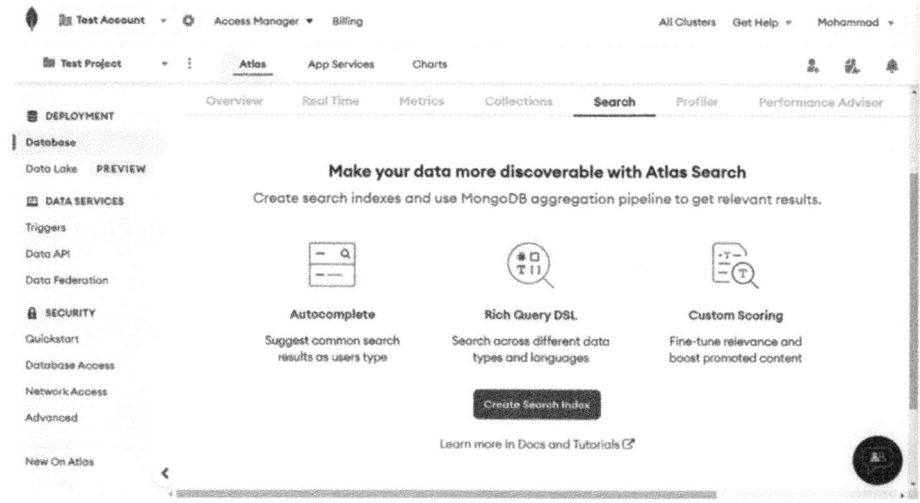

Figure 5-16. *Creating a full-text index for the database*

3. **Filter documents**

   Subsequently, we will filter the passed documents based on the user's entry for the type of cuisine. Please note that unlike fuzzy matching, at this stage, queries must exactly match the tokens in the documents for successful filtering.

```
"$match": {
    "Cuisine": f"{cuisine}"
}
```

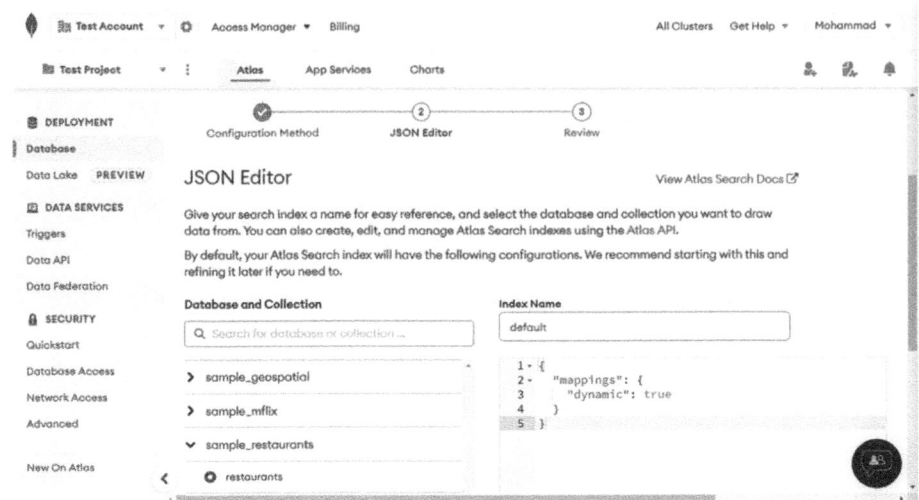

Figure 5-17. *Creating a full-text index for the database (continued)*

4. **Limit results**

Finally, at this stage, we will limit the number of results passed to the required amount:

```
"$limit": 5
```

For information regarding additional options for the aggregation pipeline, please refer to https://docs.mongodb.com/manual/reference/aggregation/.

5.2.5. Displaying Tables in Streamlit

Once the aggregation pipeline completes and returns the queried results, post-processing is necessary before rendering the table in Streamlit. Specifically, you need to convert the MongoDB query result into a Pandas DataFrame and specify the columns to retain. Additionally, parse any returned lists (such as restaurant grades) and convert them to plain text as shown in the following:

```
df = pd.DataFrame(result)[['Name','Address','Grade','Score']]
df['Grade'] = [','.join(map(str, x)) for x in df['Grade']]
```

You can refer to Listing 5-4 for the complete code in this section.
Additionally, the associated Streamlit application is shown in Figure 5-18,
displaying an example of a fuzzy matched query and the returned table in
Streamlit.

Listing 5-4. mongodb.py

```
import streamlit as st
import pandas as pd
from pymongo import MongoClient
@st.cache_resource
def create_client():
    return MongoClient('<connection_string>')
def query(cuisine,address):
    result = create_client()['sample_restaurants']
['restaurants'].aggregate([
        {
            "$search": {
                "index": "default",
                "text": {
                    "query": f"{address}",
                    "path": ["borough", "address.street"],
                    "fuzzy": {
                        "maxEdits": 2,
                        "prefixLength": 2
                    }
                }
            }
```

```
        }, {
            "$project": {
                "Name": "$name",
                "Cuisine": "$cuisine",
                "Address": "$address.street",
                "Borough": "$borough",
                "Grade": "$grades.grade",
                "Score": {
                    "$meta": "searchScore"
                }
            }
        }, {
            "$match": {
                "Cuisine": f"{cuisine}"
            }
        }, {
            "$limit": 5
        }
    ])
    try:
        df = pd.DataFrame(result)[['Name','Address','Grade','S
        core']]
        df['Grade'] = [','.join(map(str, x)) for x in
        df['Grade']]
        return df
    except:
        return None
if __name__ == '__main__':
    st.title('Restaurants Explorer')
    cuisine = st.selectbox('Cuisine',['American','Chinese','Del
    icatessen',
```

```
'Hamburgers','Ice Cream, Gelato, Yogurt, Ices','Irish'])
address = st.text_input('Address')
if st.button('Search'):
    if address != ":
        st.write(query(cuisine,address))
    else:
        st.warning('Please enter an address')
```

Figure 5-18. *Output of Listing 5-4*

5.3. Summary

In this chapter, we explored relational and nonrelational databases for storing and retrieving structured and unstructured data, respectively. We learned how to provision a PostgreSQL database and integrate it with a Streamlit application to manage and process structured datasets. Similarly, we saw how to provision a MongoDB cloud database to handle unstructured data, storing collections of documents with varying schemas, objects, and elements. We also demonstrated how MongoDB can create a full-text index, indexing every token in each document for improved querying, and how to perform fuzzy matching of query terms with document tokens to reduce the impact of typos. Finally, we wrapped up by integrating all these operations—setting up a database client, writing an aggregation pipeline, and postprocessing queried results—into a Streamlit application.

CHAPTER 6

Leveraging Backend Servers

In this chapter, we will introduce a more sophisticated and scalable approach to designing web applications. Specifically, we will explore how to offload the overhead of managing databases from the Streamlit server to an independent backend server, as is typical in a full-stack environment. The chapter will guide the developer through the process of provisioning a backend server in Python, which will act as an intermediary between the database and the frontend. Finally, the developer will be introduced to a highly modular, versatile, and secure architecture, with added security layers between the application and the database.

6.1. The Need for Backend Servers

As part of building a scalable and robust Streamlit application, certain tasks that are executed within the Streamlit app are better handled in an isolated environment that can be easily communicated with. This environment is called a backend, which is responsible for managing authentication, authorization, databases, and other gateway connections. Additionally, it handles core business logic that should not be executed on the frontend (i.e., Streamlit). Although Streamlit is a server-side web framework, isolating it from other system components improves modularity and security. Running everything, from authentication to database management, directly within Streamlit can introduce multiple security risks, such as XSS, SSRF, and potentially RCE, if not engineered properly.

While a backend-frontend architecture is not invulnerable, it adds an extra layer of protection through the use of APIs. This makes it harder for malicious actors to bypass security measures and access protected system components. Modern API design methodologies also ensure that every request is routed through a consistent mechanism, reducing the likelihood of vulnerabilities due to human error.

6.2. Frontend–Backend Communication

The backend is typically referred to as the server, while the frontend is known as the client. In this setup, the client triggers a request for resources or information based on user actions. The server then responds with the requested data. This request-response communication model is the foundation of the HTTP protocol, which consists of two main components: headers and the body.

The request and response headers contain metadata about the request and the payload in the body. This metadata includes, but is not limited to, cookies, request identifiers, keys, tokens, the body's content type, the host or IP address of the server, and data encoding or compression mechanisms. For the purposes of this book, we will focus on key aspects like keys, tokens, cookies, and the content type of the body. As an example, request body types are shown in Table 6-1. Since backends primarily handle the sending and receiving of information, JSON is the most widely used format for communication.

Table 6-1. *Common content-type header values*

Content-Type Value	Description
text/HTML	Text format but is parseable to HTML to be rendered as a web page
application/JSON	JSON format
application/xml	XML format
image/png	Image binary of type PNG

6.2.1. HTTP Methods

HTTP requests have methods, as discussed in Section 5.1. Unlike SQL, the syntax of HTTP methods does not drastically change. The main methods are GET, POST, PUT, and DELETE, which correspond to retrieving, adding, modifying, and deleting a resource, respectively. Adding and modifying resources can include a body to alter the resource, while GET and DELETE typically use resource identifiers in the request URL. These are the core functions of a RESTful API, which acts as an HTTP gateway to manage resources or data on the server side.

Visiting a website is a GET request to the URL, which includes request-specific data in its header, body, and response code. For example, requesting a page with just its domain name will by default request its HTTP version, but the backend server may redirect to the HTTPS version. For instance, Google redirects from google.com to https://google.com. You can check this by inspecting the page's network traffic or using *Curl*. Curl is a tool for making HTTP requests from the terminal or CMD, allowing you to view the response body, headers, and status code. It also helps in understanding backend commands, like following a redirect. Figure 6-1 demonstrates this with the command curl -i -L google.com, where -i displays response headers and -L follows redirects.

Figure 6-1. *Getting google.com and watching response headers and redirection*

6.3. Working with JSON Files

JSON documents can be used to represent and parse data. They can contain lists/arrays or key/value pairs, similar to dictionaries in Python. They can also include other primitive data types such as integers, floats, strings, and booleans. With these simple data types, complex data structures can be represented. A sample JSON representing one of the previously introduced examples is shown in Listing 6-1.

Listing 6-1. sample_json.json

```
[
    {
        "Name": "Adam",
        "DOB": "01/01/1990",
        "Paygrade ID": "2"
    },
```

```
{
    "Name": "Sara",
    "DOB": "01/01/1980",
    "Paygrade ID": "1"
},
{
    "Name": "Bob",
    "DOB": "01/01/1970",
    "Paygrade ID": "1"
},
{
    "Name": "Alice",
    "DOB": "01/01/2000",
    "Paygrade ID": "3"
}
]
```

6.4. Provisioning a Backend Server

To stay consistent with the Python theme of the book, we will build a Pythonic backend server. Among the options available, Flask and Django are both great choices for this task. While both can serve as frontend application servers by delivering HTML for browsers to render, *Django* is designed specifically for that purpose, thanks to its built-in web template engine, *Jinja*. On the other hand, Flask is more flexible and configurable to the developer's needs, and it is lighter in weight. To get started, install Flask using *pip*.

6.4.1. API Building

A backend will execute one or more methods or functions in response to a request to the server. These methods and functions depend on the URL and can be configured to take headers into consideration as well. A simple example of this is shown in Listing 6-2, where requesting `http://<SERVER-HOST>/server_status` will serve the page in Figure 6-2, while any other request will return a *404 Not Found* error.

Listing 6-2. flask_sample.py

```python
from flask import Flask
app = Flask(__name__)
@app.route('/server_status')
def welcome_controller():
    return {
        'message': 'Welcome to your Flask Server',
        'status': 'up',
        'random': 1 + 1
    }
app.run()
```

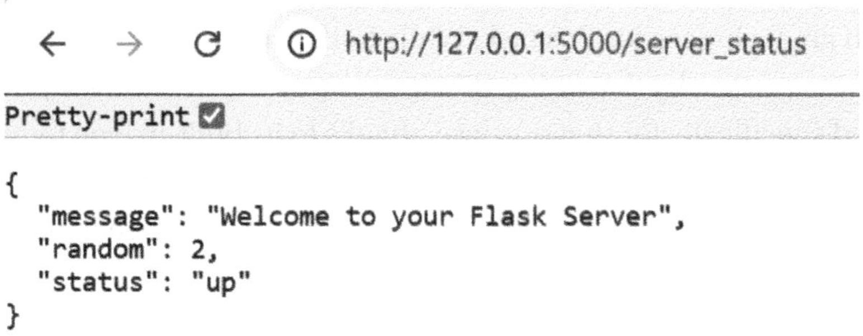

Figure 6-2. *Page returned when the /server_status route is requested for the server with Listing 6-2*

To trigger a specific function call when a route is requested, a function decorator needs to be added before it with the route name. Routes do not have to be static; they can be dynamic by using a specific string format, which Flask will map to that function. For example, /text/1 and /text/3 can map to /text/<id>. Additionally, the HTTP method can be specified in the same function decorator by adding an extra parameter, like this:

```
@app.route('/text/<id>', methods=['GET', 'PUT'])
```

Following up on the Employee and Pay Grade example from before, we will reuse the same database for this example but use *SQLAlchemy* instead of *psycopg2* to take advantage of the *ORM*, which maps SQL commands to Python class objects. To begin, we need to represent our tables as classes, along with a Base class that the other two classes will inherit SQL properties from. These properties include SQL query parameterization to prevent SQL injection (SQLI). The classes in Listings 6-4 and 6-5 will point to already existing tables in the database, with the *_tablename_* property representing the table name.

Listing 6-3. DataBase/Base.py

```
from sqlalchemy.ext.declarative import declarative_base
Base = declarative_base()
```

Listing 6-4. DataBase/PayGrades.py

```
from sqlalchemy import Column, Integer, String
from DataBase.Base import Base

class PayGrades(Base):
    __tablename__ = 'paygrades'
    id = Column(Integer, primary_key=True)

    base_salary = Column(String)
    reimbursement = Column(String, default=True)
    bonuses = Column(String)
```

```python
    def to_dict(self):
        return {
            "id": self.id,
            "base_salary": self.base_salary,
            "reimbursement": self.reimbursement,
            "bonuses": self.bonuses
        }
```

Listing 6-5. DataBase/Employees.py

```python
from sqlalchemy import Column, Integer, String
from DataBase.Base import Base

class Employees(Base):
    __tablename__ = 'persons'
    id = Column(Integer, primary_key=True)

    name = Column(String)
    date_of_birth = Column(String, default=True)
    paygrade_id = Column(Integer, unique=True, index=True)

    def to_dict(self):
        return {
            "id": self.id,
            "name": self.name,
            "date_of_birth": self.date_of_birth,
            "paygrade_id": self.paygrade_id
        }
```

Then, we can support adding and retrieving employee data through HTTP requests using Flask, as shown in Listings 6-6, 6-7, and 6-8. This backend server includes two routes: the first queries all employees using the database connection established with SQLAlchemy, and the second inserts or adds a new employee to the employees table using user-supplied properties sent in the HTTP body as a JSON document.

Listing 6-6. DataBase/__init__.py

```
from .Employees import Employees
from .PayGrades import PayGrades
```

Listing 6-7. DataBase/Connection.py

```
from contextlib import contextmanager
from sqlalchemy import create_engine
from sqlalchemy.orm import sessionmaker, Session

engine = create_engine("postgresql://
postgres:admin@127.0.0.1:5432/CompanyData")
DBSession = sessionmaker(bind=engine)

@contextmanager
def session_manager() -> Session:
    session = DBSession()
    try:
        yield session
    except Exception as e:
        session.rollback()
        raise e
    finally:
        session.close()
```

Listing 6-8. main.py

```
from flask import Flask, request
from DataBase import Employees
from DataBase.Connection import session_manager

app = Flask(__name__)
```

```python
@app.route('/employees')
def get_all_employees():
    with session_manager() as session:
        employees = session.query(Employees).all()
        employees = [employee.to_dict() for employee in
        employees]
        return {"data": employees}

@app.route('/employee', methods=["POST"])
def add_employee():
    body = request.json
    with session_manager() as session:
        session.add(Employees(**body))
        session.commit()
    return {"message": "New employee added successfully"}

app.run()
```

6.4.2. API Testing

In this example, the user will interact with the backend using an API testing platform like Postman, as shown in Figures 6-3 and 6-4. In a later section, Streamlit will directly interface with this server without the need for an API testing platform.

Figure 6-3. *Adding a new employee*

To wrap up this section, it is important to note that we did not set any headers, including the content type for the POST/employee route using a JSON payload, because Postman handled that automatically. Flask also took care of adding the JSON content type to the response, as Python's lists and dictionaries can be easily parsed into JSON, as mentioned earlier.

Figure 6-4. *Getting all employees*

173

6.5. Multithreading and Multiprocessing Requests

Once an application scales, or when one of its initial requirements involves heavy, independent computations or processes, a lot of power is wasted, whether on the backend's Flask side or Streamlit's side. This is because the full power of modern CPUs is not being utilized. Modern CPU strength comes not from faster clock cycles, but from having more cores. By default, both Streamlit and Flask are single-threaded, single-process applications. To speed them up, we can leverage *multiprocessing* and *multithreading*, which enable true parallelization. The developer can control the use of both techniques to run a function multiple times, allowing it to be executed in parallel by the CPU. An example of using both approaches in Streamlit is shown in Listing 6-9 and shown in Figure 6-5.

Listing 6-9. streamlit_main.py

```
import streamlit as st
from multiprocessing import Pool, cpu_count
import threading
import time
def func(iterations, id):
    i = 0
    for i in range(iterations):
        i += 1
    print('Finished job id =', id)
if __name__ == '__main__':
    pool = Pool(cpu_count())
    st.title('Speed You Code! ')
    jobs_count = 5
    iterations = 10 ** 3
    c1, c2 = st.columns(2)
```

```
with c1:
    if st.button('multiprocess'):
        inputs = [(iterations, i) for i in
        range(jobs_count)]
        t11 = time.time()
        pool.starmap(func, inputs)
        t21 = time.time()
        st.write(f'Finished after {t21 - t11} seconds')
with c2:
    if st.button('multithread'):
        threads = [threading.Thread(target=func,
        args=(iterations, i)) for i in range(10)]
        t12 = time.time()
        for thread in threads:
            thread.start()
        for thread in threads:
            thread.join()
        t22 = time.time()
        st.write(f'Finished after {t22 - t12} seconds')
```

Speed You Code!

Figure 6-5. *Output of Listing 6-9*

Notice that in Listing 6-9, the first code to be executed is after line 13, which is essential for the entire example to work without errors. This ensures that Streamlit knows the code block should be executed only once, meaning the processing pool will not be initialized again during reruns. A similar precaution should be taken in Flask applications.

The main difference between multiprocessing and multithreading is that multithreading reuses the existing memory space, spawning new threads within the same process, which is faster than spawning entirely new processes that add the overhead of CPU context switching. In contrast, each new process in the multiprocessing pool requires a separate memory space. Additionally, each process's inputs need to be copied or cloned, which increases memory consumption. Although multithreading may seem like the better option, it is not always true. Multiprocessing is more CPU-efficient when handling heavy tasks, as the CPU scheduler allocates more time to those processes. Figure 6-6 shows the correlation between execution time and the job iteration count in 10x from Listing 6-9.

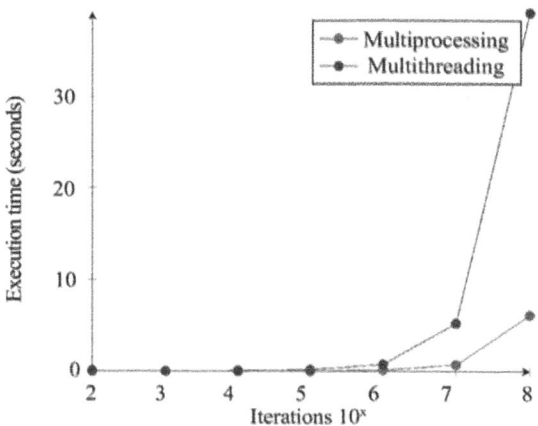

Figure 6-6. *Multiprocessing vs. multithreading for five jobs with increasing iteration count*

6.6. Connecting Streamlit to a Backend Server

Once we have optimized the backend server with multiprocessing and/or multithreading, we are ready to connect our Streamlit application to it. For this, we will need to use an HTTP client library to communicate with the backend API. Listing 6-10 uses the popular *requests* library to achieve this, with the output shown in Figure 6-7.

Listing 6-10. streamlit_api.py

```python
import streamlit as st
import requests
import datetime
url = 'http://127.0.0.1:5000'
def add_employee(name, dob, paygrade):
    data = {
        'name': name,
        'date_of_birth': dob,
        'paygrade_id': paygrade
    }
    response = requests.post(url + '/employee', json=data)
    if response.status_code == 200:
        return True
    return False
def get_employees():
    response = requests.get(url + '/employees')
    return response.json()['data']
form = st.form('new_employee')
name = form.text_input('Name')
dob = str(form.date_input('DOB', min_value=datetime.
datetime(year=1920, day=1, month=1)))
paygrade = form.number_input('paygrade', step=1)
if form.form_submit_button('Add new Employee'):
    if add_employee(name, dob, paygrade):
        st.success('Employee Added')
    else:
        st.error('Error adding employee')
st.write('___')
employees = get_employees()
st.table(employees)
```

Name

Ahmed

DOB

1985/01/01

paygrade

1   − +

Add new Employee

Employee Added

	date_of_birth	id	name	paygrade_id
0	01/01/1990	1	Adam	2
1	01/01/1980	2	Sara	1
2	01/01/1970	3	Bob	1
3	01/01/2000	4	Alice	3
4	01/01/1975	5	Karen	2
5	1985-01-01	6	Ahmed	1

Figure 6-7. *Output of Listing 6-10*

6.7. Summary

In this chapter, we learned that backend servers are the backbone of every
expanding web application, adding layers of obscurity and security to the
frontend. We also explored HTTP communication, the language of APIs,
and its structure. To ensure efficient and organized API communication,
we introduced JSON, the most widely used data format in APIs. With
these building blocks in place, we then turned to Flask as a Python
backend framework to create a well-structured server that exposes specific
endpoints to serve data from a local database. Finally, we demonstrated
ways to speed up Python code execution, both in Streamlit and the
backend server, by leveraging multiprocessing and multithreading,
comparing the performance and use cases of each.

CHAPTER 7

Implementing Session State

In order to develop more advanced Streamlit applications, it is vital to establish session-specific data that can be used to deliver an enhanced user experience. Specifically, the application will need to preserve the user's data and inputs using what is referred to as session states. These states can be set and accessed on demand whenever necessary, and they will persist when the user triggers a rerun of the Streamlit application or navigates between pages. In addition, we will establish a method to store state across multiple sessions using cookies, which can save data in the user's browser for access when they restart the associated Streamlit application. Finally, we will learn how to record and visualize rich insights into how users interact with our application, providing analytics for both the developer and product owner alike.

7.1. Implementing Session State Natively

Since Streamlit version 0.84.1, a native way to store and manage session-specific data—including but not limited to variables, widgets, text, images, and objects—has been introduced. The values of session states are stored in a dictionary format, where each value is assigned to a unique key for indexing. Previously, without this feature, all variables would be reset whenever the user triggered a rerun of the Streamlit script by interacting with the application. Similarly, widgets would also reset to their default values when the user navigated from one page to another. However, with session state, users can enjoy an enhanced and more personalized experience by accessing variables or entries previously made on other pages within the application. For instance, users can enter their username and password once and continue navigating through the application without being prompted to re-enter their credentials—until they log out. In a nutshell, session states enable us to develop far more complex applications, which will be discussed extensively in subsequent chapters.

The method to set and get session state data can be implemented as shown in Listing 7-1, with the associated output in Figure 7-1. Please note that the first two key-value entries (KeyInput1 and KeyInput2) are present even though they have not been explicitly created by the user. These keys exist to store the state of the user-modified components—in this case, the defined text input components. This means that the developer also has the ability to modify the values of any component, as long as it has a unique key assigned during its definition. Another important point is that each session state must be initialized before it can be read; otherwise, an error will occur. To prevent this, always make sure to initialize the state with a null or default value.

Listing 7-1. session_state.py

```
import streamlit as st
def get_state_value(key):
    return st.session_state.get(key)
def set_state_value(key, value):
    st.session_state[key] = value
st.title('Session State Management')
c1, c2, c3 = st.columns(3)
with c1:
```

```
    st.subheader('All')
    st.write(st.session_state)
with c2:
    st.subheader('Set Key')
    key = st.text_input('Key', key='KeyInput1')
    value = st.text_input('Value')
    if st.button('Set'):
        st.session_state[key] = value
        st.success('Success')
with c3:
    st.subheader('Get Key')
    key = st.text_input('Key', key='KeyInput2')
    if st.button('Get'):
        st.write(st.session_state.get(key))
```

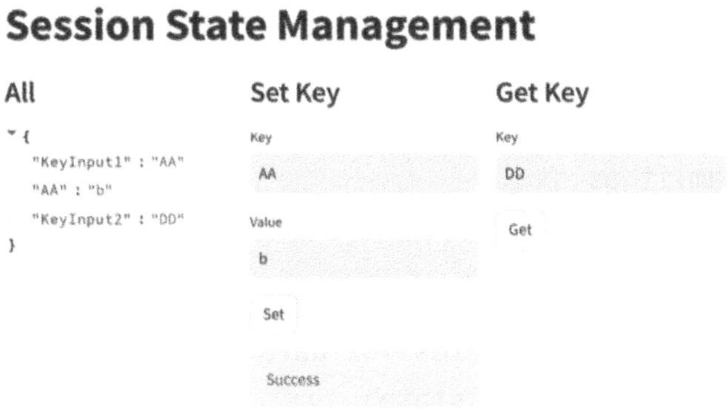

Session State Management

All	Set Key	Get Key
▾ {	Key	Key
"KeyInput1" : "AA"	AA	DD
"AA" : "b"		
"KeyInput2" : "DD"	Value	Get
}	b	
	Set	
	Success	

Figure 7-1. *Session state data display and manipulation*

7.1.1. Building an Application with Session State

To demonstrate the utility of session states, in the following example we will create a simple multipage application where the user can use states to store the key of the selected page, an uploaded dataframe, and the value of a slider widget. As shown in Listing 7-2, on our main page we first initialize

181

the state for page selection, and then use buttons to change the state to the key of the requested page. Subsequently, the associated function of the selected page is invoked directly from the session state to render the page.

In Page One of the application, shown in Listing 7-3, we use session states to store an uploaded dataframe and the value of a slider that filters the number of rows displayed in the dataframe. The user can navigate back and forth between pages and still access a previously uploaded dataframe with the same number of rows set by the slider, as shown in Figure 7-2.

Listing 7-2. main_page.py

```python
import streamlit as st

st.title('Main Page')
# Initializing session state for page selection
if 'page_state' not in st.session_state:
    st.session_state['page_state'] = 'Main Page'
```

Listing 7-3. page_1.py

```python
import streamlit as st
import pandas as pd

st.title('Page One')
# Initializing session states for dataframe and slider
if 'df' not in st.session_state:
    st.session_state['df'] = None
if 'rows' not in st.session_state:
    st.session_state['rows'] = None
file = st.file_uploader('Upload file')
# Writing dataframe to session state
if file is not None:
    df = pd.read_csv(file)
    st.session_state['df'] = df
```

```
if st.session_state['df'] is not None:
    # Creating slider widget with default value from session state
    rows = st.slider('Rows to display',value=st.session_
    state['rows'], min_value=1,max_value=len(st.session_
    state['df']))
    # Writing slider value to session state
    st.session_state['rows'] = rows
    # Rendering dataframe from session state
    st.write(st.session_state['df'].iloc[:st.session_
    state['rows']])
```

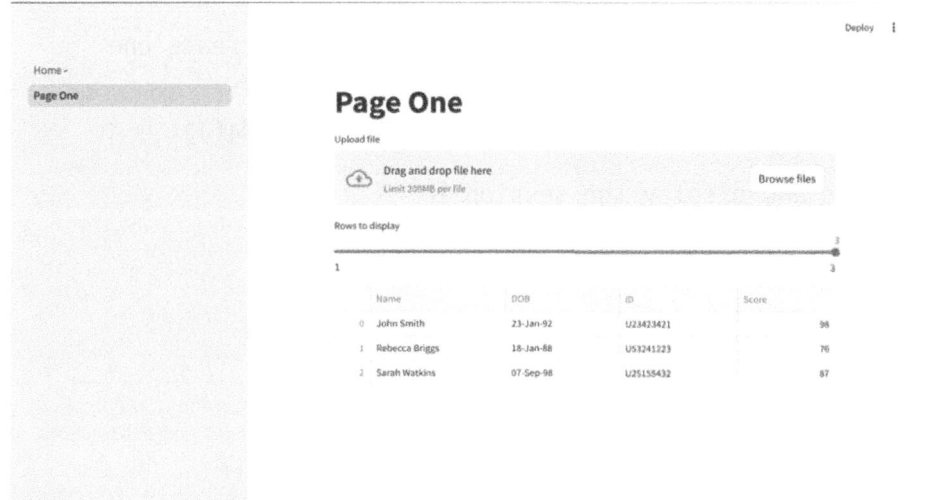

Figure 7-2. *Output of Listings 7-2 and 7-3*

7.2. Introducing Session IDs

Session IDs are unique identifiers for each new instance of a Streamlit session. A new Session ID can be established whenever a new browser page is opened, even if another connection is already active. However, each session is treated independently by the server.

These unique IDs can be used to provide the end user with a personalized experience. To achieve this, the server needs to map each user's progress and updates to their corresponding IDs. This mapping can be done by generating unique session IDs in Streamlit. In Listing 7-4, we demonstrate how to generate a session ID. The output is shown in Figure 7-3, which displays two web pages both running at http://localhost:8501/.

Listing 7-4. session_id_demo.py

```python
import streamlit as st
import uuid

# Check if session ID already exists, if not, create one
if 'session_id' not in st.session_state:
    st.session_state.session_id = str(uuid.uuid4())

# Access and display the session ID
st.title('Your session ID is:')
st.subheader(st.session_state.session_id)
```

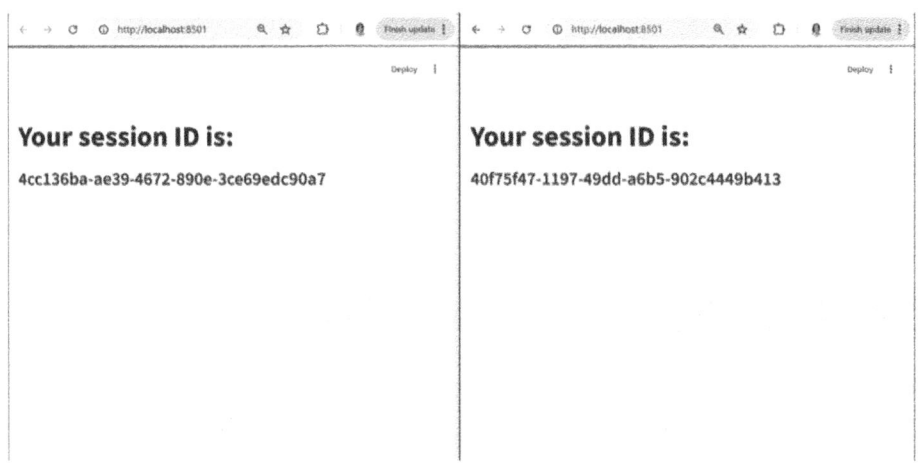

Figure 7-3. *Two different browser windows with different session IDs*

7.3. User Insights

The ability to record user interactions with a web application is often critical. Developers and product owners need access to detailed and accurate data—such as how many users are visiting the site, when they are visiting, and how they are interacting with it—in order to better tailor and improve their product or service.Consider an ecommerce web application that has been meticulously developed but is failing to convert leads into sales, and the reason is unclear. It could be a hidden bug in the interface or backend that is blocking user actions, or perhaps the server is overloaded and unable to handle incoming traffic. In either case, identifying exactly where the issue lies in the pipeline is essential—and this is where user insights become invaluable.

While Google Analytics offers robust insights at the server level—including visit counts, user demographics, and time spent on various pages—it cannot effectively capture interactions at the application level. As a result, developers must implement their own methods to track in-app user behavior.One simple approach, demonstrated in Listing 7-5, involves logging a timestamp whenever the user interacts with a specific part of the code—for example, by clicking a button or uploading a dataset, as shown in Figure 7-4—and storing this data in a PostgreSQL database, as seen in Figure 7-5. Similarly, the number of rows in the uploaded dataset can also be recorded. Each data point is stored in a separate column within a table, where the primary key is the session's unique ID. When the application restarts, a new row is created with a new session ID. By using the provided update function, you can capture and record any value at any step of your program.

```
update_row(column, new_value, session_id, mutable, engine)
```

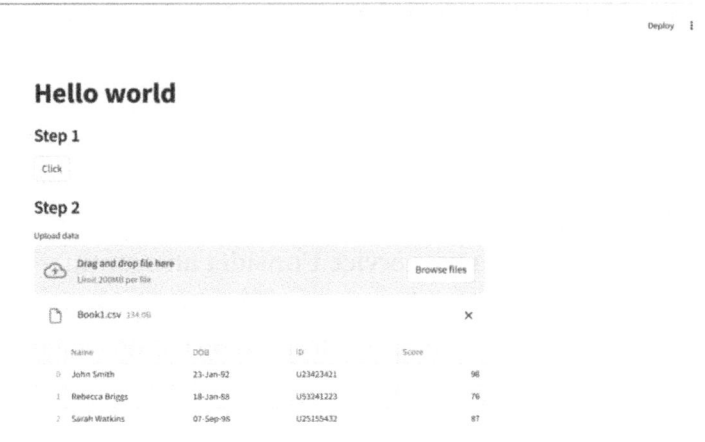

Figure 7-4. *Output of Listing 7-6*

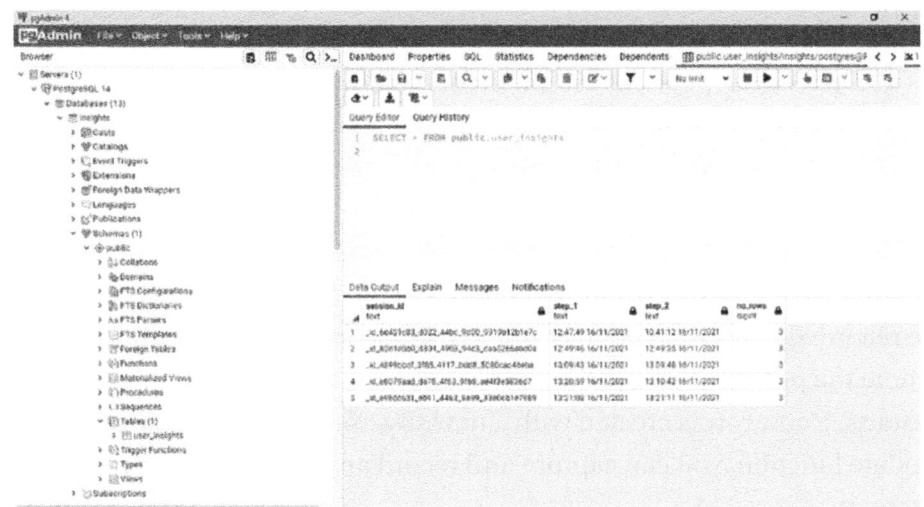

Figure 7-5. *Associated PostgreSQL database for Listing 7-5*

Please note that insights can be overwritten multiple times by setting the mutable argument to True, or left as False if you want to record a value only the first time it is generated.

Listing 7-5. record_user_insights.py

```python
import streamlit as st
import uuid
from datetime import datetime
import pandas as pd
import psycopg2
from sqlalchemy import create_engine, text

def get_session_id():
    if 'session_id' not in st.session_state:
        session_id = str(uuid.uuid4()).replace('-', '_')
        st.session_state.session_id = '_id_' + session_id
    return st.session_state.session_id

def insert_row(session_id, engine):
    with engine.connect() as conn:
        result = conn.execute(text(f'SELECT session_id FROM
        user_insights WHERE session_id = "{session_id}"')).
        fetchone()
        if result is None:
            conn.execute(text(f'INSERT INTO user_insights
            (session_id) VALUES ("{session_id}")'))
            conn.commit()

def update_row(column, new_value, session_id, mutable, engine):
    with engine.connect() as conn:
        if mutable:
            conn.execute(text(f'UPDATE user_insights SET
            {column} = "{new_value}" WHERE session_id =
            "{session_id}"'))
            conn.commit()
```

```python
        else:
            result = conn.execute(text(f'SELECT {column} FROM
            user_insights WHERE session_id = "{session_id}"')).
            fetchone()
            if result and result[0] is None:
                conn.execute(text(f'UPDATE user_insights SET
                {column} = "{new_value}" WHERE session_id =
                "{session_id}"'))
                conn.commit()

if __name__ == '__main__':
    engine = create_engine('postgresql://<username>:<password>@
    localhost:<port>/<database>')
    session_id = get_session_id()
    with engine.connect() as conn:
        conn.execute(text('CREATE TABLE IF NOT EXISTS user_
        insights (session_id text, step_1 text, step_2 text,
        no_rows bigint)'))
        conn.commit()
    insert_row(session_id, engine)
    st.title('Hello world')
    st.subheader('Step 1')
    if st.button('Click'):
        st.write('Some content')
        update_row('step_1', datetime.now().strftime('%H:%M:%S
        %d/%m/%Y'), session_id, True, engine)
    st.subheader('Step 2')
    file = st.file_uploader('Upload data')
    if file is not None:
        df = pd.read_csv(file)
        st.write(df)
```

```
update_row('step_2', datetime.now().strftime('%H:%M:%S
%d/%m/%Y'), session_id, False, engine)
update_row('no_rows', len(df), session_id,
True, engine)
```

7.3.1. Visualizing User Insights

Now that we have established how to capture insights from a Streamlit application and store them in a PostgreSQL database, the next step is to visualize the data on demand. To begin, we can use Listing 7-6 to extract the insights table into a Pandas dataframe and optionally save it locally as an Excel spreadsheet if you wish to create your own custom charts. Alternatively, we can use Listing 7-7 to visualize the data directly. In this approach, we import the previously generated Excel spreadsheet into a Pandas dataframe, convert the timestamps into hourly and daily values, group and sum the number of rows that fall within the same hour or day, and finally visualize them using Plotly charts, as shown in Figure 7-6. Additionally, we can enable filtering by allowing the user to select a column from the insights table using a st.selectbox widget.

Listing 7-6. read_user_insights.py

```
import pandas as pd
import psycopg2
from sqlalchemy import create_engine
def read_data(name,engine):
    try:
        return pd.read_sql_table(name,engine)
    except:
        return pd.DataFrame([])
if __name__ == '__main__':
    # Creating PostgreSQL engine
```

```
    engine = create_engine('postgresql://<username>:<password>@
    localhost:'
 '<port>/<database>')
    df = read_data('user_insights',engine)
    df.to_excel('C:/Users/.../user_insights.xlsx',index=False)
```

Listing 7-7. plot_user_insights.py

```python
import streamlit as st
import pandas as pd
import plotly.express as px
st.set_page_config(layout='wide')
st.title('User Insights')
df = pd.read_excel('C:/Users/.../user_insights.xlsx')
column_selection = st.selectbox('Select column', df.columns[1:-2])
df = df[column_selection]
df = pd.to_datetime(df,format='%H:%M:%S %d/%m/%Y')
df_1h = df.copy()
df_1d = df.copy()
col1, col2 = st.columns(2)
with col1:
    st.subheader('Hourly chart')
    df_1h = df_1h.dt.strftime('%Y-%m-%d %I%p')
    df_1h = pd.DataFrame(df_1h.value_counts())
    df_1h.index = pd.DatetimeIndex(df_1h.index)
    df_1h = df_1h.sort_index()
    fig = px.bar(df_1h, x=df_1h.index, y=df_1h[column_selection])
    st.write(fig)
with col2:
    st.subheader('Daily chart')
    df_1d = df_1d.dt.strftime('%Y-%m-%d')
    df_1d = pd.DataFrame(df_1d.value_counts())
```

```
df_1d.index = pd.DatetimeIndex(df_1d.index)
df_1d = df_1d.sort_index()
fig = px.line(df_1d, x=df_1d.index, y=df_1d[column_selection])
st.write(fig)
```

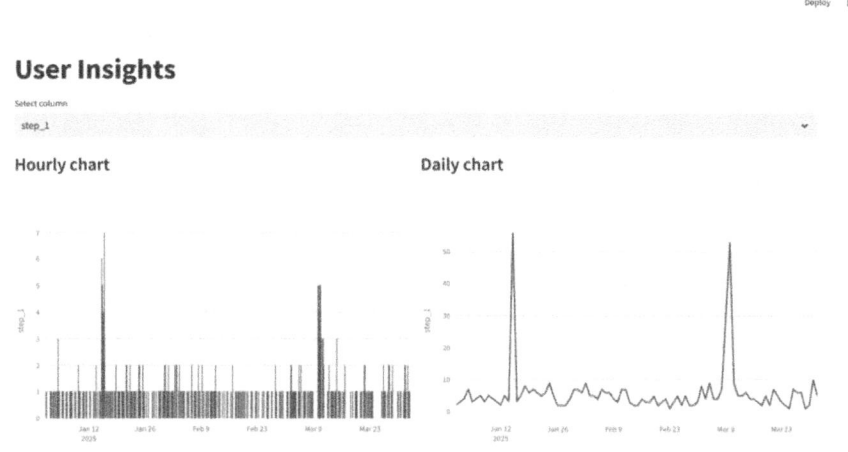

Figure 7-6. *Output of Listing 7-7*

7.4. Cookie Management

We have discussed how to store and manage data within a session using both native and workaround approaches. However, what may be missing is the ability to manage data across sessions. For example, storing a counter to track how many times a button has been clicked or, more usefully, preventing the user from having to log in every time they start a new session. To achieve this, we need to leverage cookies. And while Streamlit has implemented its own native cookie management and even authentication commands (st.context and st.login), in this book we will focus on third party components as they offer additional functionality that are yet not covered natively.

Cookies can be used to track a user's actions across multiple websites or store personal information, such as authentication tokens. They are stored and managed on the user's end, specifically in their browser, which means the server does not have direct access to their content by default. To view the cookies on any web application, simply open the developer tools in your browser and go to the console tab. Then, type `document.cookie` to display the cookies, as shown in Figure 7-7.

```
> document.cookie
< 'ajs_user_id=%22666c29e8-0a66-5f62-bdf5-b9ceaf8a6414%22; ajs_anonymous_id=%22648586…
```

Figure 7-7. *A web page cookie*

In a typical Streamlit application, there may be additional cookies— beyond the one shown in Figure 7-7—that are used for purposes such as advertisement tracking. These cookies may need to be removed depending on the cookie policy the developer adopts. In other cases, the developer may want to add additional cookies to enhance the application's user experience. Regardless, both actions require a method to manage cookies in any web application.

To manipulate cookies within a Streamlit application, we need to use a third-party module or library. For this example, we'll use *Extra-Streamlit-Components*, which can be installed via `pip install extra-streamlit-components` and imported using the alias *stx*. The *X* in the alias represents the extra capabilities that this library brings to a standard Streamlit app. This library includes a module called *Cookie Manager*, which will be our tool for managing cookies.Listing 7-8 demonstrates a simple Streamlit application with the ability to set, get, and delete cookies. The controls are customizable based on the developer's needs. For example, an expiration date can be set for any new cookie, which will automatically delete the cookie once the set date is reached. Figures 7-8 and 7-9 show examples of adding and retrieving an authentication token, respectively.

Listing 7-8. cookie_management.py

```python
import streamlit as st
import extra_streamlit_components as stx
st.title('Cookie Management Demo')
st.subheader('_Featuring Cookie Manager from Extra-Streamlit-
Components_')
cookie_manager = stx.CookieManager()
st.subheader('All Cookies:')
cookies = cookie_manager.get_all()
st.write(cookies)
c1, c2, c3 = st.columns(3)
with c1:
    st.subheader('Get Cookie:')
    cookie = st.text_input('Cookie', key='0')
    clicked = st.button('Get')
    if clicked:
        value = cookie_manager.get(cookie)
        st.write(value)
with c2:
    st.subheader('Set Cookie:')
    cookie = st.text_input('Cookie', key='1')
    val = st.text_input('Value')
    if st.button('Add'):
        cookie_manager.set(cookie, val)
with c3:
    st.subheader('Delete Cookie:')
    cookie = st.text_input('Cookie', key='2')
    if st.button('Delete'):
        cookie_manager.delete(cookie)
```

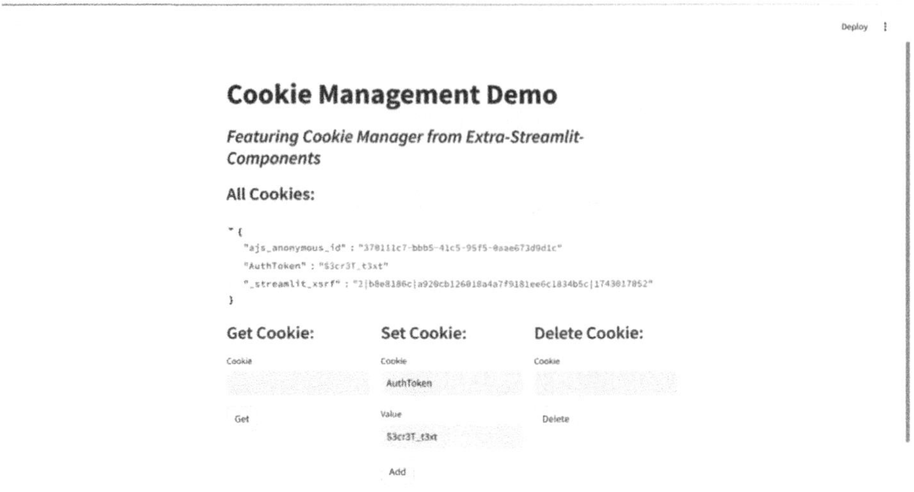

Figure 7-8. *Adding an AuthToken cookie*

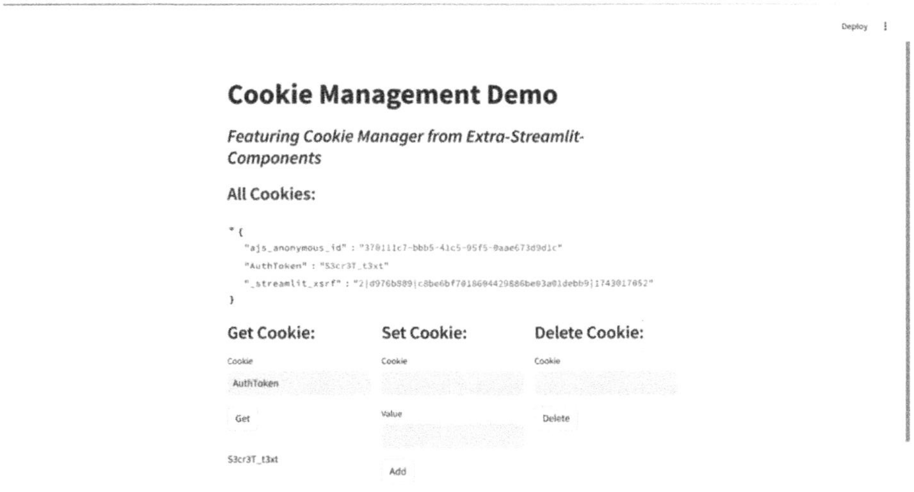

Figure 7-9. *Getting an AuthToken cookie*

Please note that the All Cookies section in Figures 7-8 and 7-9 is displayed in a well-structured JSON format, with some cookies redacted for privacy reasons. It is also important to highlight that this Streamlit application, using the newly introduced module, does not include a visual component. This is because the module is categorized as a service—hence the name *Cookie Manager*. However, this does not imply that all other Streamlit-compatible libraries behave the same way; some may indeed include visual elements as part of their functionality.

7.5. Summary

In this chapter, we explored how to store and access session states natively with Streamlit. The use of session states is crucial in many cases and will be extensively applied to develop advanced applications in the following chapters. Additionally, the reader was introduced to session IDs—unique identifiers associated with every new instance of a Streamlit application— and shown how to record and visualize user insights. Finally, we covered how to store and retrieve cookies in a browser, which is essential for maintaining session states across multiple sessions of a Streamlit application on the same browser. This is particularly useful for scenarios where the user wants to automatically log in without re-entering their credentials.

CHAPTER 8

Authenticating Users and Securing Applications

After familiarizing ourselves with the essential building blocks of a well-structured Streamlit web application, we now require an additional feature to deploy a production-ready app: a secure user authentication service. Once all users requesting access to the application are authenticated, we can ensure a secure user experience where private data remains safe and any unwelcome or malicious requests are effectively denied. In this chapter, we will learn how to establish user accounts, verify user actions, and implement other housekeeping measures expected of any proficient software engineer.

8.1. Developing User Accounts

In this chapter, we will build on the example from Chapters 5 and 6 by introducing HR admins who can view and add employees along with their pay grades. Assume there are designated admins responsible for these actions, and the company frequently changes or assigns new admins. In this case, our application needs to support the creation of multiple admin accounts and authorize them accordingly.

© Mohammad Khorasani, Mohamed Abdou, Javier Hernández Fernández 2025
M. Khorasani et al., *Streamlit for Web Development*,
https://doi.org/10.1007/979-8-8688-1826-4_8

Since these actions require authorized personnel, we need to implement three main features: adding an admin table to our database, enabling admin account creation, and authorizing users with admin privileges to access the relevant parts of the service.

8.1.1. Hashing

To add a new table to the database, we will follow a process similar to what was done previously, as shown in Figure 8-1. Notice that we are storing two key pieces of information for each admin: the username and the password hash. Instead of saving the password itself, we store a hash—a non-guessable representation of the password. This approach helps protect user privacy and credentials in the event of a data breach. If such a breach occurs, the attacker would need to spend billions of years brute-forcing the hashes to uncover even a single user's actual password. Hashing is essentially a one-way transformation of data that cannot be reversed.

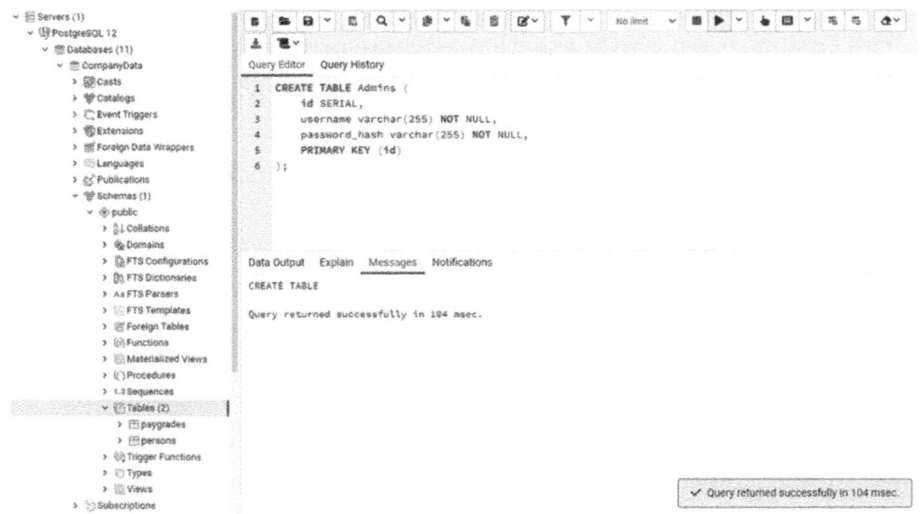

Figure 8-1. *Creating a new table to store admin credentials, using the contents of Flask/create_admins_table.sql*

After creating the new table, we will need to define a corresponding Python class to create an ORM model for SQLAlchemy, as shown in Listing 8-1. Password hashing can be performed using various algorithms, such as MD5, SHA256, SHA512, and others. However, the most commonly used algorithm in modern systems is Bcrypt. In fact, Bcrypt is the default choice for securing user passwords in many Linux environments. Before diving into how Bcrypt works, we first need to understand the methods used to make a hash more secure.

As mentioned earlier, hashing transforms data. For example, the text

```
Password123
```

maps to

```
42f749ade7f9e195bf475f37a44cafcb
```

using MD5. However, even a slight modification to the original plain text can result in a significantly different hashed output, as shown below:

```
MD5(Password1239) -> abd7fdbb048a611ea0a0937265765404
```

8.1.2. Salting

Including extra bytes in the password—also known as adding a salt— results in a completely different hash. This is especially helpful in cases where users reuse passwords across different websites and one of those sites is breached. By salting the password, attackers will not be able to tell whether the same password is used across multiple domains, making it significantly harder to crack. However, this method becomes less effective if the attacker knows the salt value and how it is applied. This is where Bcrypt stands out—it introduces a cryptographic approach that stores randomly generated salts within the hash itself. As a result, it becomes possible to verify whether a Bcrypt hash was generated from a given plaintext using an abstracted function from a Bcrypt library, as shown in Listing 8-2.

Listing 8-1. Flask/DataBase/Admins.py

```python
from sqlalchemy import Column, Integer, String
from .Base import Base
class Admins(Base):
    __tablename__ = 'admins'
    id = Column(Integer, primary_key=True)
    username = Column(String)
    password_hash = Column(String, default=True)
    def to_dict(self):
        return {
            'id': self.id,
            'username': self.username,
            'password_hash': self.password_hash
        }
```

Listing 8-2. Flask/Services/HashingService.py

```python
import bcrypt
class HashingService:
    def __init__(self, bcrypt_gen_salt: int = 12):
        self.gen_salt = bcrypt_gen_salt
    def hash_bcrypt(self, plain_text: bytes) -> bytes:
        return bcrypt.hashpw(plain_text, bcrypt.gensalt(self.
        gen_salt))
    def check_bcrypt(self, plain_text: bytes, hashed_password:
    bytes) -> bool:
        try:
            return bcrypt.checkpw(plain_text, hashed_password)
        except:
            return False
```

8.2. Verifying User Credentials

Now that we have the necessary services and storage mechanisms to manage passwords, we can proceed with refactoring the backend to support authentication for every route. This means we need to intercept each request to the server and determine whether it is authenticated. In other words, we need an independent software component to sit between the client's request and the access controller. This component is commonly referred to as *middleware* by backend developers.

The authentication process must check for a specific identifier in the request that the server can trust. This identifier is known as an *authentication token*, or simply *token*. The token should be issued by the server and must be verifiable.

Tokens are generally one of two types: custom session IDs or JWTs. In this example, we will use JWTs, as they do not require server-side storage, making them stateless. A JWT consists of three parts, encoded in Base64 and separated by periods. The first part contains metadata about the signing algorithm, the second holds the raw payload, and the third is a password-protected signature of the payload, created using the hashing algorithm specified in the first part. This structure is illustrated in more detail in Figure 8-2 from *jwt.io*.

Figure 8-2. *JSON Web Token (JWT) content*

When a new request is made, we will check the headers for a token. The token's payload will be signed, and the signature will be compared against the signature in the passed token. If they match, we can confirm that the token was issued by the server. For added security, to prevent attackers from stealing legitimate tokens, we will set an expiration date (*defaulting to 30 days from issuance*), which will require the user to log in again once it expires. Since this process involves multiple logical steps, it is best to isolate it as a dedicated service to manage tokens, as shown in Listing 8-3.

Listing 8-3. Flask/Services/JWTService.py

```python
from jwt import PyJWT
from time import time
from typing import Union
class JWTService:
    expires_in_seconds = 2592000
    signing_algorithm = 'HS256'
```

```python
def __init__(self, signing_key: str, expires_in_seconds:
int = 2592000):
    self.signing_key = signing_key
    self.expires_in_seconds = expires_in_seconds
def generate(self,
            data: dict,
            expires_in_seconds: int = expires_in_seconds) ->
            Union[str, None]:
    try:
        instance = PyJWT()
        curr_unix_epoch = int(time())
        data['iat'] = curr_unix_epoch
        if isinstance(expires_in_seconds, int):
            data['exp'] = curr_unix_epoch + expires_
            in_seconds
        token = instance.encode(
            payload=data,
            key=self.signing_key,
            algorithm=self.signing_algorithm)
        if type(token) == bytes:
            token = token.decode('utf8') # Needed for some
            versions of PyJWT
        return token
    except BaseException as _:
        return None
def is_valid(self, token: str, verify_time: bool = True)
-> bool:
    try:
        payload = self.get_payload(token)
        if payload is None:
            return False
```

```
        if verify_time and 'exp' in payload and
        payload['exp'] < int(time()):
            return False
        return True
    except:
        return False
def get_payload(self, token: str):
    try:
        instance = PyJWT()
        payload = instance.decode(
            jwt=token,
            key=self.signing_key,
            algorithms=[self.signing_algorithm])
        return payload
    except Exception as e:
        return None
```

Now that we have a way to issue and validate tokens, we can integrate this logic into our middleware class, as shown in Listing 8-4. This class includes a function responsible for checking whether the requested route requires authentication. If authentication is needed, the middleware will verify whether the provided JWT is valid. If the token is invalid or missing, it will return a standard 401 error, which indicates *Not Authorized*. Otherwise, it will return *None*, signaling that the request can proceed to the next step in the backend code—in our case, the controller.

As shown in line 8, we specify that the login and sign-up routes—both of which will be introduced later—do not require authentication. This is because, after a successful login, a token will be issued to the user. The same applies to sign-up, although we will introduce an additional layer of protection later to prevent abuse by external actors creating accounts without oversight.

Listing 8-4. Flask/Middleware/Middleware.py

```python
from flask import Request
from Services.JWTService import JWTService
from werkzeug import exceptions
class Middleware:
    def __init__(self, jwt_service: JWTService):
        self.unauthenticated_route_names = {'/api/auth/login',
        '/api/auth/sing_up'}
        self.jwt_service = jwt_service
    def auth(self, request: Request):
        is_route_unauthenticated = request.path in self.
        unauthenticated_route_names
        if is_route_unauthenticated:
            return None
        if 'token' in request.headers:
            token = request.headers['token']
            is_valid = self.jwt_service.is_valid(token)
            if is_valid:
                return None
            else:
                return exceptions.Unauthorized()
        return exceptions.Unauthorized()
```

Finally, we need to initialize the previously created services and define three additional routes for logging in, signing up, and checking login status. The last route is necessary to allow the frontend to determine whether it should display the login page. The server's main file should look like Listing 8-5.

As shown in the listing, secrets and keys are read from an external YAML file and then parsed. One of these secrets is used to ensure that only those who know it can create new accounts, as demonstrated in Figures 8-3 and 8-4 using Postman.

Listing 8-5. Flask/flask_main.py

```python
from flask import Flask, request
from DataBase import Employees, Admins
from DataBase.Connection import session_manager
from Services import JWTService, HashingService
from Middleware import Middleware
from werkzeug import exceptions
import yaml

app = Flask(__name__)

with open(".streamlit/secrets.toml") as f:
    yaml_dict = yaml.safe_load(f)
    sing_up_key = yaml_dict['sing_up_key']
    jwt_secret = yaml_dict['jwt_secret']

jwt_service = JWTService(jwt_secret)
middleware = Middleware(jwt_service)
hashing_service = HashingService()

app.before_request(lambda: middleware.auth(request))

@app.route('/api/employees')
def get_all_employees():
    with session_manager() as session:
        employees = session.query(Employees).all()
        employees = [employee.to_dict() for employee in employees]
        return {"data": employees}

@app.route('/api/employee', methods=["POST"])
def add_employee():
    body = request.json
    with session_manager() as session:
        session.add(Employees(**body))
```

```
        session.commit()
    return {"message": "New employee added successfully"}

@app.route('/api/auth/login', methods=["POST"])
def log_in():
    username, password = request.json['username'], request.
    json['password']
    with session_manager() as session:
        admin_account = session.query(Admins).filter(
            Admins.username == username).first()
        print(1)
        if admin_account is None:
            # Username doesn't exist. But don't inform the
            client with that as
            # they can use it to bruteforce valid usernames
            return exceptions.Unauthorized(
                description="Incorrect username/password
                combination")
        print(2)

        # Checking if such hash can be generated from that
        password
        is_password_correct = hashing_service.check_bcrypt(
            password.encode("utf8"), admin_account.password_
            hash.encode("utf8"))
        print(3)
        if not is_password_correct:
            return exceptions.Unauthorized(
                description="Incorrect username/password
                combination")
        print(4)

        token_payload = {"username": username}
```

```
        token = jwt_service.generate(token_payload)
        print(5)

        if token is None:
            return exceptions.InternalServerError(description="
            Login failed")
        print(6)

        return {"token": token}

@app.route('/api/auth/sing_up', methods=["POST"])
def sign_up():
    username, password = request.json['username'], request.
    json['password']
    if request.headers.get("sing_up_key") != "sing_up_key":
        exceptions.Unauthorized(description="Incorrect Key")

    with session_manager() as session:
        password_hash = hashing_service.hash_bcrypt(
            password.encode("utf-8")).decode("utf-8")
        admin = Admins(username=username, password_
        hash=password_hash)
        session.add(admin)
        session.commit()
        return {"message": "Admin account created successfully"}

@app.route('/api/auth/is_logged_in')
def is_logged_in():
    # If this controller is reached this means the
    # Auth middleware recognizes the passed token
    return {"message": "Token is valid"}

app.run()
```

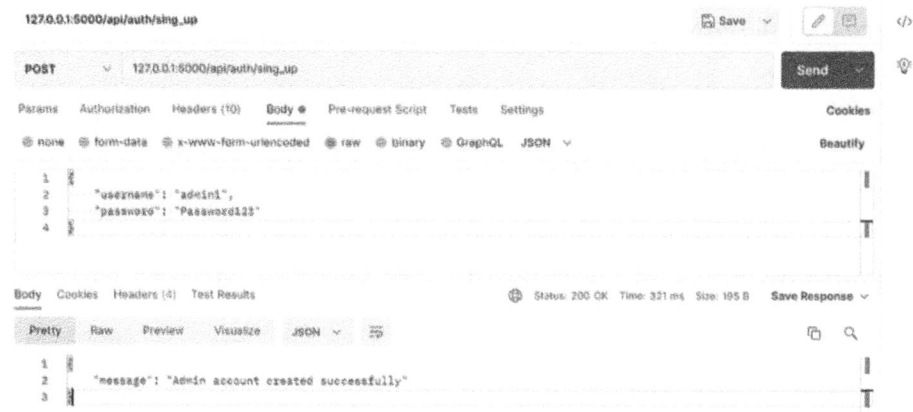

Figure 8-3. *Creating an admin account, step 1: adding a sign-up key*

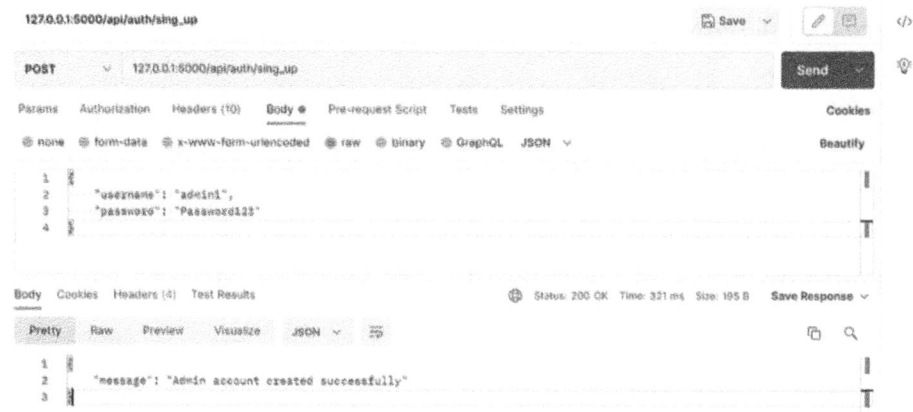

Figure 8-4. *Creating an admin account, step 2: setting the new account's credentials*

After creating the account, we can manually check the database to verify that the new credentials have been stored. This is demonstrated in Figure 8-5, where the username matches the one provided, and the other column contains a valid Bcrypt hash of the supplied password.

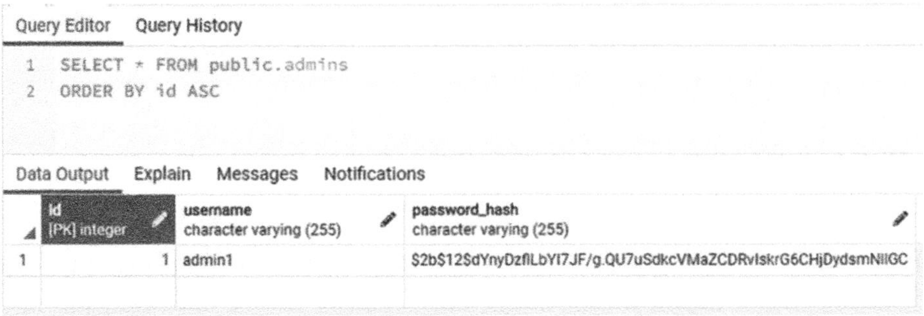

Figure 8-5. *Created account details in the database*

Now that we have admin accounts set up, we can test the login process using Postman before moving on to the next steps. By sending the same username and password used during sign-up in JSON format via a POST request to the appropriate route, we receive a token in response, as shown in Figure 8-6.

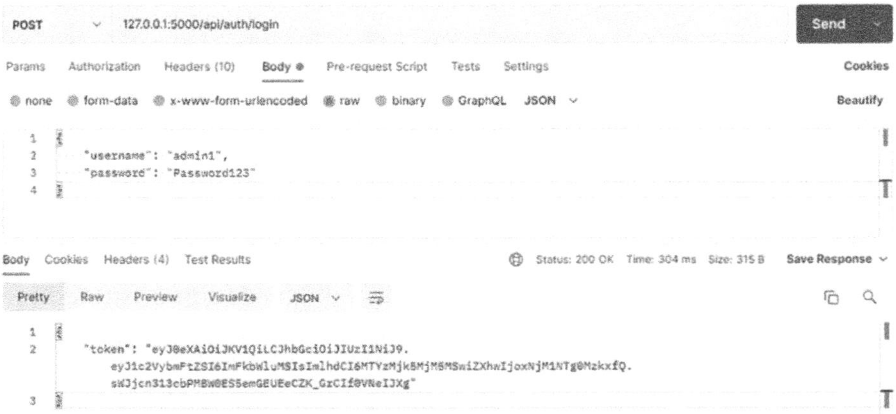

Figure 8-6. *Logging in with Postman using credentials from Figure 8-4*

Moving on to the next phase of development on the Streamlit side, we will start by refactoring Listing 8-6 to support initialization with an authentication token. This token will then be included in every request—except for the login request, where it is not yet available. It is also worth noting that the is_logged_in function is implemented to quickly check the validity of the current token, if one is provided.

Listing 8-6. Streamlit/API.py

```
import requests
class API:
    def __init__(self, base_url: str, token: str):
        self.base_url = base_url
        self.base_headers = {'token': token}
    def add_employee(self, name, dob, paygrade):
        try:
            data = {
                'name': name,
                'date_of_birth': dob,
                'paygrade_id': paygrade
            }
            response = requests.post(self.base_url + '/employee',
            json=data, headers=self.base_headers)
            if response.status_code == 200:
                return True
        except:
            return False
    def get_employees(self):
        try:
            response = requests.get(self.base_url + '/employees',
            headers=self.base_headers)
            return response.json()['data']
        except:
            return None
    def login(self, username, password):
```

```
    try:
        response = requests.post(self.base_url + '/auth/
        login', json={
            'username': username,
            'password': password
        })
        body = response.json()
        token = body.get('token') if type(body) == dict
        else None
        return token
    except:
        return None
def is_logged_in(self):
    return requests.get(self.base_url + '/auth/is_logged_
    in', headers=self.base_headers).status_code == 200
```

With our API now adapted to use authentication tokens, as shown in Listing 8-7, we can move on to the frontend by implementing cookie support to store these tokens and use them as needed, as demonstrated in Listing 8-8. Whenever Streamlit renders, it will check the local cookies for an authentication token. If the token is valid, the application will display the management portal, along with a customized welcome message, as shown in Figure 8-8. Otherwise, it will prompt the user to log in, as shown in Figure 8-7.

Listing 8-7. Streamlit/API.py

```
import requests
class API:
    def __init__(self, base_url: str, token: str):
        self.base_url = base_url
        self.base_headers = {'token': token}
    def add_employee(self, name, dob, paygrade):
```

```python
    try:
        data = {
            'name': name,
            'date_of_birth': dob,
            'paygrade_id': paygrade
        }
        response = requests.post(self.base_url + '/
        employee', json=data, headers=self.base_headers)
        if response.status_code == 200:
            return True
    except:
        return False
def get_employees(self):
    try:
        response = requests.get(self.base_url + '/
        employees', headers=self.base_headers)
        return response.json()['data']
    except:
        return None
def login(self, username, password):
    try:
        response = requests.post(self.base_url + '/auth/
        login', json={
            'username': username,
            'password': password
        })
        body = response.json()
        token = body.get('token') if type(body) == dict
        else None
        return token
```

```
        except:
            return None
    def is_logged_in(self):
        return requests.get(self.base_url + '/auth/is_logged_
        in', headers=self.base_headers).status_code == 200
```

Listing 8-8. Streamlit/streamlit_main.py

```
import streamlit as st
from Views import AddEmployee, DisplayEmployees, Login
from API import API
import extra_streamlit_components as stx
import base64, json

cookie_manager = stx.CookieManager()
cookies = cookie_manager.get_all()
authentication_token = cookies.get("token")\
    if type(cookies) == dict else cookies

api = API("http://127.0.0.1:5000/api", authentication_token)

def get_username_from_token(auth_token):
    b64 = str(auth_token).split(".")[1]
    b64 = b64 + "=" * (4 - (len(b64) % 4))
    data = base64.b64decode(b64).decode("utf8")
    username = json.loads(data)['username']
    return username

def manage_login(username, password):
    token = api.login(username, password)
    cookie_manager.set("token", token)
    return token is not None
```

```
st.title("Company Management Portal")

if st.user.is_logged_in or api.is_logged_in():
    st.subheader(f"_Welcome "
                f"**{get_username_from_token(authentication_
                token)}**_")
    if st.button("Log out"):
        cookie_manager.delete("token")
    st.write("_____")
    AddEmployee(api.add_employee)
    st.write("___")
    DisplayEmployees(api.get_employees)
else:
    Login(manage_login)
```

Company Management Portal

Login

Username

Password

Login

Log in with Google

Figure 8-7. *Login page*

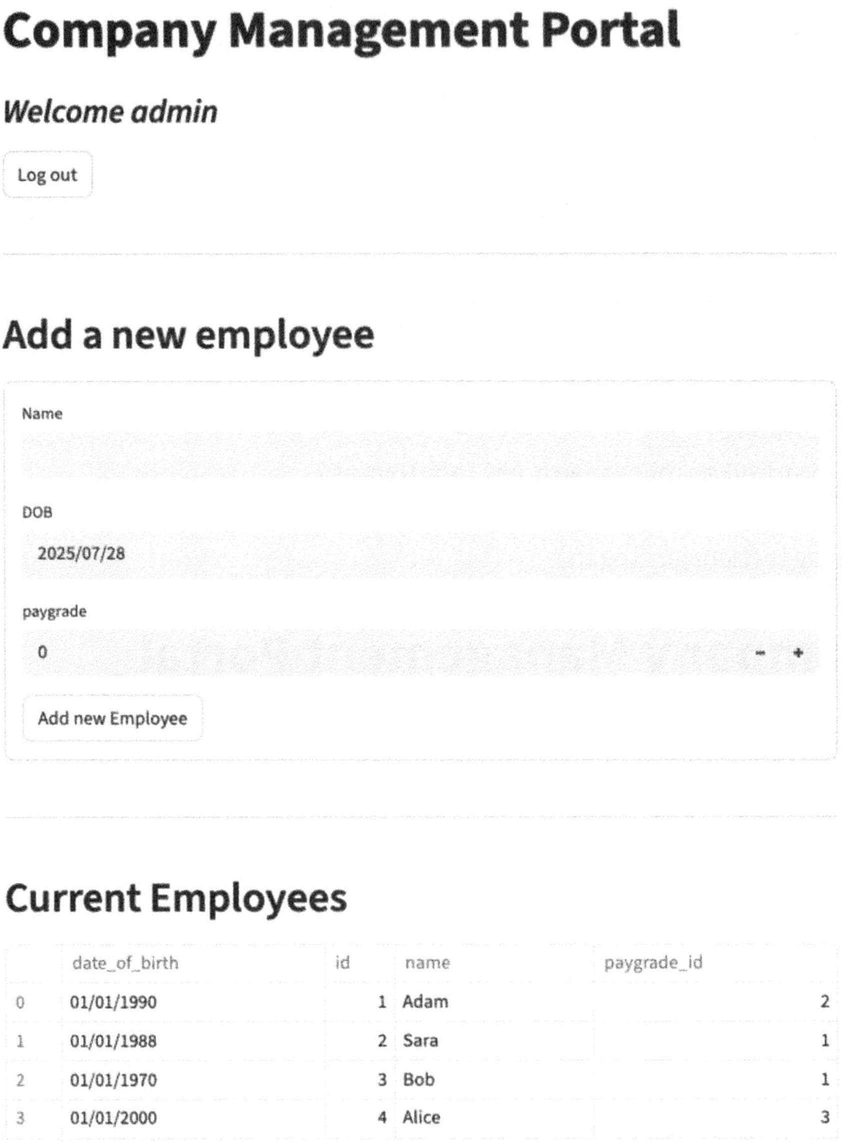

Company Management Portal

Welcome admin

Log out

Add a new employee

Name

DOB

2025/07/28

paygrade

0   -   +

Add new Employee

Current Employees

	date_of_birth	id	name	paygrade_id
0	01/01/1990	1	Adam	2
1	01/01/1988	2	Sara	1
2	01/01/1970	3	Bob	1
3	01/01/2000	4	Alice	3

Figure 8-8. *Adding and viewing the list of authenticated employees*

Looking closely at the Streamlit-side code, we can see that it follows a coding pattern similar to the backend—namely, dependency injection. This approach helps maintain coherence across the entire codebase. Essentially, the API actions are passed down to the views, which are abstracted into a class, as demonstrated in Listings 8-9, 8-10, and 8-11.

Listing 8-9. Streamlit/Views/AddEmployee.py

```python
import streamlit as st
from typing import Callable
import datetime
class AddEmployee:
    def __init__(self, on_submit: Callable[[str, str,
    int], bool]):
        st.header('Add a new employee')
        form = st.form('new_employee')
        name = form.text_input('Name')
        dob = str(form.date_input('DOB',
                    min_value=datetime.datetime(year=1920,
                    day=1, month=1)))
        paygrade = form.number_input('paygrade', step=1)
        if form.form_submit_button('Add new Employee'):
            success = on_submit(name, dob, paygrade)
            if success:
                st.success('New employee added')
            else:
                st.error('Employee not added')
```

Listing 8-10. Streamlit/Views/DisplayEmployees.py

```python
import streamlit as st
from typing import Callable
class DisplayEmployees:
```

```python
    def __init__(self, get_employees: Callable[[], list]):
        st.header('Current Employees')
        employees = get_employees()
        if employees is None:
            st.error('Error getting employees')
        else:
            st.table(employees)
```

Listing 8-11. Streamlit/Views/Login.py

```python
import streamlit as st
from typing import Callable

class Login:
    def __init__(self, on_login: Callable[[str, str], bool]):
        st.header("Login")
        username = st.text_input("Username")
        password = st.text_input("Password",type="password")

        if st.button("Login"):
            success = on_login(username, password)
            if success:
                st.success("Login successful")
            else:
                st.error("Incorrect username and password
                combination")

        st.write("___")

        if st.button("Log in with Google"):
            st.login()
```

8.3. Secrets Management

As we have already discussed how to keep a Streamlit application's secret credentials safe from external access, we will now introduce another method—commonly used in Flask—that can also be applied in a Streamlit context. Essentially, we need a file to store these secrets. This includes the JWT signing key and the sign-up header key, which should be saved on disk and then loaded into the application's memory during runtime. While there are various ways to store secrets and keys, one of the most user-friendly options is using YAML files, as shown in Listing 8-12. These files can be easily parsed and converted into a Python dictionary.

To support signing in with other one-click methods like with Google or Microsoft, you will need to add necessary credentials to the file below to allow your application to utilize these methods of signing in. Extra detail on how to set it up can be found in `https://docs.streamlit.io/ develop/api-reference/user/st.login`

Listing 8-12. Flask/secrets.yaml

```yaml
jwt_secret: "A RANDOM TEXT HERE"
sign_up_key: "ANOTHER RANDOM TEXT HERE"
auth:
    redirect_uri: "http://localhost:8501/oauth2callback"
    cookie_secret: "xxx"
    client_id: "xxx"
    client_secret: "xxx"
    server_metadata_url: "https://accounts.google.com/.well-
    known/openid-configuration"
```

8.4. Anti-SQL Injection Measures with SQLAlchemy

As a final code-implemented protection, we aim to protect the backend's SQL queries by preventing unintended actions from occurring. First, we need to identify what SQL injection is. It typically happens when user-controlled input changes the behavior of the SQL command. For example, suppose we want to support searching for employees whose names start with a string provided by the end user. This could result in a query like: `SELECT * FROM Employees WHERE name = 'input%'`. However, this poses a threat if the input is `OR 1=1 --`, which would change the final query to:`SELECT * FROM Employees WHERE name = '%' OR 1=1 --`.

This causes the database to return all employees instead of treating the input as the search string.

To prevent this problem, we use parameterization, a technique that separates the SQL command from the changing variables. So, in the example above, the query would look like: `SELECT * FROM Employees WHERE name = '@name%'`,where *@name* is a SQL variable initialized before submitting the query. As a developer, this may seem like extra work to ensure more secure SQL. However, libraries and packages can handle this for us. For this purpose, we are using SQLAlchemy, which is a library that connects to many types of databases and adapts SQL command formats based on the database architecture, origin, and version. It follows an intuitive API that is well-documented at docs.sqlalchemy.org.

8.5. Configuring Gitignore Variables

Tracking all files with a version control system like Git is essential for large projects, as it simplifies managing important files and their modification history. However, not all files should be tracked, especially those that could pose security risks. If the codebase is public, or if a private repository is compromised, secrets stored in the tracked files become vulnerable. For this reason, it is widely accepted among developers not to track secrets files in version control. Instead, secrets should be stored in a secure vault that can be accessed through various authentication methods.

While this approach adds an extra layer of security, it can negatively impact code readability, especially if an unfamiliar developer starts working on the project. To resolve this, we can add a file named *Flask/secrets.example.yaml* that contains similar content to the actual secrets file, but with the sensitive key values replaced by vague placeholders, as shown in Listing 8-13. This provides an example for developers without exposing real secrets.

Next, we can exclude the actual secrets file from Git by updating the *.gitignore* file, as shown in Listing 8-14. If necessary, any file or folder in the same directory as .gitignore can be ignored or excluded, depending on the specified syntax.

Listing 8-13. Flask/secrets.example.toml

```
jwt_secret = "<INSERT TEXT>"
sing_up_key = "<INSERT TEXT HERE>"

[auth]
redirect_uri = "http://localhost:8501/oauth2callback"
cookie_secret = "xxx"
client_id = "xxx"
client_secret = "xxx"
server_metadata_url = "https://accounts.google.com/.well-known/
openid-configuration"  # fmt: skip
```

Listing 8-14. Flask/.gitignore

```
Secrets.example.toml
```

8.6. Summary

As part of making any web application public, it is essential to manage the resources being served by verifying each user's authorization level. In this chapter, we have explained how to create and manage user accounts and use them for authentication. We introduced key security mechanisms, such as generating JSON Web Tokens, hashing passwords, and embedding secure signatures into cookies. Additionally, we covered techniques to prevent SQL injection attacks, ensuring unauthorized users cannot access the database. Finally, we explored how to secure application keys and secrets during deployment and how to exclude them from being committed to a version control system like Git.

CHAPTER 9

Deploying Locally and to the Cloud

As you approach the end of the development phase with your Streamlit application, it is time for it to see the light for the first time. In other words, you are ready to deploy the application and share your work with the world. To do that, you will need a machine to serve your application continuously, robustly, and resiliently. While it is possible to turn your local machine into a makeshift server, you are better off deploying the application to the mighty cloud—using platforms like Amazon Web Services, Microsoft Azure, Google Cloud Platform, or, last but not least, Streamlit itself.

In this chapter, we will walk through the steps required to forward your local application to the web, and more importantly, how to deploy your application on remote servers using Linux containers, Windows Server, and Streamlit's dedicated cloud service, *Streamlit Cloud*. By the end of this chapter, you will have acquired the technical know-how to serve your users both within a local network and across the World Wide Web.

© Mohammad Khorasani, Mohamed Abdou, Javier Hernández Fernández 2025
M. Khorasani et al., *Streamlit for Web Development*,
https://doi.org/10.1007/979-8-8688-1826-4_9

9.1. Exposing Streamlit to the World Wide Web

After building an application with Streamlit, you can see it in action by visiting the loopback address in your browser at `http://127.0.0.1:8501`. In addition, you can also share it locally with people and devices on your local network, which typically assigns IP addresses starting with `192.168.*`, `172.(16-31).*`, or `10.*`. To access the running Streamlit application from any device on the same network, simply prepend your IP address with `http://` and append `:8501` or whichever port Streamlit is listening on. However, there is no straightforward way to temporarily showcase your Streamlit application to anyone, anywhere, without leasing a static public IP from your ISP or renting a cloud server from a major provider. In this section, we will explore free, easy-to-configure methods to present your application globally at no extra cost.

9.1.1. Port Forwarding over a Network Gateway

Almost every household has a broadband device, which serves as the gateway to the Internet. However, the household's network and devices are not directly exposed to the Internet; instead, their Internet requests are routed through the broadband device. This device uses NAT (Network Address Translation) to map private IP addresses to a public one. However, the reverse—accessing a device from the Internet—does not work by default unless explicitly configured. With most broadband devices, a built-in web server is available to control various network settings. Usually, the first IP address on the network belongs to the broadband device. Entering this IP into a browser typically brings up a configuration page, as shown in Figure 9-1. While the interface may vary across devices, most offer options to configure *port forwarding* or *port mapping*. On that page, we want to map an internal IP and port to one of the broadband's public-facing ports. Ideally, we would map Streamlit's default port 8501 to port 80, the default for HTTP.

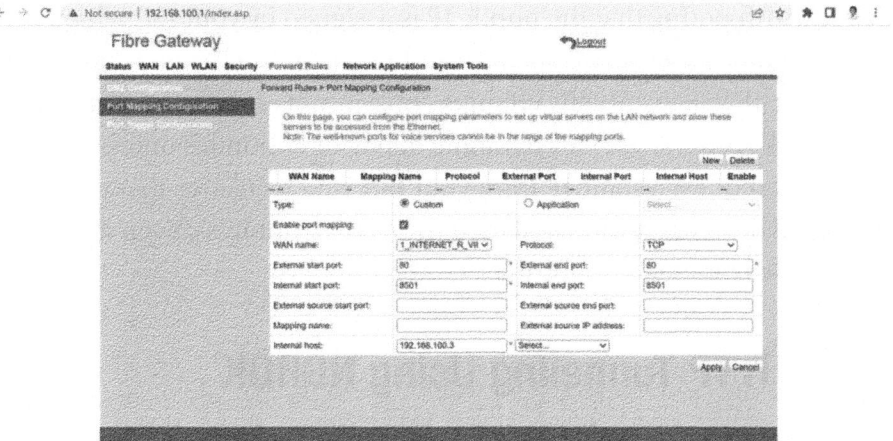

Figure 9-1. *Broadband's configuration website*

The next step is to find out the gateway's public IP address. An easy way to do this is by simply googling it, as shown in Figure 9-2. Essentially, any website you visit can detect your public IP and display it back to you. Once you have this IP, you can paste it into your browser's address bar, and—if everything is configured correctly—you will be presented with your Streamlit application.

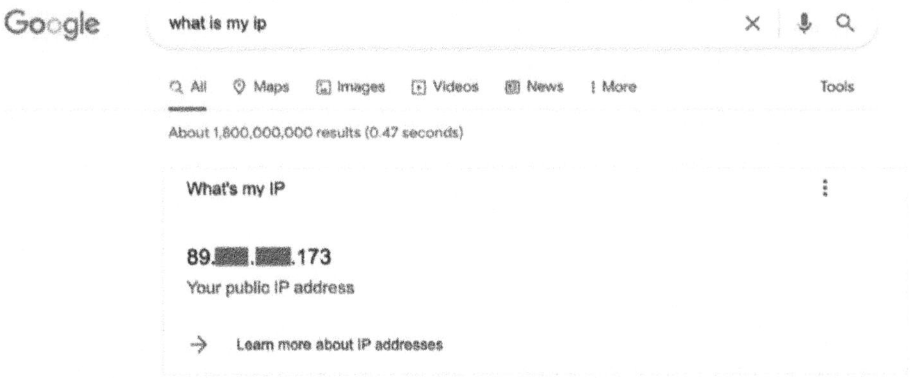

Figure 9-2. *Host's public IP address*

It is worth noting that the public IP is assigned by your ISP, which typically rotates through a pool of IP addresses for its clients. This means your public IP will eventually change—possibly every hour or when the network reconnects. This dynamic behavior continues unless you specifically request a static IP from your ISP, which ensures that your broadband device is always assigned the same IP address, even if your network goes offline temporarily.

9.1.2. HTTP Tunneling Using NGROK

The concept of tunneling is similar to establishing a VPN connection between two devices, even if they are far apart and not on the same network. Ngrok uses tunneling to allow private network devices to be accessed by the public network for a short period (usually two hours). It does this by allocating a temporary subdomain on their servers, which forwards requests to your service and exposes it on your behalf. In short, a Streamlit application running at `http://127.0.0.1:8501` can be accessed via a specific ngrok URL, which follows this format:

`http://<random-uuid-here>.ngrok-free.app`

Once the tunnel command is initiated by the Ngrok user, the connection is established, and the Ngrok URL is provided. The user can then share this URL with anyone to access their local Streamlit application for the next few hours. After installing Ngrok on your computer, you can run it by typing the following command into the CMD or terminal:

`ngrok http <port_to_tunnel_to>`

where the *<port_to_tunnel_to>* block can be replaced with 8501 to tunnel to the running Streamlit application. Listing 9-1 shows a simple Streamlit application using an iframe to display the user's public IP address. After running ngrok on port 8501 in the CMD, the user is presented with the allocated subdomain, as seen in Figure 9-3.

The subdomain's location is listed as the United States, as mentioned by ngrok. However, when visiting a public IP website, it does not show the United States as the origin, as seen in Figure 9-4. Instead, the IP displayed is the user's original ID from Qatar, even though ngrok tunneled through the United States. This is because ngrok is not a VPN but a network, and the request to the page is routed through the Streamlit host machine.

Listing 9-1. main.py

```python
import streamlit as st

st.title('Welcome, WWW')
url = 'https://www.whatismyip-address.com'
script = f"""
<iframe src='{url}' height='500' width='500'></iframe>
"""

st.write(script, unsafe_allow_html=True)
st.write(f'Check out your [public IP]({url})')
```

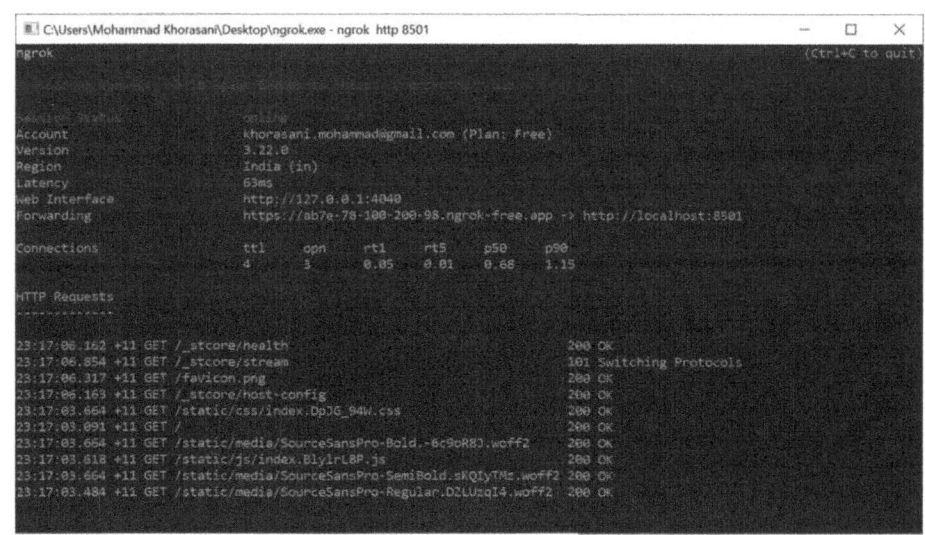

Figure 9-3. *Ngrok dashboard after tunneling to port 8501*

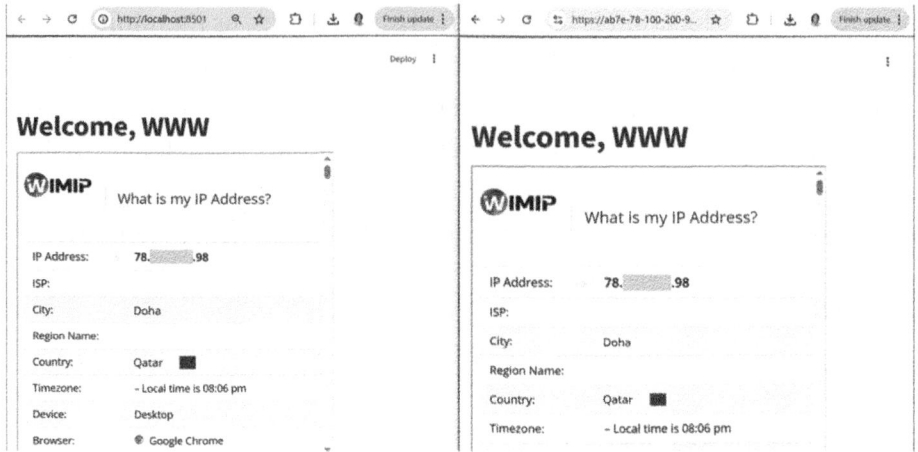

Figure 9-4. *Two browser windows, one being served locally and the other by ngrok, and both showing the same client IP*

9.2. Deployment to Streamlit Community Cloud

Deploying a web application on the cloud can be a demanding task, depending on your cloud service provider. Some, like Heroku, have made it as simple as connecting your GitHub repository, installing build packs, configuring the application, and launching it. Others require you to handle the entire process, including setting up the virtual machine, creating containers, configuring port forwarding, load balancing, and routing requests yourself. Regardless, deploying to the cloud requires at least a basic understanding of cloud computing concepts—after all, that is why we have DevOps engineers.

Streamlit, however, is democratizing this last frontier and making deployment almost a one-click process. With *Streamlit Cloud*, you can simply connect your GitHub repository and click *deploy*. Streamlit will automatically provision the application with all its required dependencies and update it each time you push a new version of your source code. No additional intervention is required from the developer. Furthermore, if you need more than one private application, additional computing resources, or enterprise-grade features, you can upgrade to Streamlit's premium packages.

9.2.1. One-Click Deployment

Before deploying your first application to Streamlit Cloud, you should create a GitHub account and push your script to a repository. Once that is done, you can follow these steps to deploy:

1. Navigate to *share.streamlit.io*, log in with your GitHub account, and click *New app*.

2. Select the repository, branch, and file where your source code is located. Then click *Deploy!* as shown in Figure 9-5.

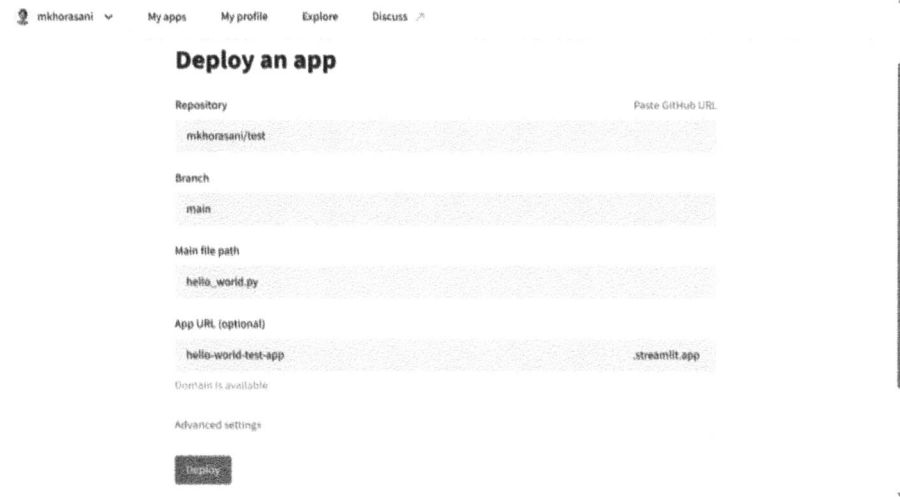

Figure 9-5. Deploying an application to Streamlit Cloud (1)

3. Sit back and relax while Streamlit Cloud provisions your application, as shown in Figure 9-6.

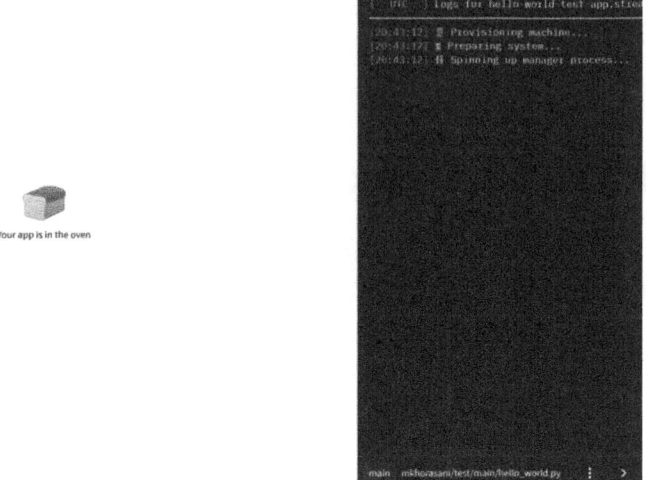

Figure 9-6. *Deploying an application to Streamlit Cloud (2)*

4. And there you have it, your first application
    deployed to Streamlit Cloud, as shown in Figure 9-7.

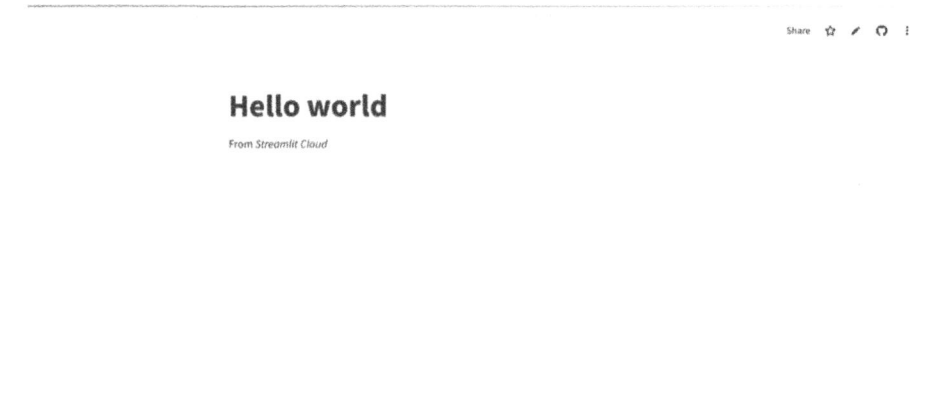

Figure 9-7. *Deploying an application to Streamlit Cloud (3)*

230

9.2.2. Streamlit Secrets

Another benefit of using Streamlit Cloud is that you can securely store private data on Streamlit's servers and easily access it in your application. This feature is particularly useful for storing user credentials, database connection strings, API keys, and other passwords—without the risk of exposing them in plain text within your code (which you should never do under any circumstances). Instead, you can follow these steps to store and access private data using Streamlit's *Secrets Management*.

1. Navigate to *share.streamlit.io* and open the settings for the application to which you want to add secrets, as shown in Figure 9-8.

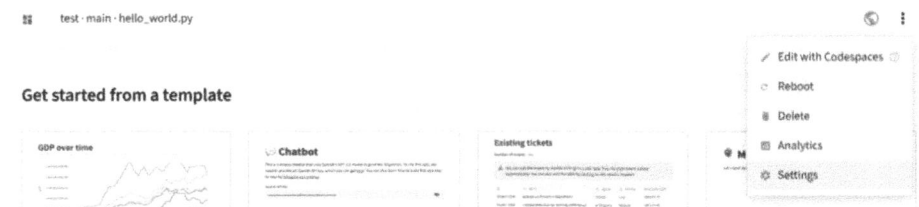

Figure 9-8. *Adding secrets to Streamlit Cloud's Secrets Management (1)*

2. Add your secrets in the form of a TOML file, as shown in Figure 9-9.

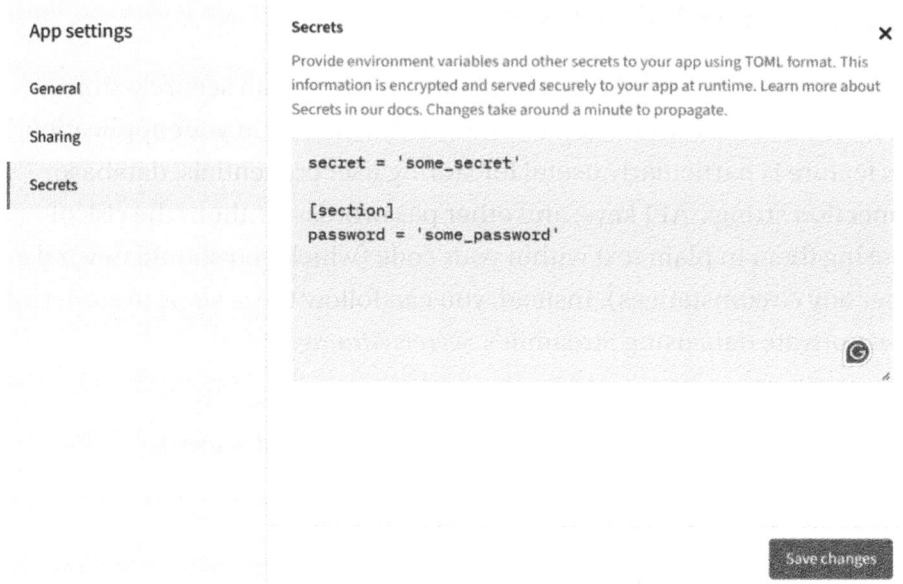

Figure 9-9. Adding secrets to Streamlit Cloud's Secrets Management (2)

3. Access your secrets in your script using the st. secrets command, as shown in the following and in Figure 9-10:

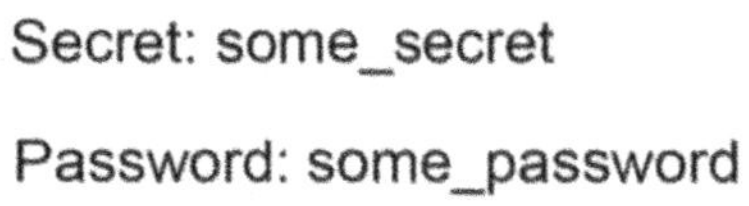

Secret: some_secret

Password: some_password

Figure 9-10. Using secrets in a Streamlit Cloud application

```
import streamlit as st
st.write('**Secret:**',st.secrets['secret'])
st.write('**Password:**',st.secrets['section']
['password'])
```

4. If you wish to replicate Secrets Management locally on your own server, you can simply add the same TOML file as secrets.toml in the .streamlit folder in your root directory. Be sure to add this folder to your .gitignore file to ensure that such files are not included in Git commits.

9.3. Deployment to Linux

Most cloud providers specialize in offering virtual machine leases to corporations and individuals for running services and apps in a Linux environment. The strength of Linux lies in its ability to process at higher speeds and make better use of computer resources due to its minimalistic kernel layers. These factors make Linux the go-to choice for cloud machines.

9.3.1. Native Deployment on a Linux Machine

With access to a Linux machine, such as Ubuntu WSL (Windows Subsystem for Linux) run on Windows, you can run Streamlit through the CLI as shown in Figure 9-11.

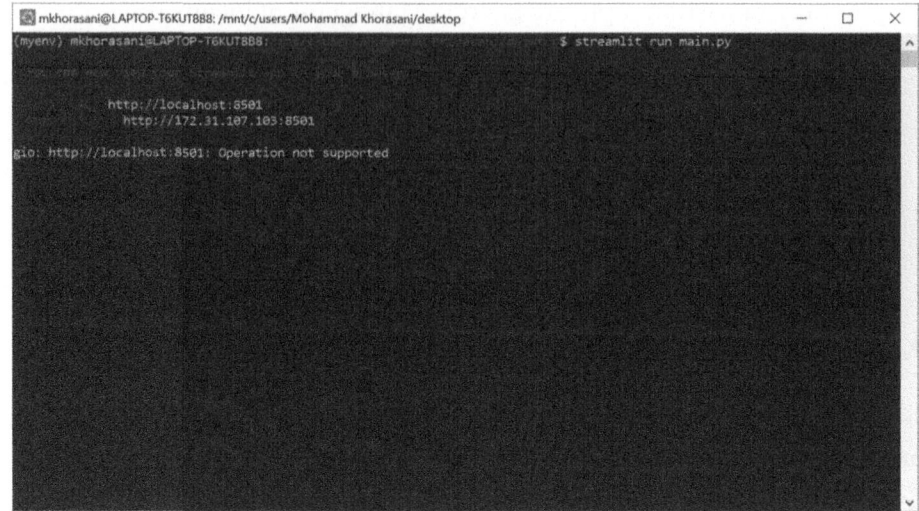

Figure 9-11. *Running Listing 9-2 in the terminal*

The output of the Streamlit application in Listing 9-2 can be seen in Figure 9-12.

Figure 9-12. *Output of Listing 9-2, showing the operating system being Linux*

To display the system platform running, you can run the script shown in Listing 9-2.

Listing 9-2. main.py

```
import os
import platform
import streamlit as st

st.title(f'Deployed on {platform.system()} ({os.name})')
st.subheader('More details: ') st.write(f'_{platform.
platform()}_')
```

9.3.2. Deployment with Linux Docker Containers

To avoid the hassle of running your Streamlit application in a specific way—and for added security—you can use a Docker container to run it. Docker allows you to host an application in any OS environment with its own variables, applications, and services, while giving you control over the computer resources it can access. Moreover, if the application is compromised by a malicious actor, they are unlikely to escape the Docker container and further compromise the host machine, provided the container is configured correctly.

Now that we understand the benefits of deploying services in a containerized environment, we can proceed to create Docker's main file, as shown in Listing 9-3. Assuming Docker is already installed, this file initiates a Linux environment with Python 3.8 pre-installed, then creates a folder to hold your Streamlit/Python files. Next, it copies your existing *requirements.txt* file (as shown in Listing 9-4) into Docker's working directory, where the dependencies will be installed. Once Streamlit is installed, the Docker container is instructed to expose port 8501 to allow access from outside the container—this is Streamlit's default port. Finally, your Streamlit files are copied into the working directory and executed.

Listing 9-3. Dockerfile

```
FROM python:3.10

# Set working directory
WORKDIR /app

# Install dependencies
COPY requirements.txt ./requirements.txt
RUN pip install --no-cache-dir -r requirements.txt

# Expose Streamlit port
EXPOSE 8501

# Copy app files
COPY . /app

# Add a simple healthcheck (tries to curl the Streamlit app
every 30s)
HEALTHCHECK --interval=30s --timeout=10s --start-period=
30s --retries=3 \
  CMD curl -f http://localhost:8501/_stcore/health || exit 1

# Explicit entrypoint with host binding
ENTRYPOINT ["streamlit", "run", "main.py", "--server.
address=0.0.0.0"]
```

Listing 9-4. requirements.txt

```
streamlit==1.41.1 # Latest version as of writing this book
```

With our files ready, we need to build a custom Docker image from our project—similar to what is shown in Figure 9-13—by running the command in Listing 9-5 from the project's root folder, where the Dockerfile should reside.

Listing 9-5. Building a Docker image

```
docker build -t <CUSTOM_IMAGE_NAME>:latest .
```

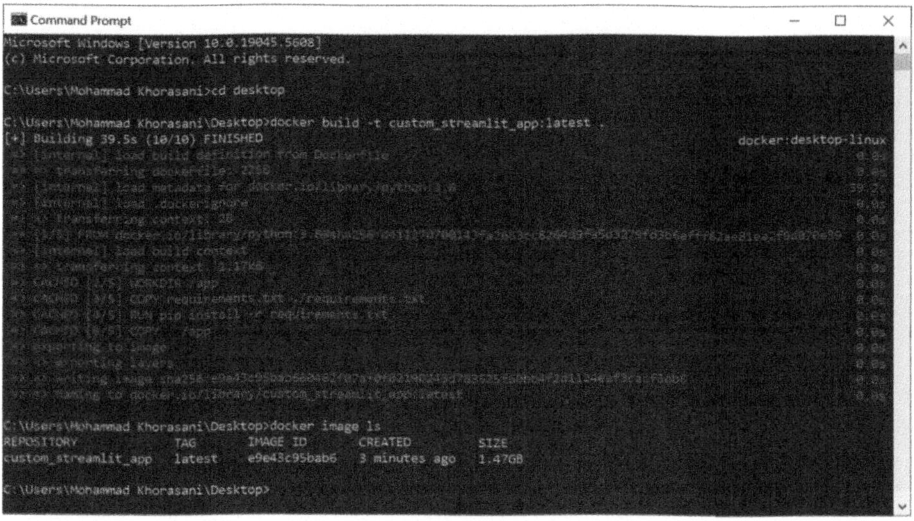

Figure 9-13. *Building image and verifying its existence*

Running the image is done by executing the code shown in Listing 9-6; the -d option is to detach the process from the command line, similar to the disown command in Linux. Figure 9-14 shows how the process is not detached and therefore stops reusing the same command-line window. Now we have a running container overriding the current machine's port 8501 with its own, which means the Streamlit application can be visited from localhost as seen in Figure 9-15.

You can run the image by executing the command shown in Listing 9-6. The -d option detaches the process from the command line, similar to the disown command in Linux. Figure 9-14 demonstrates what happens when the process is not detached—it remains tied to the same command-line window. Now, with a running container overriding the host machine's port 8501 with its own, the Streamlit application can be accessed via localhost, as shown in Figure 9-15.

Listing 9-6. Making a container out of a Docker image

```
docker run -d -p 8501:8501 <CUSTOM_IMAGE_NAME>:latest
```

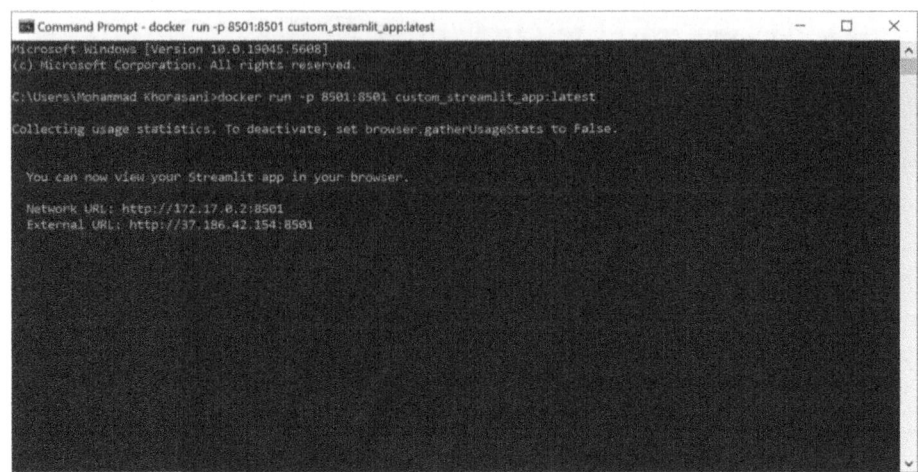

Figure 9-14. *Running the Docker image*

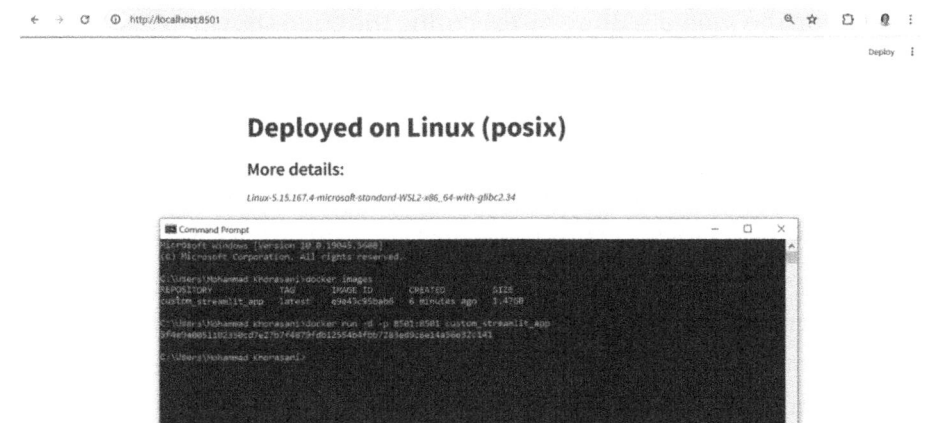

Figure 9-15. *Streamlit application running from a Docker container*

Finally, we can destroy the container, without affecting the image, by running Listing 9-8. First, we need to know the container ID by running Listing 9-7, then apply the stopping action as seen in Figure 9-16.

Listing 9-7. Displaying all running Docker container metadata

```
docker ps
```

Listing 9-8. Stopping a specific Docker container

```
docker stop <CONTAINER_ID>
```

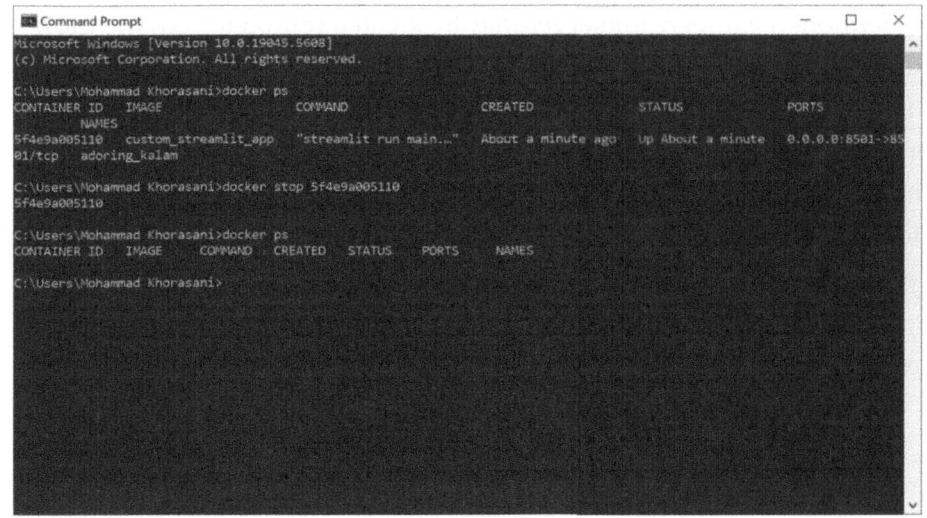

Figure 9-16. *Checking active containers and closing a specific container*

9.4. Deployment to Windows Server

Given the corporate world's affinity for Microsoft, if you are deploying your Streamlit application on a corporate server, chances are you will be using Windows Server. Fortunately, the process to provision your application is simple and straightforward. While this section focuses on Windows

Server, the steps can also be followed for deploying on a standard Windows operating system. Before we proceed, however, we will make a few assumptions: your corporate server is located remotely, and you only have local Intranet access with no Internet connectivity. As a result, additional steps will be required to overcome these assumptions, and these will be explained in the following sections.

9.4.1. Establishing a Remote Desktop Connection

As mentioned earlier, your server may be located remotely, and the most likely way to connect to it will be through the Remote Desktop Protocol (RDP). RDP provides a graphical user interface to access the remote server over a network connection. The Microsoft client for RDP is Remote Desktop Connection, as shown in Figure 9-17. To connect, enter the IP address of the remote server in the *Computer* field, and if required, append the domain to the username in the *User name* field in the format *domain/username*. Then, click *Connect*, and you will be prompted to enter your password to log in to the server.

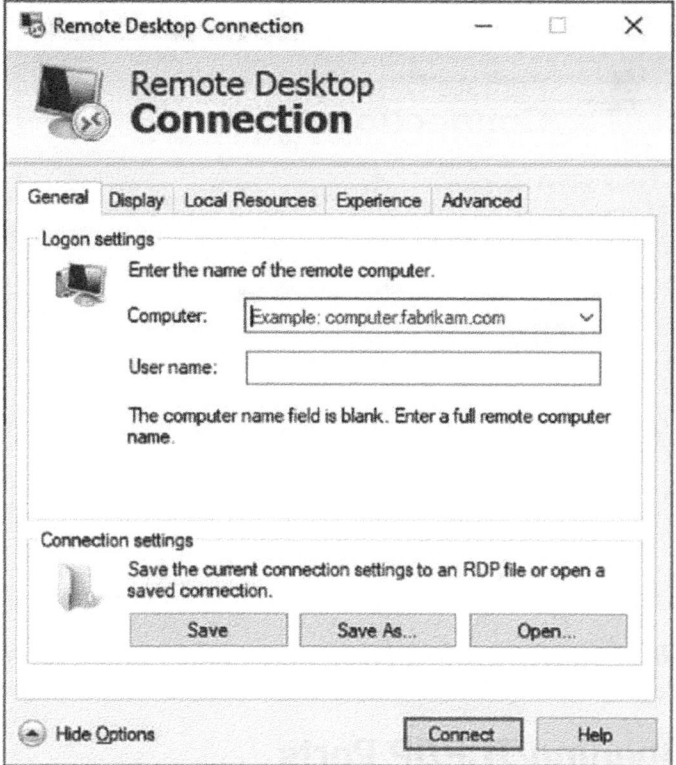

Figure 9-17. *Establishing a RDP connection to the remote server*

Since your remote server might not have Internet access, you can use RDP to transfer files from your local disk to the server by selecting the *Drives* checkbox in the Local Resources tab, as shown in Figure 9-18. This feature also allows you to provide access to other local resources, such as I/O devices and peripherals, on the server if needed.

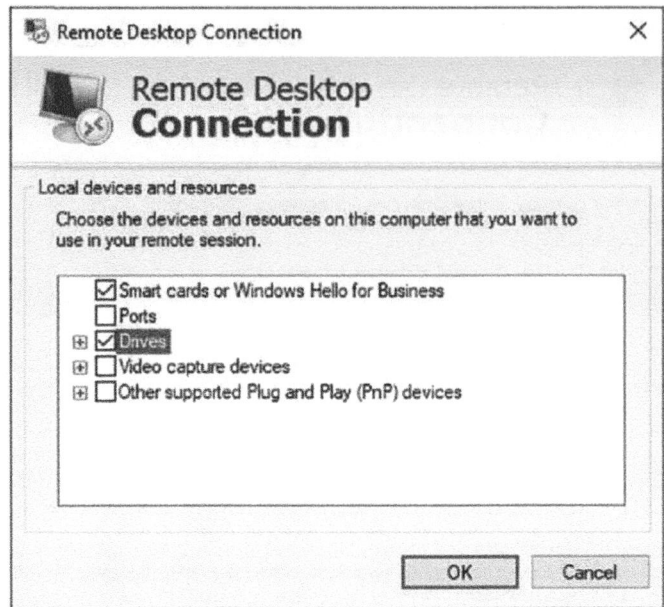

Figure 9-18. *Transferring local resources to the remote server*

9.4.2. Opening TCP/IP Ports

Before proceeding, make sure that all relevant inbound and outbound TCP/IP ports on the server are open, allowing the Streamlit application to be forwarded across the local network:

1. Open *Windows Defender Firewall with Additional Security.*

2. Select *Inbound Rules* or *Outbound Rules* in the left pane.

3. Click *New Rule* in the right pane to open the *New Rule Wizard* window.

4. Select the *Port* option and then click next as shown in Figure 9-19.

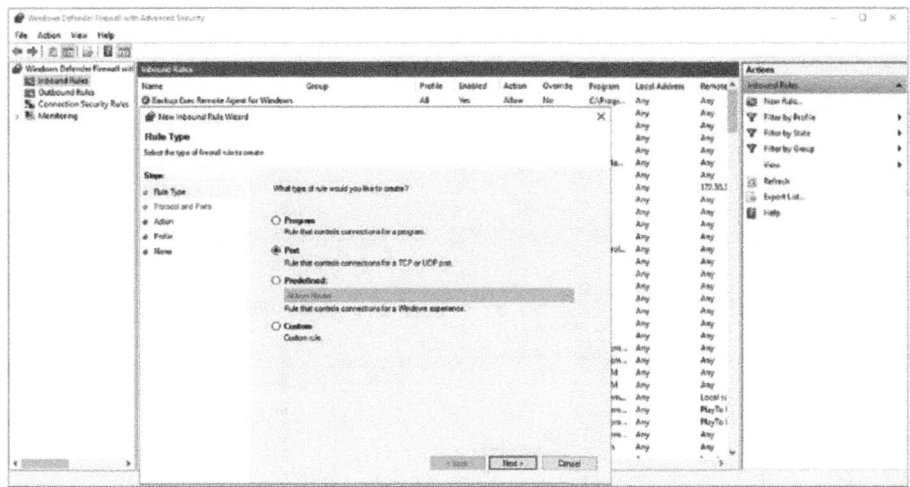

Figure 9-19. *Opening TCP/IP ports (1)*

5.   Select *TCP* and enter the port number that your
     Streamlit application will be served on, for example,
     8501, as shown in Figure 9-20.

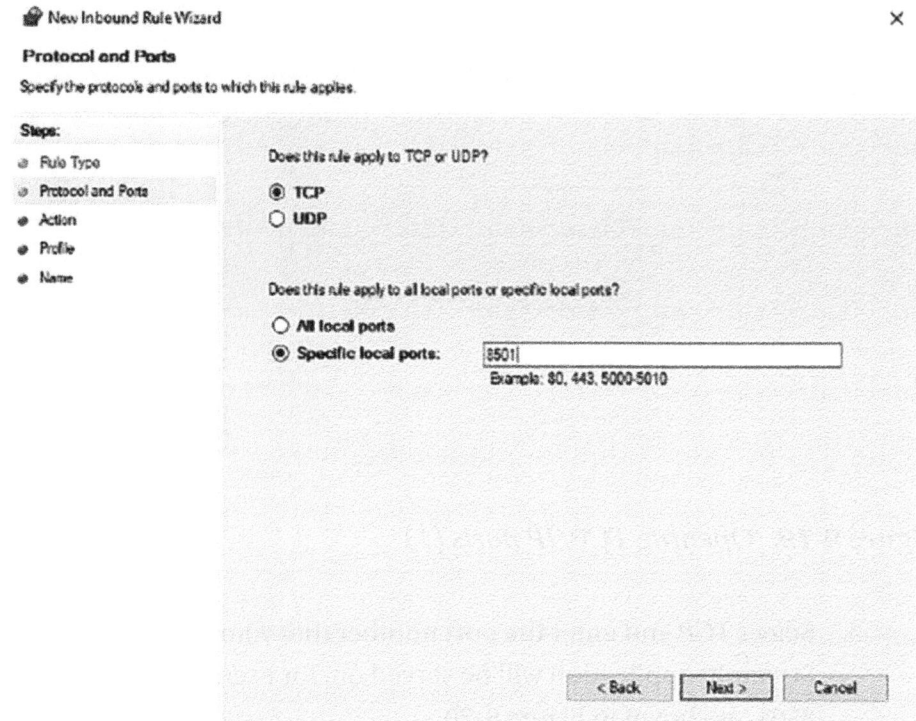

Figure 9-20. *Opening TCP/IP ports (2)*

6. Select *Allow the connection* to serve the port to all
    users, or alternatively select *Allow the connection*
    if it is secure to serve the port to specific users, as
    shown in Figure 9-21.

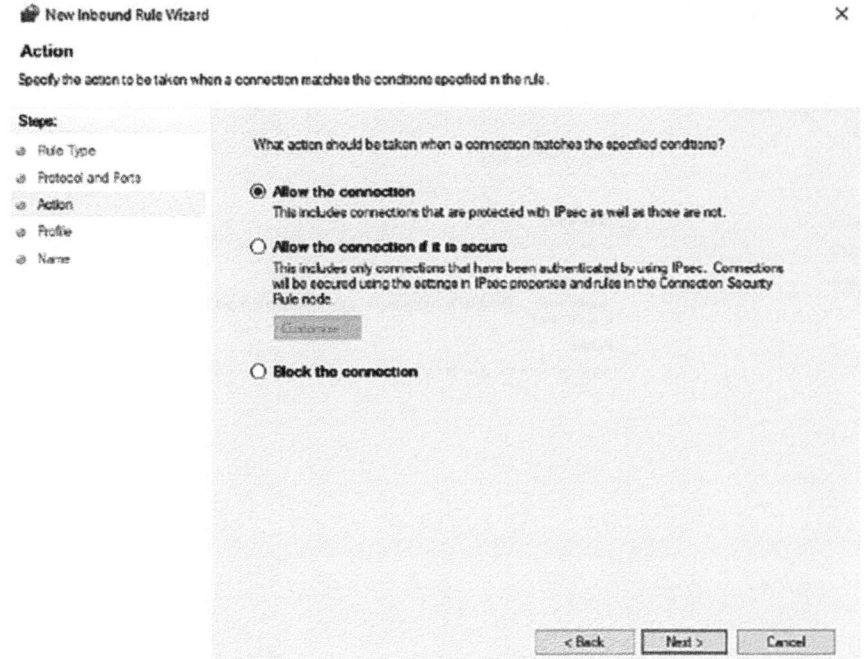

Figure 9-21. *Opening TCP/IP ports (3)*

7. Next, select *Domain* and *Private* to serve the port to
    secure networks, as shown in Figure 9-22.

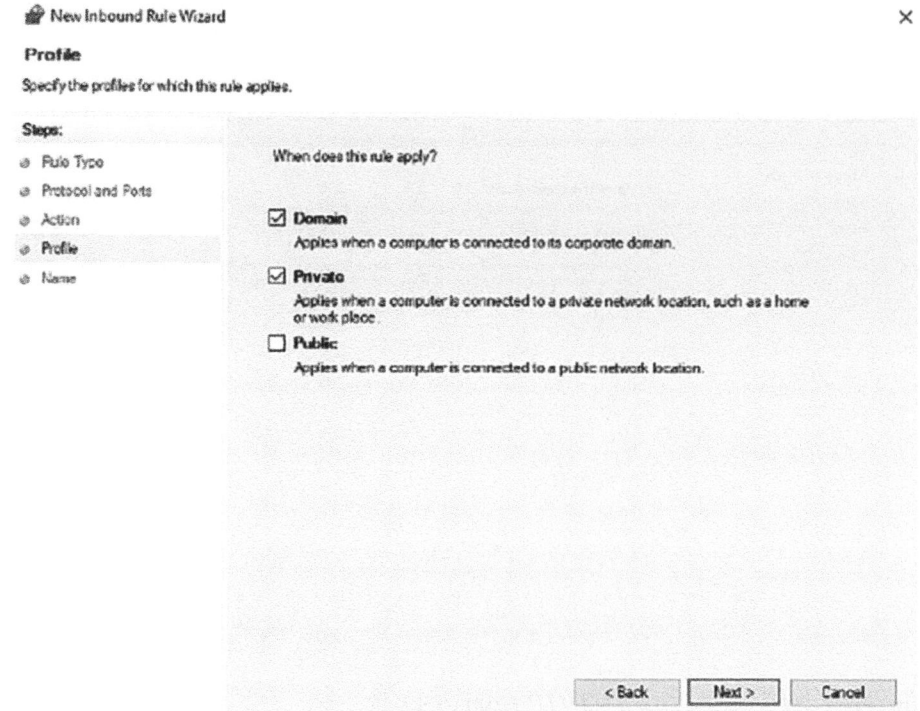

Figure 9-22. *Opening TCP/IP ports (4)*

8. Finally, enter a name for your rule and follow the same steps to open the same port for both inbound and outbound communication.

9.4.3. Anaconda Offline Package Installation

Since your server may not have Internet access, you will not be able to install Python packages and their dependencies using Pip as usual. Instead, you will need to perform an offline installation by following these steps:

1. Open Anaconda Prompt on a computer with access to the Internet.

2. To download the required Python package with all of its related dependencies, type the following command, specifying the file path of where to save the package:

```
pip download <package name> -d '<folder path>'
```

3. Once the package has been downloaded, zip the files and transfer them to the server using RDP or any other available method.

4. Unzip the files and type the following command into Anaconda Prompt on the server to change the root directory to the location where the package is stored:

```
cd <folder path>
```

5. Enter the following command into Anaconda Prompt to initiate an offline installation of the required package:

```
pip install <package name> -f ./ --no-index
```

9.4.4. Adding Anaconda to System Path

To run your Streamlit application as an executable batch file (explained in the following section), you first need to add Anaconda or any other Python interpreter of your choice to the system path in Windows. Follow these steps:

1. Determine the location of Anaconda.exe by typing the following command into Anaconda Prompt:

```
where anaconda
```

2. Open the Windows search bar and select *Edit the system environment variables*.

3. Once the *System Properties* window opens, click the *Advanced* tab and select *Environment Variables*.

4. Next, highlight *Path* and click *Edit* to add the path for Anaconda, as shown in Figure 9-23.

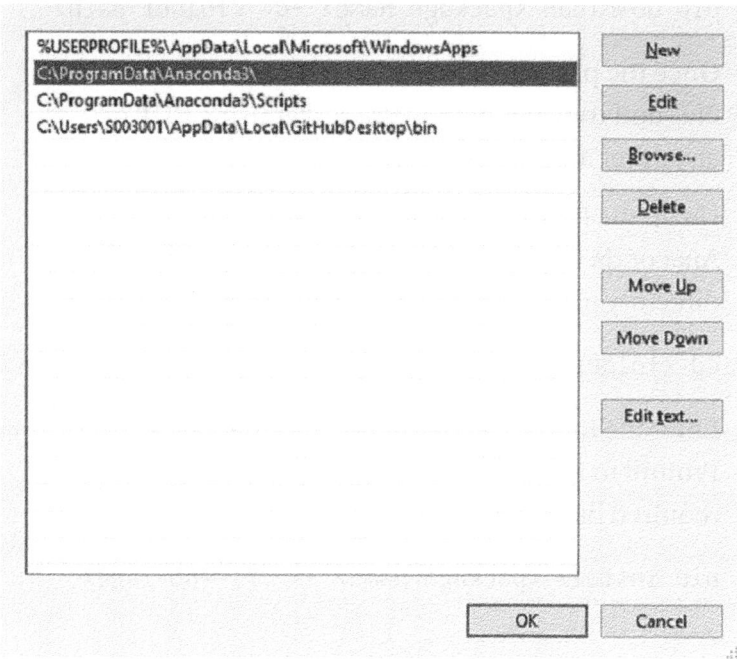

Figure 9-23. Adding Anaconda to the system path

5. If the necessary paths do not already exist, add the path that was found in step 1 by entering the following two:

    ```
    C:\...\Anaconda3\
    ```

    and

    ```
    C:\...\Anaconda3\Scripts\
    ```

6. To verify that Anaconda has been successfully added to the system path, open Windows Command Prompt and type anaconda. If Anaconda has not been added, an error will appear. Otherwise, you should be able to use any Anaconda command, such as conda list.

9.4.5. Running Application As an Executable Batch File

To run your Streamlit application as a Windows service (explained in the following section), you first need to create an executable batch file. Batch files are similar to .exe files and can be run by double-clicking, just like any other application. Follow these steps to create a batch file for your Streamlit application:

1. Open notepad or any other text editor of your choice.

2. Type the following commands on separate lines:

```
call activate <environment name>
cd <folder path>
streamlit run <script name.py>
pause
```

3. Save the file with a *.bat* extension to create the batch file.

4. Run the batch file to ensure that the application launches as expected.

9.4.6. Running Application As a Persistent Windows Service

The final step in preparing for deployment on Windows Server is to run your Streamlit application persistently as a Windows service. While you can still serve it as you would normally with any Streamlit application, running it as a Windows service offers several benefits, including the following:

1. Your application will be run in the background without opening a console.

2. The application will remain independent of the RDP session, ensuring it continues to run even when the RDP connection is terminated.

3. You can schedule your application to run on Windows startup or based on any other trigger.

For a robust setup, consider using a tool like **NSSM (the Non-Sucking Service Manager)**. NSSM allows you to run any executable, such as python.exe running your Streamlit app, as a Windows service. It provides better control over logging, process priority, and automatic restarts, making your deployment more reliable and easier to manage.

To configure your application as a persistent Windows service, please follow these steps:

1. Open *Windows Task Scheduler* and click *Create Task* on the right pane, as shown in Figure 9-24.

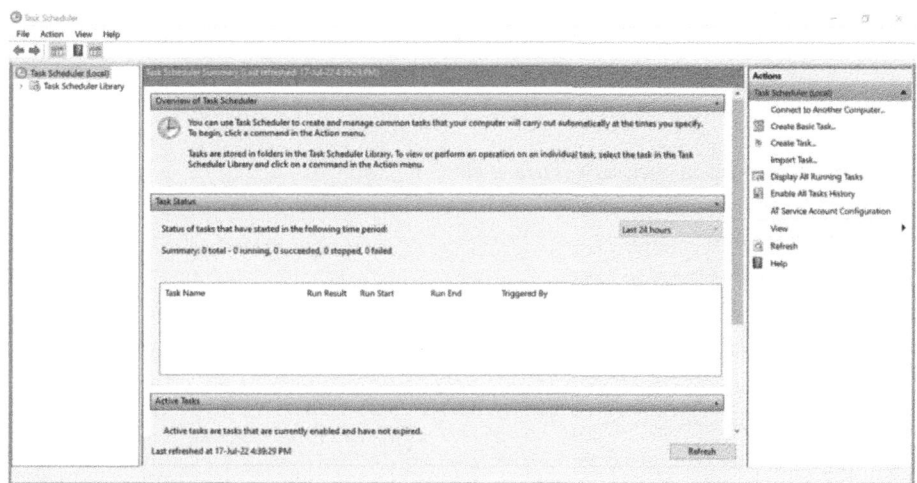

Figure 9-24. *Running application as a persistent Windows service (1)*

2. Enter a name for the task, then select the *Run whether user is logged on or not* and *Run with highest privileges* options, as shown in Figure 9-25.

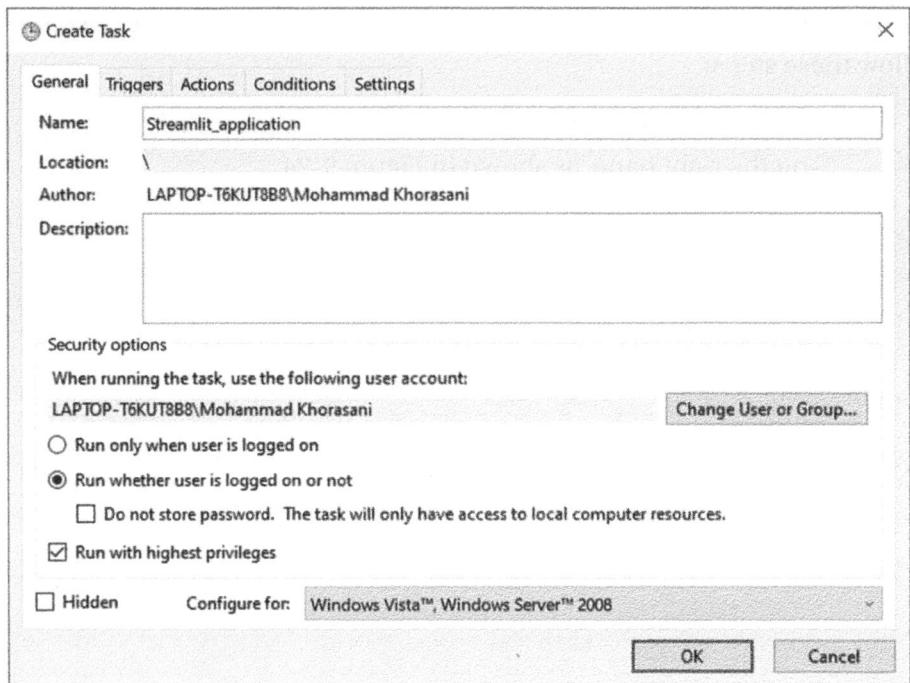

Figure 9-25. Running application as a persistent Windows service (2)

3.   Navigate to the *Actions* tab and select *Start a
     program* from the action menu, then browse to
     the location of the batch file you created for your
     Streamlit application (explained in the previous
     section), as shown in Figure 9-26.

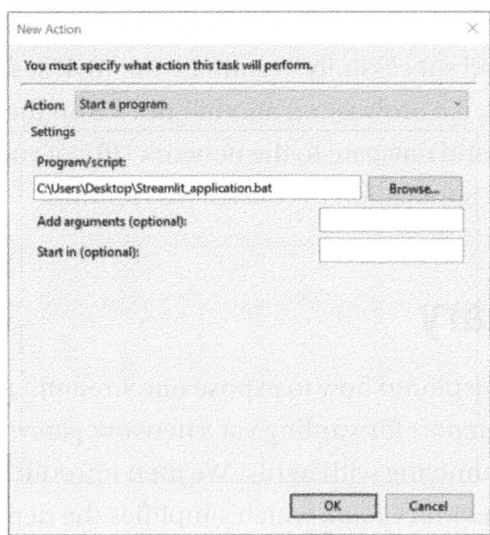

Figure 9-26. *Running application as a persistent Windows service (3)*

4. Open the *Task Scheduler Library* on the left pane,
   select your created task in the list, and select *Run* on
   the right pane, as shown in Figure 9-27.

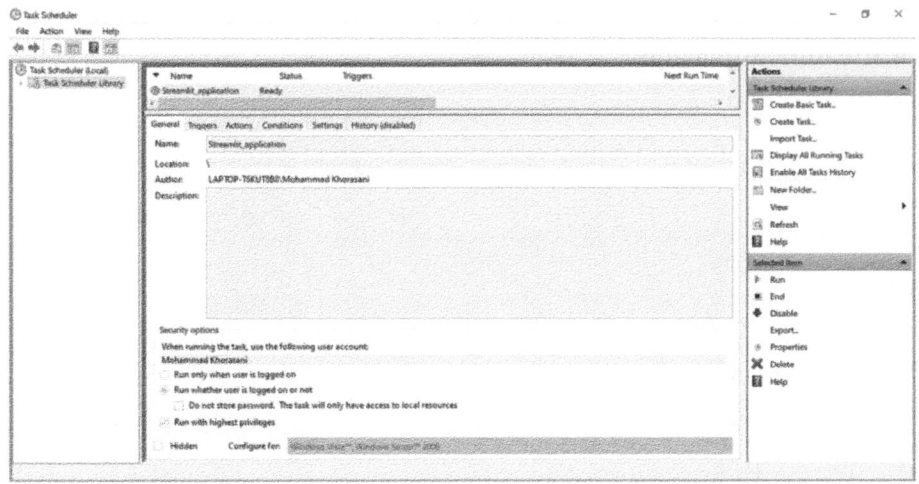

Figure 9-27. *Running application as a persistent Windows service (4)*

5. To verify that your Windows service task has been configured successfully, terminate the RDP session. Then, open a browser on another device on the local network and navigate to the network URL of your Streamlit application to check if it's running.

9.5. Summary

In this chapter, we explored how to expose our Streamlit application to the Internet through port forwarding via a network gateway, as well as leveraging HTTP tunneling with ngrok. We then introduced Streamlit's cloud platform, *Streamlit Cloud*, which simplifies the deployment process. With Streamlit Cloud, developers can deploy their applications with just a click by connecting their GitHub repository. Additionally, we learned how to securely integrate private data into our applications using Streamlit's *Secrets Management*, both locally and in the cloud. Finally, we covered the process of deploying our applications to Linux containers and Windows Server, which are the foundation of most remote servers worldwide. With that, we have completed the entire development-to-deployment life cycle of a Streamlit application.

## CHAPTER 10

Building Streamlit Components

Streamlit continuously expands its feature set to offer developers new capabilities with just a few lines of code. However, there comes a time when developers need to customize their applications to meet specific user needs. Whether it is modifying the user interface or providing a tailored user experience, Streamlit allows developers to create custom components as needed. Moreover, Streamlit supports the use of ReactJS to build components that can either function as a live web server or be deployed with production-ready code. In this chapter, we will guide you through the process of creating custom Streamlit components, integrating them into a Pythonic context, and sharing them with the broader community.

10.1. Introduction to Streamlit Custom Components

Fundamentally, Streamlit acts as a backend server, delivering web page updates to client browsers using DG. While HTML and JavaScript can be generated by various web frameworks, Streamlit is capable of serving components from any web application framework. For instance, frameworks like ReactJS allow developers to code in JSX, which is then

M. Khorasani et al., *Streamlit for Web Development*,
https://doi.org/10.1007/979-8-8688-1826-4_10

compiled into a combination of static files that can be served from disk. In a production environment, it is highly recommended to serve static files from disk, as shown in Figure 10-1. However, Streamlit also allows for components hosted locally. The trade-off here is that the component, when imported into a Streamlit app, may behave differently. For example, if you print the current URL from the custom component, it will not reflect the same URL where the Streamlit application is hosted.

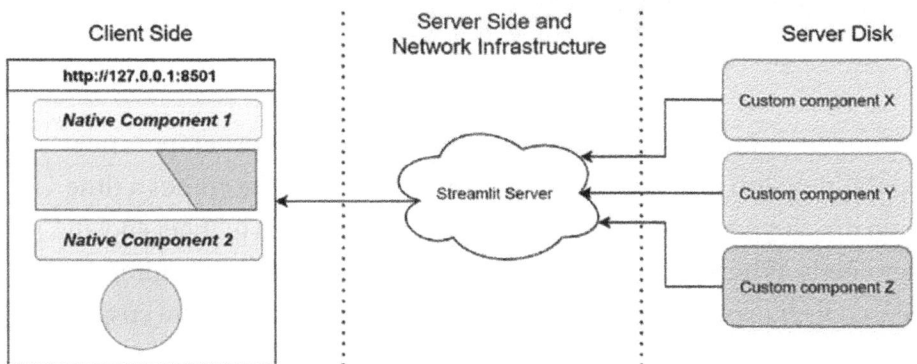

Figure 10-1. *How custom components are served through Streamlit*

10.2. Using ReactJS to Create Streamlit Custom Components

In this section, we will demonstrate how to create a ReactJS-based component for use in Streamlit. Additionally, we will showcase how to facilitate bidirectional data sharing between Streamlit and the component. This feature can be used to send initial values, trigger user actions, or even pass styling themes and colors to the custom component.

10.2.1. Making a ReactJS Component

To begin, you need to install Node.js and npm from *NodeJS.org*. After that, we will use Streamlit's official GitHub template to create custom components. In this subsection, we will walk through the process of building a ReactJS component. For this example, we will create a rating stars widget, as shown in Figure 10-2, using ReactJS. The ReactJS developer community is significantly larger than that of other frameworks, making it a valuable investment to create components within this ecosystem.

Figure 10-2. *Interactive rating star view from Material UI*

By copying the content from `component-template/template/my_component` into our working directory, we will set up a ReactJS application with a single file module located at `src/MyComponent.tsx`. This is the file we need to modify to create our rating star component. The changes made to this file will result in the code shown in Listing 10-1.

Listing 10-1. stars_demo/rating_stars/frontend/src/CleanedTemplate.tsx

```
import {
    Streamlit,
    StreamlitComponentBase,
    withStreamlitConnection,
} from 'streamlit-component-lib'
import React, { ReactNode } from 'react'
interface State {}
class MyComponent extends StreamlitComponentBase<State> {
  public state = {}
```

```
  public render = (): ReactNode => {
   return (
    <div></div>
   )
  }
}
export default withStreamlitConnection(MyComponent)
```

Use the following command to install the Material UI library:

```
npm i @mui/material
```

Then run the following command to install other packages in the
package.json file:

```
npm i
```

After running both commands, make sure to change the name in
package.json to be your component's reference name in Streamlit down
the road as shown in Listing 10-2.

Listing 10-2. Updated Package.json

```
{
   "name": "rating_star",
   "version": "0.1.0",
   "private": true,
   "dependencies": {
     "@mui/material": "^5.0.6",
     ...
   },
   "scripts": ...,
   "eslintConfig": ...,
   "browserslist": ...,
   "homepage": ". "
}
```

With the necessary packages in place and a basic understanding of JavaScript/TypeScript (or with a bit of googling), we can begin creating our first ReactJS module to be used as a custom Streamlit component. We will modify Listing 10-1 to display the rating stars, as documented on the Material UI website. The final result will be the content shown in Listing 10-3, which should reside in frontend/src/. Also, do not forget to update the file to run in index.tsx.

Listing 10-3. Initial version of RatingStar.tsx

```
import {
    Streamlit,
    StreamlitComponentBase,
    withStreamlitConnection,
} from 'streamlit-component-lib'
import React, { ReactNode } from 'react'
import { Rating } from '@mui/material';
interface State {}
class RatingStar extends StreamlitComponentBase<State> {
  public state = {}
  public render = (): ReactNode => {
   return (
     <Rating size='large' defaultValue={3} />
   )
  }
}
export default withStreamlitConnection(RatingStar)
```

10.2.2. Using a ReactJS Component in Streamlit

To prepare the React application, run the following command. If any errors appear regarding missing packages, install them using the command provided earlier.

```
npm start
```

Now, on Streamlit's side, we will integrate the running ReactJS application as a component by using Streamlit's API for including external components. Before doing that, we need to populate the __init__.py file, as shown in Listing 10-4.

Listing 10-4. Initial version of __init__.py

```
import os
import streamlit.components.v1 as components
IS_RELEASE = False
if IS_RELEASE:
    absolute_path = os.path.dirname(os.path.abspath(__file__))
    build_path = os.path.join(absolute_path, 'frontend/build')
    _component_func = components.declare_component('rating_
    stars', path=build_path)
else:
    _component_func = components.declare_component('rating_
    stars', url='http://localhost:3001')
def rating_stars():
    _component_func()
```

The previous code snippet uses a live component running locally on port 3001, which, in this case, refers to the ReactJS app. It then exposes a function to be used by any other Python source, allowing it to be run as a Streamlit module. Running Listing 10-5 with Streamlit's CLI tool will result in the output shown in Figure 10-3.

Listing 10-5. Initial version of main.py

```
import streamlit as st
from rating_stars import rating_stars
st.title('Rating stars demo! ')
rating_stars()
```

Rating stars demo!

Figure 10-3. *First custom component!*

Having accomplished that, we successfully displayed a live ReactJS application within the Streamlit context. However, as we become more creative and develop additional custom components, it could become cumbersome to navigate to each component's folder and run it as a ReactJS application before launching the Streamlit app. This approach may also lead to running out of ports, as each custom component requires its own unique local URL. To overcome this, we can build the ReactJS application into static files after development by running

```
npm run build
```

Once you run the `build` command, a new folder named build will appear inside the `frontend` folder. This folder will contain the necessary JavaScript, CSS, and HTML files required by Streamlit to load the component into an application. After building the static version of the component, you need to set `IS_RELEASE` to `True`, which will instruct Streamlit to load the custom component from the `frontend/build/` folder. This process is illustrated in Figure 10-1.

10.2.3. **Sending Data to the Custom Component**

At this point, we can display ReactJS applications within a Streamlit context, though without a communication mechanism between the frontend and backend. In the next section, we will demonstrate how to send dynamic data from Streamlit to ReactJS, enabling the transmission of information with each rerender. This will allow Streamlit to send data to the ReactJS application whenever the app is updated.

To enhance the functionality of our rating star custom component, we will add support for setting the total star count and the number of selected stars, all through Streamlit's Python code. First, it is important to understand that Streamlit converts the parameters passed from Python (via _component_func) into properties in ReactJS. Therefore, our goal is to refactor the component's __init__.py file to accept these new parameters, as shown in Listing 10-6, and then read them in RatingStar.tsx, where they will be assigned to the view's properties, as demonstrated in Listing 10-7.

Listing 10-6. Second version of __init__.py

```
import os
import streamlit.components.v1 as components
IS_RELEASE = False
if IS_RELEASE:
    absolute_path = os.path.dirname(os.path.abspath(__file__))
    build_path = os.path.join(absolute_path, 'frontend/build')
    _component_func = components.declare_component('rating_
    stars', path=build_path)
else:
    _component_func = components.declare_component('rating_
stars', url='http://localhost:3001')
def rating_stars(stars_count: int, selected: int):
    _component_func(stars_count=stars_count, selected=selected)
```

Listing 10-7. Second version of RatingStar.tsx

```
import {
   Streamlit,
   StreamlitComponentBase,
   withStreamlitConnection,
} from 'streamlit-component-lib'
import React, { ReactNode } from 'react'
import { Rating } from '@mui/material'
interface State {}
class RatingStar extends StreamlitComponentBase<State> {
  public state = {}
  public render = (): ReactNode => {
    const {selected, stars_count} = this.props.args
    return <Rating size='large' defaultValue={selected}
    max={stars_count}/>
  }
}
export default withStreamlitConnection(RatingStar)
```

To put this update into action, we will create a Streamlit application as shown in Listing 10-8, which demonstrates both native and custom components side by side. Figure 10-4 illustrates the seamless integration between our newly created configurable component and the default components provided by Streamlit.

Listing 10-8. Second version of main.py

```
import streamlit as st
from rating_stars import rating_stars
st.title('Rating stars demo! ')
total_stars = st.slider(label='Total Stars', min_
value=0, max_value=20, value=10, step=1) selected_stars =
```

```
st.slider(label='Selected Stars', min_value=0, max_value=total_
stars, step=1) rating_stars(total_stars, selected_stars)
```

Figure 10-4. *Using native and custom components*

10.2.4. Receiving Data from the Custom Component

After experimenting with the sliders to configure our custom rating component, it becomes apparent that the Streamlit application's view becomes cluttered with additional widgets solely used to control another view's behavior. Ideally, users should be able to set the number of selected stars simply by hovering over and clicking them. To enable this, however, the Streamlit application needs to be aware of the selected value—and this is where data retrieval from custom components comes into play.

Streamlit not only provides an API to embed ReactJS applications but also enables bidirectional communication between Streamlit and these components. Sending data from ReactJS back to Streamlit can be achieved using a library that is already included in the component template's package.json. While this library offers several ReactJS-specific actions, we will focus on the Streamlit.setComponentValue function. This function allows us to set the return value of a component in the Streamlit Python context based on the parameter passed to it.

To implement this, we will add the function call within the rating component's callback in ReactJS, as shown in Listing 10-9. Then, we will update the __init__.py file accordingly to propagate the return value back to the running Streamlit script, as shown in Listing 10-10.

Listing 10-9. Final version of RatingStar.tsx

```
import {
   Streamlit,
   StreamlitComponentBase,
   withStreamlitConnection,
} from 'streamlit-component-lib'
import React, { ReactNode } from 'react'
import { Rating } from '@mui/material'
interface State {}
class RatingStar extends StreamlitComponentBase<State> {
  public state = {}
  public render = (): ReactNode => {
    const { selected, stars_count } = this.props.args
    return (
     <Rating
       size='large'
       defaultValue={1}
       max={stars_count}
       onChange={(_, stars_count) => Streamlit.
       setComponentValue(stars_count)}
     />
    )
  }
}
export default withStreamlitConnection(RatingStar)
```

Listing 10-10. Final version of __init__.py

```
import os
import streamlit.components.v1 as components
IS_RELEASE = False
if IS_RELEASE:
   absolute_path = os.path.dirname(os.path.abspath(__file__))
   build_path = os.path.join(absolute_path, 'frontend/build')
   _component_func = components.declare_component('rating_
   stars', path=build_path)
else:
   _component_func = components.declare_component('rating_
   stars', url='http://localhost:3001')
def rating_stars(stars_count: int):
   stars_selected = _component_func(stars_count=stars_count)
   if stars_selected is None:
     stars_selected = 0
   return stars_selected
```

In our main Streamlit file, we remove the slider used to select the star count and replace it with the output of our custom component. Finally, we display the selected number of stars on the application, as shown in Listing 10-11, with the output illustrated in Figure 10-5.

Listing 10-11. main.py, Streamlit file to be run

```
import streamlit as st
from rating_stars import rating_stars
st.title('Rating stars demo!')
total_stars = st.slider(label='Total Stars', min_value=0,
max_value=20, value=10, step=1) selected_stars = rating_
stars(total_stars)
st.write(str(selected_stars) + ' star(s) have been selected')
```

Figure 10-5. *Result of communicating back and forth with a custom Streamlit component*

10.3. Publishing Components As Pip Packages

Once you create your first custom component, you will likely want to share it with friends or contribute it to the open source community, as many developers do. Simply sending a zip file of the source code or uploading the component to a version control service like GitHub may not be the most scalable solution to reach a large number of developers. This method can add unnecessary overhead for others to get it up and running.

A more developer-friendly and professional way to share Python packages is by compressing them into a pip wheel format. This format can be easily installed in the Python interpreter by running

```
pip install <PIP_PACKAGE_NAME>.whl
```

Continuing with the example in this chapter, we do not need to install any additional packages to accomplish this, as Python natively supports wheel building. The goal is to package the rating_stars/ folder into a file that can then be installed and referenced from any script, just like a local package.

Building a pip file is as simple as running the following command:

```
python setup.py sdist bdist_wheel
```

Before creating the pip wheel, ensure that the ReactJS part of the custom component is built, as it won't be run live on the user's end. Instead, it should offer a seamless plug-and-play experience with the new component. To do this, navigate to the `rating_stars/frontend/` directory and run

```
npm run build
```

However, the wheel builder requires additional information, such as the exact folder to package and other metadata, including the version number and description. There is no need to explicitly mention the folder to be packaged, as Python automatically looks for all `Python packages` in the current directory. For a folder to be recognized as a Python package, it must contain an `__init__.py` file, which we already have. However, by default, the wheel builder does not include non-Python files and folders unless they contain at least one Python file. This becomes an issue in our case because our component relies on the `ReactJS build` folder, which contains the necessary static web files. To resolve this, we need to add a new file, as shown in Listing 10-12, in the project's root directory. This will ensure the inclusion of the `build` folder and its contents.

Listing 10-12. MANIFEST.in

```
recursive-include rating_stars/frontend/build *
```

Now that we have half of the requirements for creating a pip wheel, we can address the final part by creating a `setup.py` file with the content shown in Listing 10-13. This file should be placed in the same folder as the `MANIFEST.in`. The `setup.py` file will include the version number of your custom component, a description, and other details, such as the pip download name if the package is uploaded to pypi.org.

Listing 10-13. setup.py

```
import setuptools
setuptools.setup(
    name='rating_stars',
    version='0.1',
    author='YOUR-NAME',
    author_email='YOU-EMAIL@DOMAIN.com',
    description='INSERT-DESCRIPTION-HERE',
    long_description='INSERT-LONGER-DESCRIPTION-HERE',
    packages=setuptools.find_packages(),
    include_package_data=True,
    classifiers=[
        'Programming Language :: Python :: 3',
        'License :: OSI Approved :: MIT License',
        'Operating System :: OS Independent',
    ],
    keywords=['Python', 'Streamlit', 'React', 'JavaScript',
    'Custom'],
    python_requires='>=3.6',
    install_requires=[
        'streamlit >= 0.86',
    ],
)
```

And for better dependency management and Streamlit Cloud integration we need to create a pyproject.toml file as shown in Listing 10-14.

Listing 10-14. pyproject.toml

```
[build-system]
requires = ["setuptools", "wheel"]
build-backend = "setuptools.build_meta"

[project]
name = "rating_stars"
version = "0.1"
authors = [{name = "YOUR-NAME", email = "YOU-EMAIL@DOMAIN.com"}]
description = "INSERT-DESCRIPTION-HERE"
requires-python = ">=3.6"
dependencies = [
    "streamlit>=0.86",
]
classifiers = [
    "Programming Language :: Python :: 3",
    "License :: OSI Approved :: MIT License",
    "Operating System :: OS Independent",
]
keywords = ["Python", "Streamlit", "React", "JavaScript", "Custom"]
```

After running the Python package command, three new folders will
appear in the project's root directory, as shown in Figure 10-6. The file
of interest is the rating_stars-0.1-py3-none-any.whl in the second
folder. This file can be sent to others and easily installed, provided that the
package requirements are met. The other created folders also have their
benefits. For example, the dist/ folder can be used by *twine*, the tool for
uploading pip wheels to the global pip repository. If you wish to share your
package with the public, sign up at pypi.org and then run the following
command:

```
python -m twine upload dist/* --verbose
```

after building the wheel to upload it.

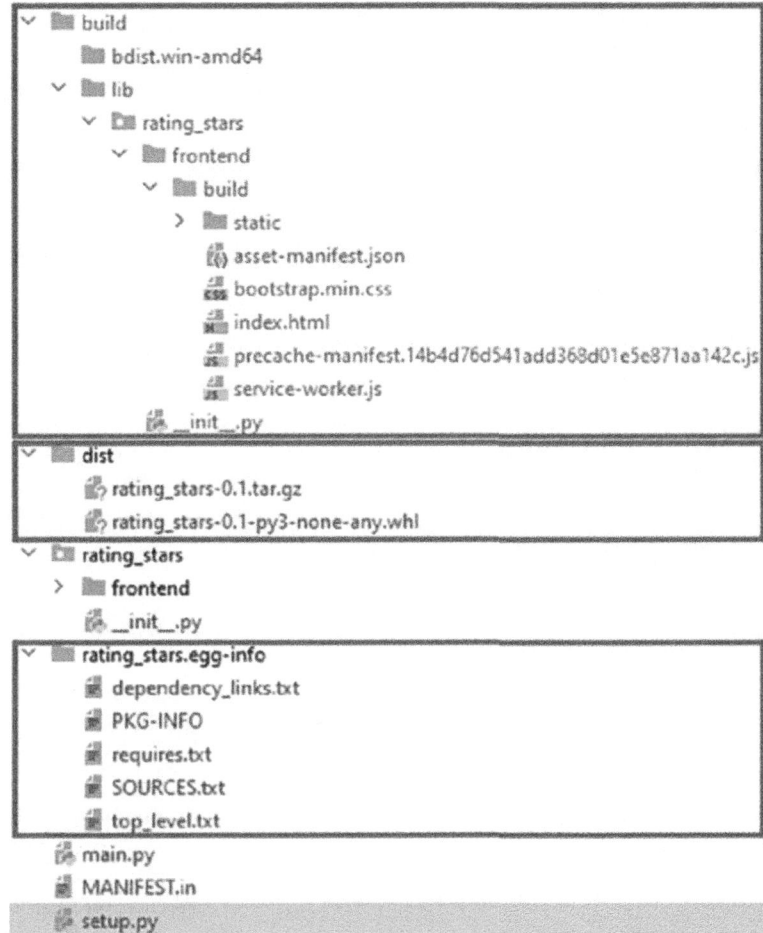

Figure 10-6. *New folders after building the custom component*

10.4. Component in Focus: Extra-Streamlit-Components

Streamlit, as a framework, is continuously evolving. However, it may not always provide certain bespoke features needed for a production-ready web application. Features like application routing, custom URLs for multiple views, or saving user-related data on the browser side may not be natively supported. Additionally, you might want to offer a unique look and feel for your application or add widgets that are not yet part of Streamlit's standard library. When it comes to components, the possibilities are endless. In this chapter, we will introduce *Extra-Streamlit-Components (STX)*, an open source collection of sophisticated Streamlit components and services. We will also dive into how each subcomponent is built from both the Streamlit and ReactJS perspectives, hoping to inspire creative developers to build their own unique components.

10.4.1. Stepper Bar

This component is inspired by Material UI's Stepper. As previously mentioned, ReactJS's developer community offers a wide range of useful components that can be seamlessly integrated into the Streamlit ecosystem. The stepper bar, in particular, can be highly beneficial for most Streamlit applications, especially those that involve sequential steps in a data science workflow. It allows users to navigate through stages in a specific order. The stepper is a simple component that returns the index of the stage the user has reached, as demonstrated in Figures 10-7, 10-8, and 10-9. As a developer, you are not limited to just three phases. You can provide a list of tab names, and the component will return the index of the selected item, as shown in Listing 10-15. The numbering and animations are already handled for you.

Phase #0

Figure 10-7. *Stepper bar phase 3*

Phase #1

Figure 10-8. *Stepper bar phase 3*

Phase #2

Figure 10-9. *Stepper bar phase 3*

On the ReactJS side, the stepper package needs to be installed via *npm* and then imported into the source file, as shown in Listings 10-15 and 10-16. This file is responsible for detecting user clicks, returning the corresponding index of the current step, and managing the theme of each step based on the user's position within the sequence.

Listing 10-15. StepperBar/frontend/src/StepperBar.jsx

```
import {
   Streamlit,
   StreamlitComponentBase,
   withStreamlitConnection,
} from 'streamlit-component-lib'
import React from 'react'
import { withStyles, createStyles } from '@material-ui/
core/styles'
import Stepper from '@material-ui/core/Stepper'
import Step from '@material-ui/core/Step'
import StepLabel from '@material-ui/core/StepLabel'
const styles = createStyles((theme) => ({
   root: {
     width: '100%',
     backgroundColor: 'transparent',
   },
   icon: {
     color: 'grey',
     cursor: 'pointer',
     '&$activeIcon': {
       color: '#f63366',
      },
     '&$completedIcon': {
       color: '#f63366',
     },
   },
   activeIcon: {},
   completedIcon: {},
}))
```

```
class StepperBar extends StreamlitComponentBase {
  state = { activeStep: 0, steps: [] }
  componentDidMount() {
    this.setState((prev, state) => ({
      steps: this.props.args.steps,
      activeStep: this.props.args.default,
    }))
  }
  onClick = (index) => {
    const { activeStep } = this.state
    if (index == activeStep + 1) {
      this.setState(
        (prev, state) => ({
          activeStep: activeStep + 1,
        }),
        () => Streamlit.setComponentValue(this.state.
        activeStep)
      )
    } else if (index < activeStep) {
      this.setState(
        (prev, state) => ({
          activeStep: index,
        }),
        () => Streamlit.setComponentValue(this.state.
        activeStep)
      )
    }
  }
  getLabelStyle = (index) => {
    const { activeStep } = this.state
    const style = {}
```

```
    if (index == activeStep) {
        style.color = '#f63366'
        style.fontStyle = 'italic'
     } else if (index < activeStep) {
        style.color = '#f63366'
        style.fontWeight = 'bold'
      } else {
        style.color = 'grey'
      }
     return style
  }
  render = () => {
    let { classes } = this.props
    const { activeStep } = this.state
    const steps = this.state.steps
    return (
      <div className={classes.root}>
        <Stepper
          activeStep={activeStep}
          alternativeLabel
          className={classes.root}
        >
          {steps.map((label, index) => (
           <Step key={label} onClick={() => this.
           onClick(index)}>
             <StepLabel
               StepIconProps={{
                 classes: {
                   cursor: 'pointer',
                   root: classes.icon,
```

```
                        active: classes.activeIcon,
                        completed: classes.completedIcon,
                      },
                    }}
                  >
                    <p style={this.getLabelStyle(index)}>{label}</p>
                  </StepLabel>
                </Step>
              ))}
          </Stepper>
        </div>
      )
    }
}
export default withStreamlitConnection(withStyles(styles)
(StepperBar))
```

Listing 10-16. StepperBar/__init__.py

```
import os
import streamlit.components.v1 as components
from streamlit.components.v1.components import CustomComponent
from typing import List
from extra_streamlit_components import IS_RELEASE
if IS_RELEASE:
    absolute_path = os.path.dirname(os.path.abspath(__file__))
    build_path = os.path.join(absolute_path, 'frontend/build')
    _component_func = components.declare_component('stepper_
    bar', path=build_path)
```

```
else:
    _component_func = components.declare_component('stepper_
    bar', url='http://localhost:3001')
def stepper_bar(steps: List[str]) -> CustomComponent:
    component_value = _component_func(steps=steps, default=0)
    return component_value
```

10.4.2. Bouncing Image

This component provides zooming animations for an image with a
bouncing effect. It can be useful during loading moments or as a splash
screen. While it may not be a frequently used component, when needed,
parameters like animation duration, control switches, and dimensions
are essential for its functionality, as seen in Listing 10-17. The ReactJS side
is slightly more complex than the Python side, as it manages animation
cycles and reports the widget's state back to Streamlit with each cycle.
Although JavaScript is not the primary focus of this book, Listing 10-18
should be relatively straightforward to understand. The final result will
resemble something like Figure 10-10.

Listing 10-17. BouncingImage/__init__.py

```
import os
import streamlit.components.v1 as components
from extra_streamlit_components import IS_RELEASE
if IS_RELEASE:
    absolute_path = os.path.dirname(os.path.abspath(__file__))
    build_path = os.path.join(absolute_path, 'frontend/build')
    _component_func = components.declare_component('bouncing_
    image', path=build_path)
```

```
else:
  _component_func = components.declare_component('bouncing_
  image', url='http://localhost:3001')
def bouncing_image(image_source: str, animate: bool, animation_
time: int, height: float, width: float):
  _component_func(image=image_source, animate=animate,
animation_time=animation_time, height=height, width=width)
```

Listing 10-18. BouncingImage/frontend/src/BouncingImage.jsx

```
import {
  Streamlit,
  StreamlitComponentBase,
  withStreamlitConnection,
} from 'streamlit-component-lib'
import React from 'react'
import { withStyles, createStyles } from '@material-ui/
core/styles'
import Grow from '@material-ui/core/Grow'
import CardMedia from '@material-ui/core/CardMedia'
const styles = createStyles((theme) => ({
  root: {
    height: 180,
  },
  container: {
    display: 'flex',
  },
  paper: {
    margin: 1,
  },
```

```
    svg: {
      width: 100,
      height: 100,
    },
    polygon: {
      fill: 'white',
      stroke: 'red',
      strokeWidth: 1,
    },
}))
class BouncingImage extends StreamlitComponentBase {
    state = {
      animationTimeRoundTrip: 1750,
      isAnimating: true,
      keepAnimating: false,
    }
    constructor(props) {
      super(props)
    }
    componentDidMount() {
      const { animation_time, animate } = this.props.args
      Streamlit.setComponentValue(animate)
      this.setState(
        () => ({
          animationTimeRoundTrip: animation_time,
          keepAnimating: animate,
        }),
        () =>
          setInterval(
            () =>
              this.state.keepAnimating &&
```

```
    this.setState(
      () => ({
        isAnimating:
          !this.state.isAnimating && this.state.
          keepAnimating,
      }),
      () => Streamlit.setComponentValue(this.state.
      keepAnimating)
    ),
    this.state.animationTimeRoundTrip / 2
  )
  )
}
render = () => {
  const isAnimating = this.state.isAnimating
  let {
    classes,
    args: { image, height, width },
  } = this.props
  return (
    <div className={classes.root}>
      <div className={classes.container}>
        <Grow
          in={isAnimating}
          style={{ transformOrigin: '0 0 0' }}
          {...(isAnimating
            ? { timeout: this.state.
            animationTimeRoundTrip / 2 }
            : {})}
        >
```

```
            <CardMedia image={image} style={{ height, width }} />
          </Grow>
        </div>
       </div>
     )
   }
 }
export default withStreamlitConnection(withStyles(styles)
(BouncingImage))
```

Bouncing Image

Figure 10-10. *Bouncing image demo (a snapshot from the zoom animation)*

10.4.3. Tab Bar

Instead of using a Streamlit column widget to host multiple buttons that act as a tab bar, you can leverage this custom component. It organizes the title, description, and ID of each button in a clean and structured way. Additionally, it provides a horizontal scroll view when the tabs exceed the window's width, ensuring a seamless user experience. Figures 10-11 and 10-12 demonstrate the behavior when a tab button is clicked and the resulting output in Streamlit. To create the tabs, you need to pass a list of specific Python objects, as shown in Listing 10-20. These objects will then be converted into JSON and processed by the TypeScript ReactJS component in Listing 10-19.

Listing 10-19. TabBar/frontend/src/TabBar.tsx

```
import {
    Streamlit,
    StreamlitComponentBase,
    withStreamlitConnection,
} from 'streamlit-component-lib'
import React, { ComponentProps, ReactNode } from 'react'
import ScrollMenu from 'react-horizontal-scrolling-menu'
interface State {
    numClicks: number
    selectedId: number
}
interface MenuItem {
    id: number
    title: string
    description: string
}
class TabBar extends StreamlitComponentBase<State> {
public state = { numClicks: 0, selectedId: 1, list: [] }
    constructor(props: ComponentProps<any>) {
        super(props)
        this.state.list = this.props.args['data']
        this.state.selectedId = this.props.args['selectedId']
    }
    MenuItem = ({ item, selectedId }: { item: MenuItem;
    selectedId: number }) => {
        return (
            <div className={'menu-item ${selectedId == item.id ?
            "active" : ""}'}>
                <div>{item.title}</div>
```

```
        <div style={{ fontWeight: 'normal', fontStyle:
        'italic' }}>
            {item.description}
        </div>
      </div>
    )
  }
  Menu(list: Array<MenuItem>, selectedId: number) {
    return list.map((item) => (
      <this.MenuItem item={item} selectedId={selectedId}
      key={item.id} />
    ))
  }
  Arrow = ({ text, className }: { text: string; className:
  string }) => {
    return <div className={className}>{text}</div>
  }
  ArrowLeft = this.Arrow({ text: '<', className:
  'arrow-prev' })
  ArrowRight = this.Arrow({ text: '>', className:
  'arrow-next' })
  public render = (): ReactNode => {
    return (
      <div>
        <ScrollMenu
          alignCenter={false}
          data={this.Menu(this.state.list, this.state.
          selectedId)}
          wheel={true}
          scrollToSelected={true}
          selected={'${this.state.selectedId}'}
```

```
          onSelect={this.onSelect}
        />
        <hr
          style={{
            borderColor: 'var(--streamlit-primary-color) ',
          }}
        />
      </div>
    )
  }
  onSelect = (id: any) => {
    this.setState(
      (state, props) => {
        return { selectedId: id }
      },
      () => Streamlit.setComponentValue(id)
    )
  }
}
export default withStreamlitConnection(TabBar)
```

Listing 10-20. TabBar/__init__.py

```python
import os
import streamlit.components.v1 as components
from dataclasses import dataclass
from typing import List
from extra_streamlit_components import IS_RELEASE
if IS_RELEASE:
    absolute_path = os.path.dirname(os.path.abspath(__file__))
    build_path = os.path.join(absolute_path, 'frontend/build')
    _component_func = components.declare_component('tab_bar',
    path=build_path)
```

```python
else:
    _component_func = components.declare_component('tab_bar',
    url='http://localhost:3001')
@dataclass(frozen=True, order=True, unsafe_hash=True)
class TabBarItemData:
    id: int
    title: str
    description: str
    def to_dict(self):
        return {'id': self.id, 'title': self.title,
        'description': self.description}
def tab_bar(data: List[TabBarItemData], default=None, return_
type=str, key=None):
    data = list(map(lambda item: item.to_dict(), data))
    component_value = _component_func(data=data,
    selectedId=default, key=key, default=default)
    try:
        if return_type == str:
            return str(component_value)
        elif return_type == int:
            return int(component_value)
        elif return_type == float:
            return float(component_value)
        except:
            return component_value
```

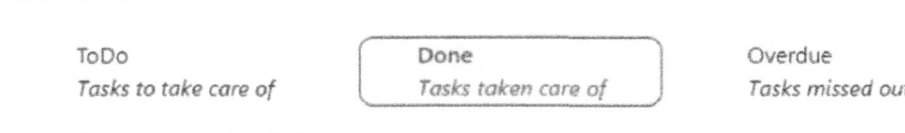

Figure 10-11. *Tab bar with first element selected*

Tab Bar

ToDo
Tasks to take care of

Done
Tasks taken care of

Overdue
Tasks missed out

chosen_id = 2, type = <class 'int'>

Figure 10-12. *Tab bar with first element selected*

10.4.4. Cookie Manager

This concept was introduced in the previous chapter as a black box that simply stores data on the client browser side. However, the Cookie Manager is more than just a custom component; it also serves as a Python service. It handles data management in a Pythonic context, with CRUD operations on a ReactJS-based component. If you are a web developer, you are likely familiar with setting cookies on the client side, which is straightforward. Fortunately, in Streamlit, we can write both server-side and client-side code within the same script. By creating a React custom component, we can execute it on the browser and set it up to control cookies on the client's side, as shown in Figure 10-13.

287

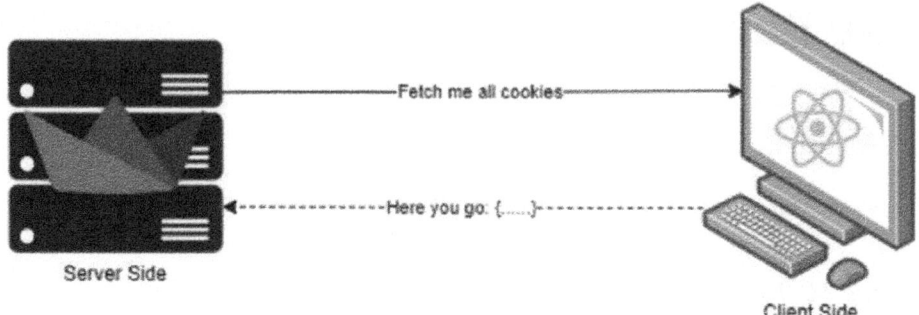

Figure 10-13. *Using Streamlit to control client-side data*

By leveraging the knowledge introduced in this chapter, we can establish bidirectional communication between Streamlit's server-side and the custom ReactJS component running on the client's browser. This enables us to instruct the component to gather, delete, or add cookies on the browser and even listen for any return values. Starting with the ReactJS side, as shown in Listing 10-21, we first read the expected arguments, such as the required operation and the data to act on. Based on these inputs, we perform the necessary actions on the cookies using the npm package universal-cookie, and finally, we send back a response indicating the status of the operation.

On the Python side, Listing 10-22 encapsulates the entire communication method with the browser's component. It also stores all cookies in memory for the user once initialized to reduce network traffic. However, if the class's constructor is not cached after the initial run, it will not provide any added value, as it will be executed each time Streamlit reruns. Therefore, it is recommended to use the snippet in Listing 10-23 when implementing the Cookie Manager. Figure 10-14 demonstrates this custom component in action.

Listing 10-21. CookieManager/frontend/src/CookieManager.tsx

```
import {
  Streamlit,
  ComponentProps,
  withStreamlitConnection,
} from 'streamlit-component-lib'
import React, { useEffect, useState } from 'react'
import Cookies from 'universal-cookie'
let last_output = null
const cookies = new Cookies()
const CookieManager = (props: ComponentProps) => {
  const setCookie = (cookie, value, expires_at) => {
    cookies.set(cookie, value, {
      path: '/',
      samesite: 'strict',
      expires: new Date(expires_at),
    })
    return true
  }
  const getCookie = (cookie) => {
    const value = cookies.get(cookie)
    return value
  }
  const deleteCookie = (cookie) => {
    cookies.remove(cookie, { path: '/', samesite: 'strict' })
    return true
  }
  const getAllCookies = () => {
    return cookies.getAll()
  }
```

```
const { args } = props
const method = args['method']
const cookie = args['cookie']
const value = args['value']
const expires_at = args['expires_at']
let output = null
switch (method) {
  case 'set':
    output = setCookie(cookie, value, expires_at)
    break
  case 'get':
    output = getCookie(cookie)
    break
  case 'getAll':
    output = getAllCookies()
    break
  case 'delete':
    output = deleteCookie(cookie)
    break
  default:
    break
}
if (output && JSON.stringify(last_output) != JSON.
stringify(output)) {
  last_output = output
  Streamlit.setComponentValue(output)
  Streamlit.setComponentReady()
}
useEffect(() => Streamlit.setFrameHeight())
  return <div></div>
}
export default withStreamlitConnection(CookieManager)
```

Listing 10-22. CookieManager/__init__.py

```
import os
import streamlit.components.v1 as components
import datetime
from extra_streamlit_components import IS_RELEASE
if IS_RELEASE:
    absolute_path = os.path.dirname(os.path.abspath(__file__))
    build_path = os.path.join(absolute_path, 'frontend/build')
    _component_func = components.declare_component('cookie_
    manager', path=build_path)
else:
    _component_func = components.declare_component('cookie_
    manager',
        url='http://localhost:3001')
class CookieManager:
    def __init__(self, key='init'):
        self.cookie_manager = _component_func
        self.cookies = self.cookie_manager(method='getAll',
        key=key, default={})
    def get(self, cookie: str):
        return self.cookies.get(cookie)
    def set(self, cookie, val,
        expires_at=datetime.datetime.now() + datetime.
        timedelta(days=1), key='set'):
        if cookie is None or cookie == '':
            return
        expires_at = expires_at.isoformat()
        did_add = self.cookie_manager(method='set',
        cookie=cookie, value=val, expires_at=expires_at, key=key,
        default=False)
        if did_add:
```

```
            self.cookies[cookie] = val
    def delete(self, cookie, key='delete'):
        if cookie is None or cookie == '':
            return
        did_add = self.cookie_manager(method='delete',
        cookie=cookie, key=key, default=False)
        if did_add:
            del self.cookies[cookie]
    def get_all(self, key='get_all'):
        self.cookies = self.cookie_manager(method='getAll',
        key=key, default={})
        return self.cookies
```

Listing 10-23. How to initialize and use Cookie Manager

```
@st.cache_resource
def get_manager():
    return stx.CookieManager()
cookie_manager = get_manager()
```

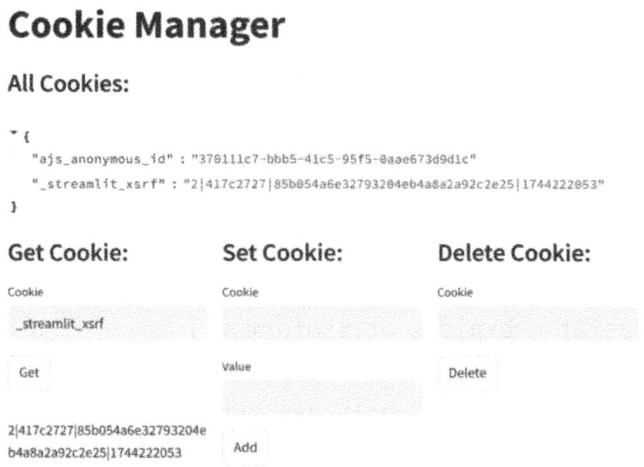

Figure 10-14. *Cookie Manager demo from Extra-Streamlit-Components*

10.5. Summary

As you reach the end of this chapter, you now possess the knowledge needed to create innovative and exciting custom components for Streamlit. By using a simplified version of the ReactJS template and referring to online resources, you can not only replicate ReactJS's Material UI views in Streamlit but also control browser functionalities to integrate a native web application UX into your app. This chapter also covered how to customize various aspects of the Streamlit user interface, adding versatility and uniqueness to your application. The techniques shared in building this library can be scaled and adapted by any developer for a wide range of purposes. Lastly, it is important to remember that no component reaches its full potential without being shared with the open source community, where it can be improved iteratively with feedback and suggestions from fellow developers.

CHAPTER 11

Streamlit Use Cases

In this chapter, we will explore several real-world use cases of Streamlit, including applications in data visualization, real-time dashboards, and time-series analysis. We will also demonstrate how to interface Streamlit applications with external subsystems such as Arduino microcontrollers, infrared temperature sensors, and sonar modules. By integrating with physical devices and peripherals, Streamlit can be extended beyond digital dashboards to support embedded systems and IoT applications. For example, we could develop an operations dashboard to remotely monitor a building's temperature or control a valve motor on a factory line. The possibilities are virtually limitless. As the culmination of the concepts covered throughout this book, the final section of this chapter will guide readers through the development of an advanced machine learning application that ties together many of the techniques discussed previously.

11.1. Dashboards and Real-Time Applications

A small yet invaluable niche within web applications consists of dashboards—whether or not they interface with real-time devices. Examples include meteorological applications that report live weather data, or control panels that allow users to operate motors with real-time feedback. The possibilities are vast, and the utility, unmatched. Thanks

© Mohammad Khorasani, Mohamed Abdou, Javier Hernández Fernández 2025
M. Khorasani et al., *Streamlit for Web Development*,
https://doi.org/10.1007/979-8-8688-1826-4_11

to Streamlit's versatility—particularly in handling data visualizations and dynamic placeholders—we are well-equipped to build such applications. In the following sections, we will examine two representative examples from this category.

11.1.1. Temperature Data Recorder Application

Given the need for real-time insights into physical parameters, numerous entities—including energy firms, research institutions, and meteorological departments—are rapidly adopting SCADA systems, often at exorbitant costs, to enhance data accessibility. While large corporations can afford to allocate significant budgets for such systems, smaller enterprises or private individuals may lack the same financial resources. Fortunately, they can develop cost-effective alternatives using Arduino microcontrollers, hobbyist-grade peripherals, and, most importantly, Streamlit to create intuitive dashboards and control systems.

In this section, we will demonstrate the implementation of a basic temperature data recording system. Specifically, an *MLX90614* infrared thermometer will be connected to an Arduino UNO microcontroller to sample ambient temperature, as illustrated in Figure 11-1. Before uploading the measurement code to the microcontroller, you must install the infrared thermometer's library `Adafruit_MLX90614` within the *Arduino IDE*, as shown in Figure 11-2. Once installed, you can upload the code provided in Listing 11-1 to the microcontroller via a USB connection. The corresponding COM port used for interfacing can also be determined through the Arduino IDE.

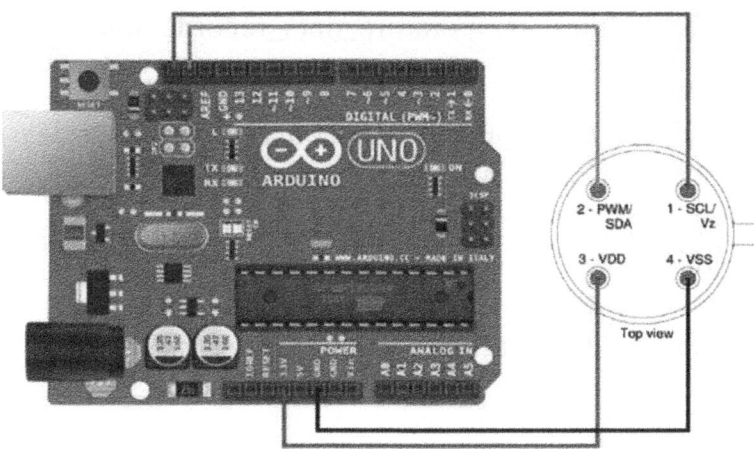

Figure 11-1. *Arduino microcontroller and infrared thermometer wiring schematic [19]*

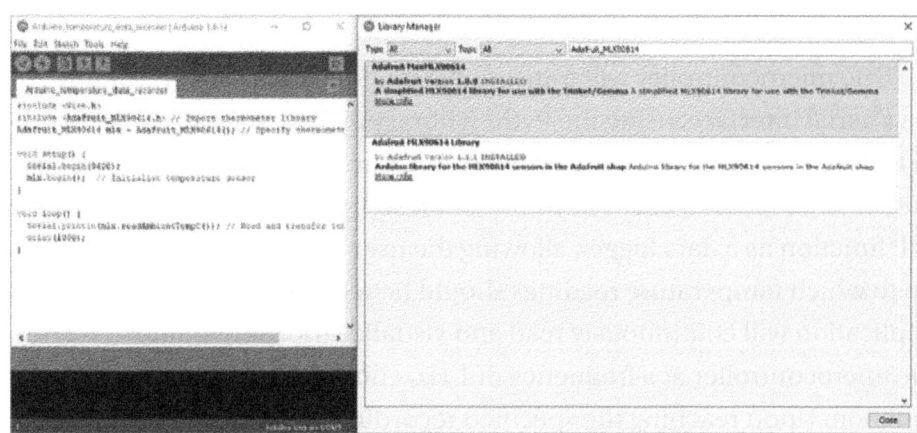

Figure 11-2. *Arduino IDE with library manager*

Listing 11-1. Arduino_temperature_data_recorder.ino

```
#include <Wire.h>
#include <Adafruit_MLX90614.h> // Import thermometer library
Adafruit_MLX90614 mlx = Adafruit_MLX90614(); // Specify
thermometer type
void setup() {
    Serial.begin(9600);
    mlx.begin(); // Initialize temperature sensor
}
void loop() {
    Serial.println(mlx.readAmbientTempC()); // Read and
    transfer temperature data
    delay(1000);
}
```

The microcontroller will transmit data to the Streamlit application via a serial interface, using the Python library pySerial, as demonstrated in Listing 11-2. Ensure that the correct COM port is specified when initializing the serial client in your Python script. The Streamlit application will function as a data logger, allowing the user to set an end date and time up to which temperature readings should be recorded. Once initiated, the application will continuously read and visualize the temperature data from the microcontroller at a frequency of 1 Hz, controlled by the time.sleep function. Upon reaching the specified recording end time, all collected readings will be presented in a table and made available for download, as illustrated in Figure 11-3.

Listing 11-2. temperature_data_recorder_app.py

```
import serial
import time
import streamlit as st
import plotly.graph_objects as go
```

```python
import plotly.express as px
from datetime import datetime
import pandas as pd
# Plotly temperature gauge visualization function
def temperature_gauge(temperature, previous_temperature, gauge_
placeholder):
    fig = go.Figure(go.Indicator(
        domain = {'x': [0, 1], 'y': [0, 1]},
        value = temperature,
        mode = 'gauge+number+delta',
        title = {'text': 'Temperature (C) '},
        delta = {'reference': previous_temperature},
        gauge = {'axis': {'range': [0, 40]}}))
    fig.update_layout(
        width=300,
    )
    gauge_placeholder.write(fig)
# Plotly time-series temperature visualization
def temperature_chart(df, chart_placeholder):
    fig = px.line(df, x='Time', y='Temperature (C)')
    chart_placeholder.write(fig)
if __name__ == '__main__':
    st.sidebar.title('Temperature Data Recorder')
    recording = False
    # End date and time form for temperature recording
    with st.sidebar.form('form_1'):
        col1, col2, = st.columns(2)
        with col1:
            end_date = st.date_input('Recording end date')
        with col2:
            end_time = st.time_input('Recording end time')
```

```
    if st.form_submit_button('Start recording'):
        recording = True
        arduino = serial.Serial(port='COM4', baudrate=9600)
previous_temperature = 0
temperature_record = pd.DataFrame(columns=['Time','Temperat
ure (C)'])
gauge_placeholder = st.sidebar.empty()
chart_placeholder = st.empty()
# Recording data while current date and time is less than
specified end
while recording and (datetime.now() < datetime.combine(end_
date, end_time)):
    current_time = datetime.now().strftime('%H:%M:%S')
    temperature = round(float(arduino.readline().decode().
    strip('\r\n')),1)
    temperature_record.loc[len(temperature_record),
    ['Time','Temperature (C)']] = [current_time, temperature]
    temperature_gauge(temperature, previous_temperature,
    gauge_placeholder)
    temperature_chart(temperature_record, chart_placeholder)
    time.sleep(1)
    previous_temperature = temperature
# Display and download temperature date if end date and
time exceeded
if recording and (datetime.now() > datetime.combine
(end_date, end_time)):
    arduino.close()
    if len(temperature_record) > 0:
        st.write(temperature_record)
        st.download_button(
            label='Download data',
```

```
        data=temperature_record.to_csv(index=False).
        encode('utf-8'),
        file_name='temperature_record.csv',
        mime='text/csv',
    )
else:
    st.warning('Please select a future end date and time')
```

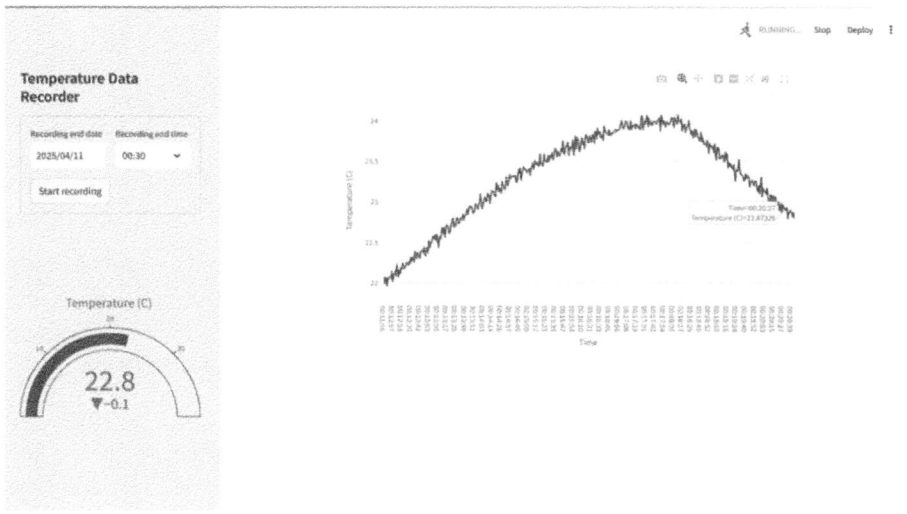

Figure 11-3. *Output of Listing 11-2*

11.1.2. Motor Command and Control Application

Electric motors play a critical role in a wide range of industrial and non-industrial applications—from operating control valves on a factory floor to adjusting flight surfaces on a remote-controlled aircraft. Given their versatility, developers frequently require dashboards that enable both motor control and performance visualization, often through the use of gauges.

In this example, we will control the speed and direction of a motor using a USB joystick and an Arduino UNO microcontroller. The motor selected for this demonstration is the *SM-S3317SR*, a compact continuous servo motor, connected as illustrated in Figure 11-4. Both the joystick and the microcontroller will interface with the computer hosting the Streamlit server via USB. To begin, upload the sketch in Listing 11-3 to the microcontroller using the *Arduino IDE*. This script is designed to receive speed and direction commands from the Streamlit application over a serial interface and execute them accordingly.

Listing 11-3. Arduino_motor_control.ino

```
#include <Servo.h>
Servo motor;
String input;
int target_speed;
void setup() {
    motor.attach(3);
    Serial.begin(9600);
}
void loop()
{
  if(Serial.available()) // Check if data available in
                            serial port
    {
    input = Serial.readStringUntil('\n'); // Read data
                                    until newline
    target_speed = input.toInt();
    motor.write(target_speed);    // Move motor at target speed
    }
}
```

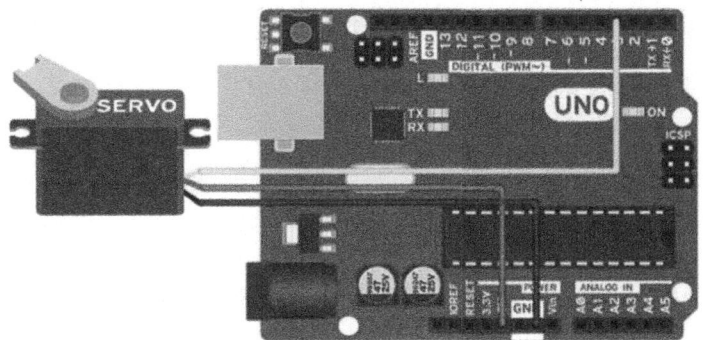

Figure 11-4. _Arduino microcontroller and servo motor wiring schematic [20]_

To begin, you can use either the Arduino IDE or your computer's device manager to identify the serial COM port associated with the microcontroller. Make sure to use the same port when creating the serial client in your Streamlit application, utilizing the Python library pySerial as shown in Listing 11-4. In this script, we will also integrate the Pygame library to interface with the joystick controller. The forward axis values of the joystick will control the speed and direction of the servo motor. Additionally, one of the joystick buttons will function as a kill switch to immediately stop the motor. To continuously update the motor's target speed, a Plotly gauge visualization will be displayed within a Streamlit placeholder, as demonstrated in Figure 11-5. This approach can be easily scaled to connect and simultaneously visualize and control other motors, actuators, sensors, and peripherals, making it ideal for more complex systems.

Please note that using Pygame to interface with a joystick is not recommended for applications without a display, because Pygame requires initializing a video system, which can lead to errors or unnecessary overhead. For headless setups or applications running on devices without a screen, it is better to use a modern, lightweight, and cross-platform library like hidapi for direct controller input.

Listing 11-4. motor_control_app.py

```python
import serial
import pygame as pg
import streamlit as st
import plotly.graph_objects as go
import time
# Plotly speed gauge visualization function
def speed_gauge(target_speed, placeholder):
    fig = go.Figure(go.Indicator(
        domain = {'x': [0, 1], 'y': [0, 1]},
        value = int(target_speed)-90,
        mode = 'gauge+number+delta',
        title = {'text': 'Speed'},
        delta = {'reference': 0},
        gauge = {'axis': {'range': [-30, 30]}}))
    placeholder.write(fig)
if __name__ == '__main__':
    st.sidebar.title('Motor Command & Control')
    info_bar = st.empty()
    speedometer = st.empty()
    # Create Arduino serial client
    arduino = serial.Serial(port='COM5', baudrate=9600)
    # Create PyGame client
    pg.init()
    # Create a list of available joysticks to initialize
    joysticks = [pg.joystick.Joystick(x) for x in range(pg.
    joystick.get_count())]
    for joystick in joysticks:
        joystick.init()
    if st.sidebar.button('Start motor'):
        info_bar.info('Motor started')
```

```python
# Connect to Arduino
try:
    arduino.open()
except Exception as e:
    print(e)
if st.sidebar.button('Stop motor'):
    info_bar.warning('Motor stopped')
    arduino.write(bytes('90' +'\n', 'utf-8'))
    arduino.close()
    pg.quit()
while True:
    # Report all joystick events
    for event in pg.event.get():
        print(event)
    for joystick in joysticks:
        if joystick.get_id() == 0: # Access the first
        connected joystick
            axes = joystick.get_numaxes()
            for x in range(axes): # Check all inputs of
            the joystick
                target_speed = str(int(((joystick.get_
                axis(1)*-1)*30 + 90)))
                press = joystick.get_button(0)
                time.sleep(0.01)
    arduino.flushInput()
    arduino.flushOutput()
    arduino.flush()
    arduino.write(bytes(target_speed +'\n', 'utf-8')) #
    Send speed to Arduino
    speed_gauge(target_speed, speedometer)
    # Disconnect Arduino if joystick button pressed
```

```
        if press == 1:
            try:
                arduino.write(bytes('90' +'\n', 'utf-8'))
                arduino.close()
            except Exception as e:
                print(e)
            break
# Disconnect Arduino if 'Stop motor' button pressed
info_bar.warning('Motor stopped')
try:
    arduino.write(bytes('90' +'\n', 'utf-8'))
    arduino.close()
except Exception as e:
    print(e)
pg.quit()
```

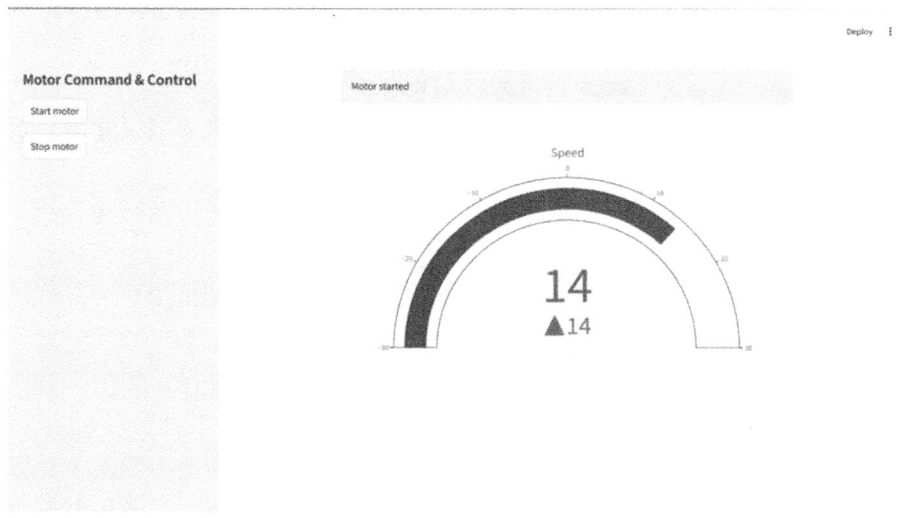

Figure 11-5. *Output of Listing 11-4*

11.2. Time-Series Applications

Time-series data is one of the most commonly used forms of data, as it is indexed by time, date, or both. Examples include temperature readings from a thermostat or signals from a SCADA system. However, time-series datasets come with their own set of challenges, such as filtering, aggregating, and visualizing the data effectively. Fortunately, Streamlit provides the tools to easily build applications that can address these needs, enabling developers to create powerful solutions for handling time-series data, as demonstrated in the following sections.

11.2.1. Date-Time Filter Application

Filtering data based on a time range is a common function in nearly every data science application. Often, you may only need a subset of the data, which can be easily achieved by selecting a leading or trailing date-time to truncate the dataset. However, timestamps often come in various formats, and sometimes the date and time are split into separate columns, making it challenging to create a one-size-fits-all solution.

In this example, we will build a date-time filter for one of the most widely used date-time formats: DD/MM/YYYY HH:MM, with the date in the first column and arbitrary measurements in the second column. Using Streamlit's st.slider, we will allow users to truncate the leading and trailing edges of the time-series data. The filtered data will then be visualized using a Plotly line chart, as shown in Listing 11-5 and Figure 11-6. This application can be adapted to other date-time formats by simply adjusting the timestamp format in the code.

Listing 11-5. datetime_filter.py

```python
import pandas as pd
import streamlit as st
from datetime import datetime
import plotly.express as px
# Streamlit slider function used to truncate leading and
trailing edges of dataset
def datetime_filter(datetime_col, df, format):
    lead, trail = st.sidebar.slider('Date-time filter', 0,
    len(df)-1, [0,len(df)-1], 1)
    df[datetime_col] = pd.to_datetime(df[datetime_col],
    format=format)
    sd = df.loc[lead][datetime_col].strftime('%d %b %Y,
    %I:%M%p')
    ed = df.loc[trail][datetime_col].strftime('%d %b %Y,
    %I:%M%p')
    st.sidebar.info(f'Start: **{sd}**')
    st.sidebar.info(f'End: **{ed}**')
    filtered_df = df.iloc[lead:trail+1][:]
    return filtered_df
# Plotly time-series visualization function
def timeseries_chart(df, datetime_col, value_col):
    df[datetime_col] = df[datetime_col].dt.strftime(' %H:%M on
    %B %-d, %Y')
    df = df.sort_values(by=datetime_col)
    fig = px.line(df, x=datetime_col, y=value_col,
                hover_data={datetime_col: '|%d/%m/%Y %H:%M'})
    st.write(fig)
if __name__ == '__main__':
    st.sidebar.title('Date-time Filter')
```

```
uploaded_file = st.sidebar.file_uploader('Upload a time-
series dataset')
if uploaded_file is not None:
    df = pd.read_csv(uploaded_file)
    df_filtered = datetime_filter('datetime', df,
    '%d/%m/%Y %H:%M')
    st.header('Filtered Chart')
    timeseries_chart(df_filtered, 'datetime', 'value')
    st.download_button(
        label='Download filtered data',
        data=df_filtered.to_csv(index=False).encode('utf-8'),
        file_name='filtered_data.csv',
        mime='text/csv',
    )
```

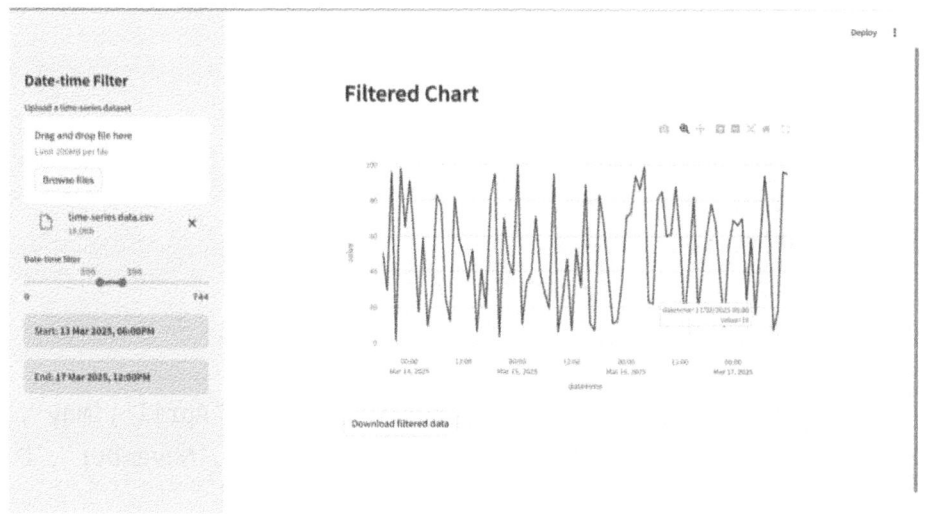

Figure 11-6. *Output of Listing 11-5*

11.2.2. Time-Series Heatmap Application

Another commonly used form of time-series data visualization is the monthly-hourly heatmap. These visualizations allow data points to be grouped into averages for each hour of each month, providing valuable insights for time-series analytics. For example, you might want to track the average temperature over the course of a year or measure website traffic within a one-year period.

In this application, we begin by parsing our date-time column (formatted as DD/MM/YYYY HH:MM) into two separate columns: one for the month (e.g., January) and another for the hour (e.g., 12AM). Using Pandas's groupby command, we aggregate the data into monthly and hourly averages across the entire dataset. Finally, we visualize the aggregated data using Plotly's heatmap in our Streamlit application, as shown in Listing 11-6 and Figure 11-7.

Listing 11-6. timeseries_heatmap.py

```
import pandas as pd
import streamlit as st
from datetime import datetime
import plotly.express as px
# Month-hours dictionary generator
def month_hours_dict():
    month_hours = {}
    month_names = ['January','February','March','April','May',
    'June','July','August','September','October','November','D
    ecember']
    for month_name in month_names:
        month = {month_name: {'12AM': None, '01AM': None,
        '02AM': None,
```

```
                       '03AM': None, '04AM': None, '05AM': None,
                        06AM': None, '07AM': None, '08AM': None,
                       '09AM': None, '10AM': None, '11AM': None,
                       '12PM': None, '01PM': None, '02PM': None,
                       '03PM': None, '04PM': None, '05PM': None,
                       '06PM': None, '07PM': None, '08PM': None,
                       '09PM': None, '10PM': None, '11PM': None}}
        month_hours.update(month)
    return month_hours
# Aggregating data into monthly-hourly averages
def aggregate(df, datetime_col, format):
    df[datetime_col] = pd.to_datetime(df[datetime_col],
    format='%d/%m/%Y %H:%M')
    for i in range(0,len(df)):
        df.loc[i,'Month'] = df.loc[i][datetime_col].
        strftime('%B')
        df.loc[i,'Hour'] = df.loc[i][datetime_col].
        strftime('%I%p')
    return df.groupby(['Month','Hour'],sort=False,as_
    index=False).mean().round(4)
# Plotly heatmap visualization
def heatmap(df, month_hours, value_col):
    for i in range(len(df)):
        month_hours[df.iloc[i][0]][df.iloc[i][1]] = df.loc[i]
        [value_col]
    data_rows = list(month_hours.values())
    data = []
    for i in range(0,len(data_rows)):
        data.append(list(data_rows[i].values()))
    fig = px.imshow(data,
```

```
                    labels=dict(x='Hour', y='Month',
                    color='Value'),
                            x=['12AM','01AM','02AM','03AM'
                            ,'04AM','05AM','06AM','07AM',
                            '08AM','09AM','10AM','11AM',
                            '12PM','01PM','02PM','03PM','0
                            4PM','05PM','06PM','07PM',
                            '08PM','09PM','10PM','11PM'],
                            y=['January','February','March'
                            ,'April','May','June','July',
                            'August','September','October',
                            'November','December']
                            )
    st.write(fig)
if __name__ == '__main__':
    st.sidebar.title('Time-series Heatmap')
    uploaded_file = st.sidebar.file_uploader('Upload a time-
    series dataset')
    if uploaded_file is not None:
        month_hours = month_hours_dict()
        df = pd.read_csv(uploaded_file)
        df_aggregate = aggregate(df, 'datetime',
        '%d/%m/%Y %H:%M')
        heatmap(df_aggregate, month_hours, 'value')
```

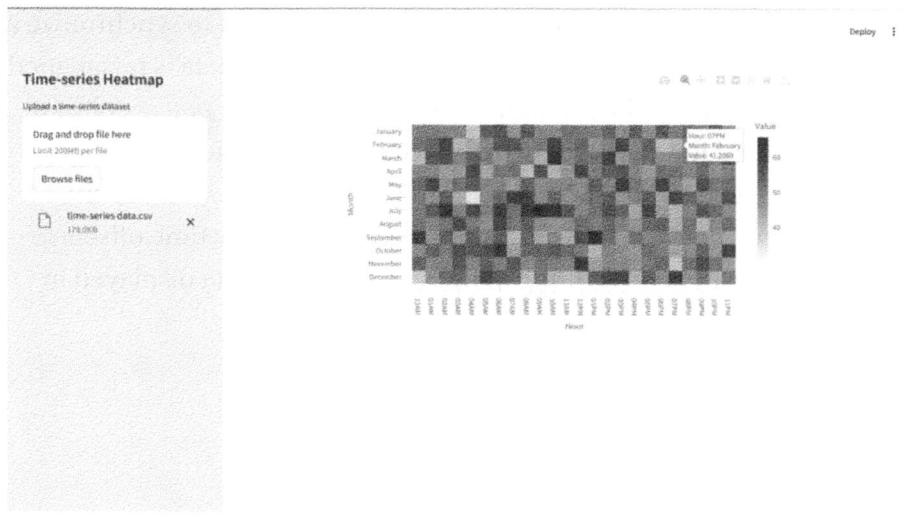

Figure 11-7. *Output of Listing 11-6*

11.2.3. Time Synchronization Application

One of the classical challenges when working with time-series data is the lack of synchronization between datasets. Even if two datasets represent the same information at the same moment, they might have different timestamps, leading to a variety of unintended problems. These discrepancies can arise from several factors, such as different time zones—where one zone observes daylight savings while the other does not—or errors in the SCADA systems during data recording. Regardless of the cause, it is essential to synchronize time-series datasets to ensure accurate analysis and interpretation of the data.

To address this issue, a technique known as *dynamic time warping* (DTW) can be employed. DTW synchronizes misaligned datasets by applying dynamic time offsets wherever necessary to maximize the correlation between the two. The advantage of this method is its ability to adjust time offsets as needed to achieve the highest possible correlation at each timestamp. Moreover, DTW can be applied to datasets of varying lengths. The only caveat is that missing values must be filled in before DTW can be executed without errors.

In this example, we will create a Streamlit application to synchronize a dataset of power vs. voltage readings, where the voltage data is misaligned by two hours. As shown in Listing 11-7, we will define the *power* column as the reference dataset, which will be used to synchronize the *voltage* column, the target dataset. The synchronization function will take the unsynchronized data (as shown in Figure 11-8) and apply time offsets to the target's timestamps, resulting in the synchronized data displayed in Figure 11-9.

Listing 11-7. timeseries_synchronization.py

```
import numpy as np
import pandas as pd
import streamlit as st
from fastdtw import *
import plotly.express as px
from sklearn.metrics import r2_score
from scipy.spatial.distance import *
# Dynamic Time Warping synchronization function
def synchronize(df, datetime_col, reference, target):
    x = np.array(df[reference].fillna(0))
    y = np.array(df[target].fillna(0))
    distance, path = fastdtw(x, y)

    result = [
        [df[datetime_col].iloc[path[i][0]], df[reference].
        iloc[path[i][0]], df[target].iloc[path[i][1]]]
        for i in range(len(path))
    ]

    df_synchronized = pd.DataFrame(result, columns=[datetime_
    col, reference, target])
    df_synchronized = df_synchronized.drop_
    duplicates(subset=[datetime_col])
```

```
    return df_synchronized
# Plotly time-series visualization function
def timeseries_chart(df, datetime_col):
    df_columns = list(df)
    df[datetime_col] = pd.to_datetime(df[datetime_
    col],format='%d-%m-%y %H:%M')
    df = df.sort_values(by=datetime_col)
    fig = px.line(df, x=datetime_col, y=df_columns,
                    hover_data={datetime_col: '|%d-%m-%Y %H:%M'})
    st.write(fig)
if __name__ == '__main__':
    st.sidebar.title('Time-series Synchronization')
    uploaded_file = st.sidebar.file_uploader('Upload a time-
    series dataset')
    if uploaded_file is not None:
        df = pd.read_csv(uploaded_file).
        dropna(subset=['datetime'])
        df_synchronized = synchronize(df, 'datetime', 'power',
        'voltage')
        timeseries_chart(df, 'datetime')
        st.subheader(f'Correlation: {round(r2_
        score(df["power"], df["voltage"]), 3)}')
        timeseries_chart(df_synchronized, 'datetime')
        st.subheader(f'Correlation: {round(r2_
        score(df_synchronized["power"], df_
        synchronized["voltage"]), 3)}')
        st.download_button(
            label='Download synchronized data',
        data=df_synchronized.to_csv(index=False).encode('utf-8'),
            file_name='synchronized_data.csv',
            mime='text/csv')
```

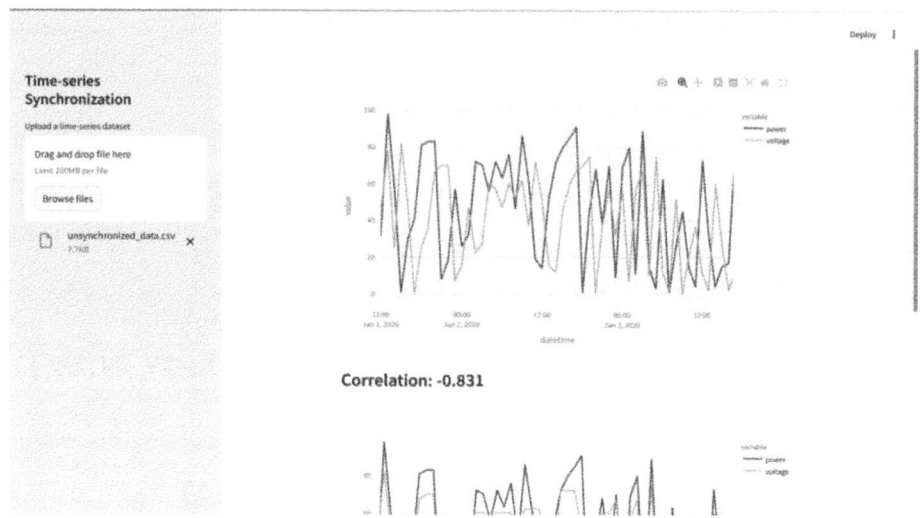

Figure 11-8. *Output of Listing 11-7 (unsynchronized dataset)*

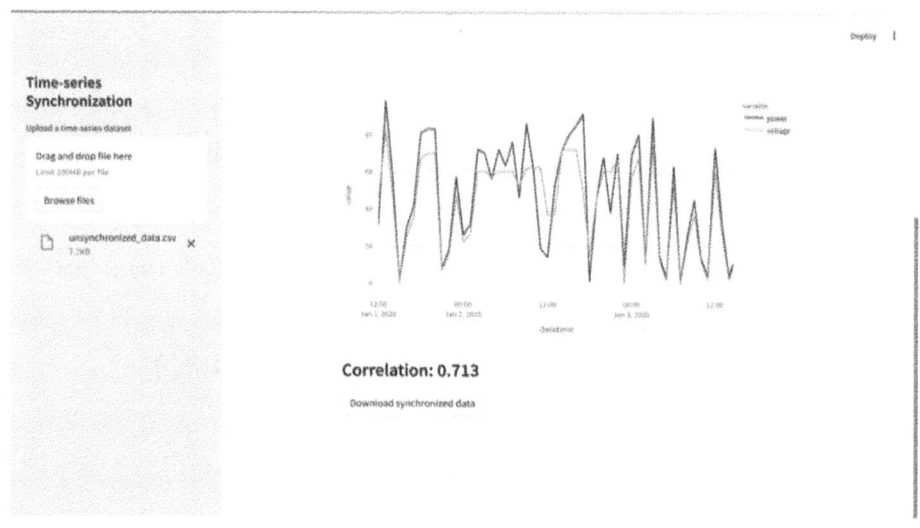

Figure 11-9. *Output of Listing 11-7 (synchronized dataset)*

11.3. Data Management and Machine Learning Applications

Undoubtedly, one of the most popular use cases for Python-based web applications is data management and machine learning. This is where Streamlit truly excels. With its extensive library of widgets for data wrangling and visualization, Streamlit empowers developers to effortlessly create powerful data analytics applications.

11.3.1. Data Warehouse Application

In this section, we will outline the foundational components for building a data warehousing application. While *warehousing* typically refers to the structured storage of data, in this case, we will leverage Streamlit to provide a rich graphical interface for managing databases and tables. Users will be able to create, read, update, and delete data, and visualize stored data on demand, all within a single application. With this tool, users can connect to either a local or remote SQL database and manage their data without needing to write SQL queries or any code.

For this example, we will use a local *PostgreSQL* database; however, you can choose any local or remote SQL database by simply modifying the database credentials and client configurations as shown in Listings 11-8 and 11-10. To enhance security, it's recommended to store your credentials in a local configuration file and ensure that this file is added to your *.gitignore* file when pushing to remote repositories. Next, use Listing 11-9 to define the functions for creating, reading, updating, and deleting data within your databases and tables. This utility file will also enable the interactive CRUD table widget, as discussed in Section 4.1, and allow for data visualization through a line chart.

Listing 11-8. config.py

```
username = "<username>"
password = "<password>"
port = "<port>"
```

Listing 11-9. warehouse_utils.py

```
from sqlalchemy import create_engine, text
import psycopg2
from psycopg2.extensions import ISOLATION_LEVEL_AUTOCOMMIT
import pandas as pd
import streamlit as st
from st_aggrid import AgGrid
from st_aggrid.shared import GridUpdateMode
from st_aggrid.grid_options_builder import GridOptionsBuilder
import plotly.express as px
# Function to create a new database
def create_database(database_name, connection):
    connection.set_isolation_level(ISOLATION_LEVEL_AUTOCOMMIT)
    cursor = connection.cursor()
    try:
        cursor.execute(f"""CREATE DATABASE {'warehouse_db_' +
        database_name} WITH OWNER = postgres ENCODING =
        'UTF8' CONNECTION LIMIT = -1;""")
        cursor.close()
        return True
    except:
        return False
# Function to return a list of databases
def read_databases(engine):
    with engine.connect() as conn:
```

```
        result = conn.execute(text('SELECT datname FROM pg_
        database'))
        result = [x[0].replace('warehouse_db_', '') for x
        in result
        if 'warehouse_db_' in x[0]]
        return result
# Function to rename a selected database
def update_database(database_name_old, database_name_new,
connection):
    connection.set_isolation_level(ISOLATION_LEVEL_AUTOCOMMIT)
    cursor = connection.cursor()
    try:
        cursor.execute(f"""SELECT pg_terminate_backend (pg_
        stat_activity.pid)
        FROM pg_stat_activity WHERE pg_stat_activity.datname =
        '{"warehouse_db_" + database_name_old}';""")
        cursor.execute(f"""ALTER DATABASE {'warehouse_db_'
        + database_name_old} RENAME TO {'warehouse_db_' +
        database_name_new};""")
        cursor.close()
        return True
    except Exception as e:
        print(e)
# Function to delete a selected database
def delete_database(database_name, connection):
    connection.set_isolation_level(ISOLATION_LEVEL_AUTOCOMMIT)
    cursor = connection.cursor()
    try:
        cursor.execute(f"""SELECT pg_terminate_backend (pg_
        stat_activity.pid)
```

```
        FROM pg_stat_activity WHERE pg_stat_activity.datname =
        '{"warehouse_db_" + database_name}';""")
        cursor.execute(f"""DROP DATABASE {'warehouse_db_' +
        database_name};""")
        cursor.close()
        return True
    except Exception as e:
        print(e)
# Function to create a table in the selected database
def create_table(table_name, table, engine):
    table.to_sql(table_name, engine, index=False, if_
    exists='replace', chunksize=1000)
# Function to return a list of tables in the selected database
def list_tables(engine):
    with engine.connect() as conn:
        tables = conn.execute(text("""SELECT table_name FROM
        information_schema.tables
        WHERE table_schema = 'public' ORDER BY table_
        name;""")).fetchall()
        return [x[0] for x in tables]
# Function to read the selected table within the selected
database
def read_table(table_name, engine):
    try:
        return pd.read_sql_table(table_name,engine)
    except Exception as e:
        print(e)
# Function to delete the selected table within the selected
database
def delete_table(table_name, engine):
    with engine.begin() as conn:
```

```
        conn.execute(text(f'DROP TABLE IF EXISTS "{table_name}"'))
# Function to render an interactive 'create, read, update and
delete' table
def crud(table_name, engine):
    df = read_table(table_name, engine)
    df = df.fillna('None')
    index = len(df)
    # Initiate the streamlit-aggrid widget
    gb = GridOptionsBuilder.from_dataframe(df)
    gb.configure_side_bar()
    gb.configure_default_column(groupable=True, value=True,
    enableRowGroup=True,
     aggFunc='sum', editable=True)
    gb.configure_selection(selection_mode='multiple', use_
    checkbox=True)
    gridOptions = gb.build()
    # Insert the dataframe into the widget
    df_new = AgGrid(df,gridOptions=gridOptions,enable_
    enterprise_modules=True,
    update_mode=GridUpdateMode.MODEL_CHANGED)
    # Add a new row to the widget
    if st.button('-----------Add a new row-----------'):
        df_new['data'].loc[index,:] = 'None'
        create_table(table_name, df_new['data'], engine)
        st.rerun()
    # Save the dataframe to disk if the widget has been
    modified
    if df.equals(df_new['data']) is False:
        create_table(table_name, df_new['data'], engine)
        st.rerun()
    # Remove selected rows from the widget
    if st.button('-----------Remove selected rows-----------'):
```

```
        if len(df_new['selected_rows']) > 0:
            exclude = pd.DataFrame(df_new['selected_rows'])
            create_table(table_name, pd.merge(df_new['data'],
            exclude, how='outer',
            indicator=True).query('_merge == "left_only"').
            drop('_merge', 1), engine)
            st.rerun()
        else:
            st.warning('Please select at least one row')
    # Check for duplicate rows
    if df_new['data'].duplicated().sum() > 0:
        st.warning(f'**Number of duplicate rows:** { df_
        new['data'].duplicated().sum()}')
        if st.button('---------Delete duplicates---------'):
            df_new['data'] = df_new['data'].drop_duplicates()
            create_table(table_name, df_new['data'], engine)
            st.rerun()
# Function to render a line chart for the selected table
def chart(df, columns):
    if len(columns) > 0:
        fig = px.line(df.sort_index(), df.index, columns)
        st.write(fig)
```

Finally, you can use Listing 11-10 to render the frontend interface for your data warehousing application. The output of this script, as shown in Figures 11-10, 11-11, and 11-12, is divided into three sections:

1. Database Manager: This section provides the user with the ability to create, read, rename, and delete databases.

2. Table Manager: In this section, the user can upload a table in CSV format, update it using the interactive CRUD widget, and delete the table.

3. Data Visualizer: This section allows the user to visualize any numeric table by selecting one or more columns and displaying them within a range-indexed line chart.

Listing 11-10. warehouse_app.py

```
from warehouse_utils import *
import config # Credentials file
# PostgreSQL credentials
username = config.username
password = config.password
port = config.port
if __name__ == '__main__':
    # Creating PostgreSQL client
    connection = psycopg2.connect(f"user={username}
    password='{password}'")
    engine = create_engine(
        f'postgresql://{username}:{password}@
        localhost:{port}/')
    st.title('Data Warehouse')
    st.write('___')
    st.subheader('Database Manager')
    col1, col2 = st.columns(2)
    with col1:
        st.write('**Create database**')
        database_name = st.text_input('Please enter
        database name')
        if st.button('Create database'):
            status = create_database(database_name, connection)
            if status is True:
                st.success(f'Database **{database_name }**
                created successfully')
```

```
        elif status is False:
            st.warning('Database with this name already exists')
    st.write('**Rename database**')
    database_name_old = st.selectbox('Please select a
    database to rename',
    read_databases(engine))
    if database_name_old is not None:
        database_name_new = st.text_input('Please enter new
        database name')
        if st.button('Rename database'):
            status = update_database(database_name_old,
            database_name_new, connection)
            if status is True:
                st.success(f'Database renamed from
                **{database_name_old}** to **{database_
                name_new}**')
with col2:
    st.write('**List databases**')
    database_selection = st.selectbox('Databases
    list',read_databases(engine))
    st.write('**Delete database**')
    database_selection = st.selectbox('Please select a
    database to delete',
    read_databases(engine))
    if database_selection is not None:
        if st.button('Delete database'):
            status = delete_database(database_selection,
            connection)
            if status is True:
                st.success(f'Database **{database_
                selection}** deleted successfully')
```

```
st.write('___')
st.subheader('Table Manager')
st.write('**Select database**')
database_selection = st.selectbox('Please select a
database',
read_databases(engine))
if database_selection is not None:
    engine_database = create_engine(f'postgresql://
    {username}:{password}@localhost:{port}/{'warehouse_db_'
    + database_selection}')
    col1_2, col2_2 = st.columns(2)
    with col1_2:
        st.write('**Create table**')
        table = st.file_uploader('Please upload data')
        if table is not None:
            table = pd.read_csv(table)
            table_name = st.text_input('Please enter
            table name')
            if st.button('Save table'):
                if len(table_name) > 0:
                    create_table(table_name, table, engine_
                    database)
                    st.success(f'**{table_name}** saved to
                    database')
                else:
                    st.warning('Please enter table name')
    with col2_2:
        st.write('**Delete table**')
        table_selection = st.selectbox('Please select table
        to delete',
        list_tables(engine_database))
```

```
            if table_selection is not None:
                if st.button('Delete table'):
                    delete_table(table_selection, engine_
                    database)
                    st.success(f'**{table_selection}** deleted
                    successfully')
        st.write('**Read and update table**')
        table_selection = st.selectbox('Please select table to
        reade and update',
        list_tables(engine_database))
        if table_selection is not None:
            crud(table_selection, engine_database)
st.write('___')
st.subheader('Data Visualizer')
st.write('**Select database**')
database_selection = st.selectbox('Please select a database
to visualize',
read_databases(engine))
if database_selection is not None:
    engine_database = create_engine(f'postgresql://
    {username}:{password}@localhost:{port}/{'warehouse_db_'
    + database_selection}')
    col1_3, col2_3 = st.columns(2)
    with col1_3:
        table_selection = st.selectbox('Please select table
        to visualize',
        list_tables(engine_database))
        table = read_table(table_selection, engine_database)
    if table_selection is not None:
        with col2_3:
            columns = st.multiselect('Please select
            columns', table.columns)
```

```
    table[columns] = table[columns].apply(pd.to_
    numeric, errors='coerce')
chart(table, columns)
```

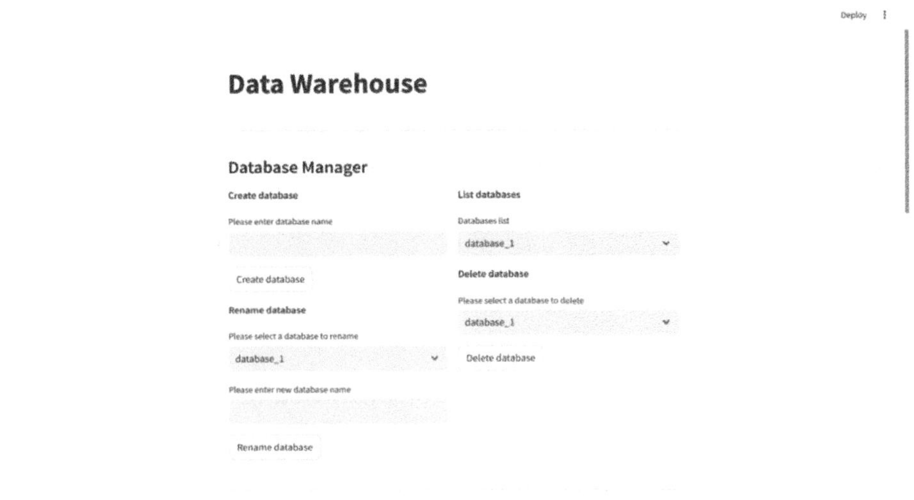

Figure 11-10. *Output of Listing 11-10*

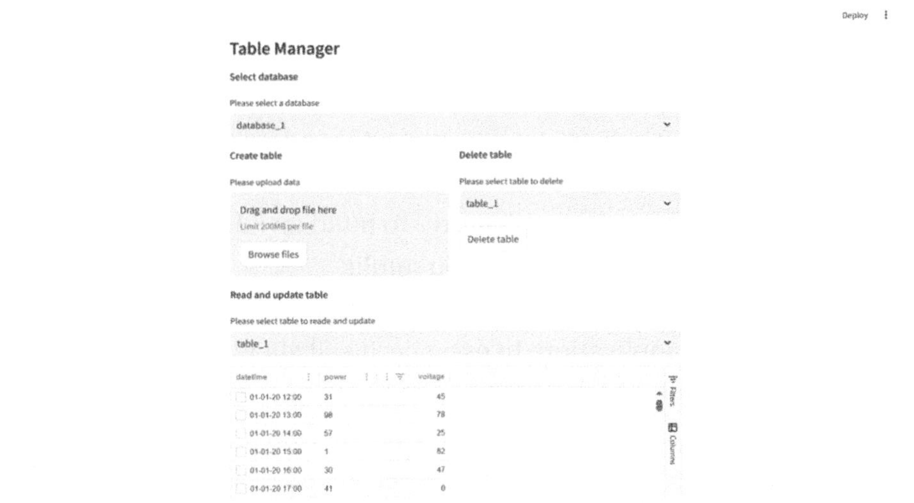

Figure 11-11. *Output of Listing 11-10 continued (1)*

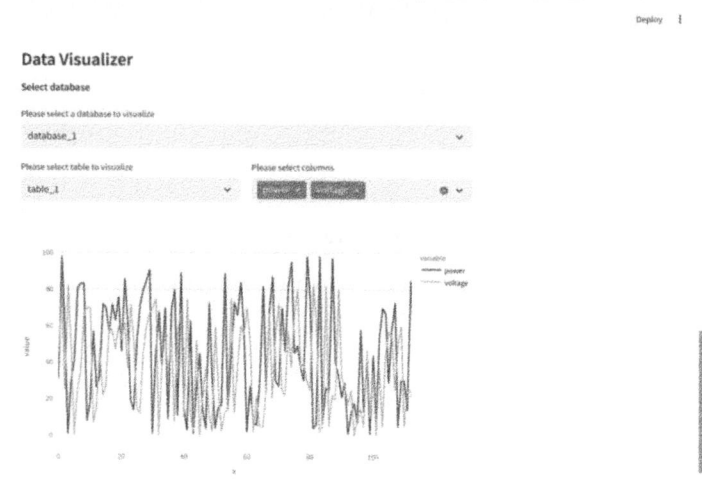

Figure 11-12.   Output of Listing 11-10 continued (2)

11.3.2. Advanced Application Development: Machine Learning As a Service

The final use case for this chapter is a *Machine Learning as a Service* (MLaaS) application. This example will integrate many of the key concepts covered in this book, showcasing how to combine databases, caching, session state, user authentication, traffic insights, data visualization, subpages, modularity, and other features to build an advanced, production-ready web application in Streamlit.

Before diving into the details, it is important to explain the functionality of this application. In essence, it will allow users to train a logistic regression model on an uploaded dataset and then use the trained model to classify a test dataset. While the core utility might seem simple, the implementation will leverage the full capabilities of Streamlit, PostgreSQL, Pandas, Plotly, and other technologies. This use case is also highly scalable, having been extended to support additional classifiers such as decision trees, support vector machines, Naive Bayes, and K-nearest neighbors.

User Authentication Without a Backend Server

In Chapter 8, we discussed implementing user authentication with a backend server. However, it is also possible to implement authentication without a server using the Streamlit component *Streamlit-Authenticator*. While Streamlit possesses its own native authentication command `st.login` which provides OIDC authentication, the *Streamlit-Authenticator* component provides a lightweight local authentication service, with a whole host of additional features such as

- User registration

- Retrieving a forgotten username

- Resetting a forgotten password

- Authenticating with OAauth2

- Two-factor authorization

Therefore, we will use this component to demo authentication in this chapter.

With Streamlit-Authenticator, the first step is to create a *config.yaml* file that will store your users' credentials as well as other configuration parameters for authentication as shown in Listing 11-11. Please note that plain text passwords will be hashed automatically unless specified otherwise. Next, you will provide the credentials to the `stauth.Authenticate` and create a login widget using the `login` command as shown in Listing 11-12. Each time a user enters their plain-text password (as shown in Figure 11-13), it is hashed and compared to the previously stored hashed password to authenticate the user.

Additionally, you can enable passwordless reauthentication by using the cookie_expiry_days argument in the stauth.Authenticate command. This will store a secure *JWT* (JSON Web Token) on the user's browser, allowing them to remain authenticated for the specified number of days before the token expires. You can check the user's authentication status at any point in your application by accessing st.session_state['authentication_status']. For further information, please refer to https://github.com/mkhorasani/Streamlit-Authenticator.

Listing 11-11. config.yaml

```yaml
cookie:
  expiry_days: 30
  key: # To be filled with any string
  name: # To be filled with any string
credentials:
  usernames:
    jsmith:
      email: jsmith@gmail.com
      failed_login_attempts: 0 # Will be managed automatically
      first_name: John
      last_name: Smith
      logged_in: False # Will be managed automatically
      password: abc # Will be hashed automatically
      roles: # Optional
      - admin
      - editor
      - viewer
    rbriggs:
      email: rbriggs@gmail.com
      failed_login_attempts: 0 # Will be managed automatically
      first_name: Rebecca
      last_name: Briggs
```

```
    logged_in: False # Will be managed automatically
    password: def # Will be hashed automatically
    roles: # Optional
    - viewer
```

Listing 11-12. Streamlit-Authenticator.py

```python
import streamlit as st
import streamlit_authenticator as stauth
import yaml
from yaml.loader import SafeLoader

with open('../config.yaml') as file:
    config = yaml.load(file, Loader=SafeLoader)

authenticator = stauth.Authenticate(
    config['credentials'],
    config['cookie']['name'],
    config['cookie']['key'],
    config['cookie']['expiry_days']
)

try:
    authenticator.login()
except Exception as e:
    st.error(e)
if st.session_state.get('authentication_status'):
    authenticator.logout()
    st.write(f'Welcome *{st.session_state.get("name")}*')
    st.title('Some content')
elif st.session_state.get('authentication_status') is False:
    st.error('Username/password is incorrect')
elif st.session_state.get('authentication_status') is None:
    st.warning('Please enter your username and password')
```

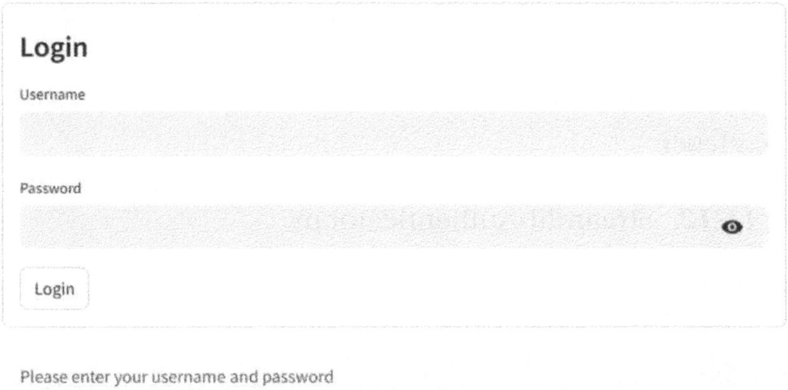

Figure 11-13. *Output of Listing 11-12*

Utilities Script

Modularizing application development is a good practice, as it helps organize and streamline the codebase. Commonly used classes, functions, database connections, and other objects should be relocated to a shared file, often named *Utils.py*. In our case, we will place functions for querying the user-insights table, generating a session ID, creating a file upload widget, and establishing a PostgreSQL connection within this file, as shown in Listing 11-13. Moreover, a valuable optimization technique is to use the `st.cache_resource` command to cache the database connection object. This will save a significant amount of time whenever a call is made to the database, improving the overall performance of the application.

Listing 11-13. Utils.py

```
import pandas as pd
from sqlalchemy import create_engine, text
import streamlit as st
import uuid
# Inserting new row in traffic insights table
```

```python
def insert_row(session_id, engine):
    with engine.connect() as conn:
        if conn.execute(text(f"SELECT session_id FROM session_state
        WHERE session_id = '{session_id}'")).fetchone() is None:
            conn.execute(text(f"INSERT INTO session_state
            (session_id) VALUES ('{session_id}')"))
# Updating row in insights table
def update_row(column, new_value, session_id, engine):
    with engine.connect() as conn:
        if conn.execute(text(f"SELECT {column} FROM session_
        state WHERE session_id = '{session_id}'")).first()[0]
        is None:
            conn.execute(text(f"UPDATE session_state SET {column}
            = '{new_value}' WHERE session_id = '{session_id}'"))
# Session state function
def get_session():
    if 'session_id' not in st.session_state:
        session_id = str(uuid.uuid4())
        session_id = session_id.replace('-', '_')
        session_id = '_id_' + session_id
        st.session_state.session_id = session_id
    return st.session_state.session_id
# File uploader function
def file_upload(name):
    uploaded_file = st.sidebar.file_uploader(name, key=name,
    accept_multiple_files=False)
    status = False
    if uploaded_file is not None:
        try:
            uploaded_df = pd.read_csv(uploaded_file)
            status = True
            return status, uploaded_df
```

```
        except:
            try:
                uploaded_df = pd.read_excel(uploaded_file)
                status = True
                return status, uploaded_df
            except:
                st.error('Please ensure file is .csv or .xlsx
                format and/or
                reupload file')
                return status, None
    else:
        return status, None
@st.cache_resource
def db_engine(username, password, port):
    return create_engine(f'postgresql://{username}:{password}@
localhost:{port}/')
```

Config Script

As mentioned in earlier sections, another best practice is to store credentials in dictionaries within a *config.py* file as shown in Listing 11-14, which is then imported and used in your main code. To ensure security, remember to add the *config.py* file to your .gitignore file, preventing it from being pushed to any remote repositories.

Listing 11-14. config.py

```
# Traffic insights database credentials dictionary
database_credentials = {
"username": "<username>",
"password": "<password>",
"port": "<port>"
}
```

Main Script

Now that we have covered the logistics, we can start developing the main script of our application. This script will act as the central hub, connecting the various pages and handling some housekeeping tasks. As shown in Listing 11-15, we start by importing the scripts for other pages, following the approach discussed in Section 3.3. Next, we use the Streamlit-Authenticator component to authenticate users based on the credentials stored in a *config.yaml* file. After authentication, we enable navigation between pages using the st.selectbox command, which selects the function for the chosen page from a dictionary of key-value pairs, where the key is the page's name and the value is the corresponding function. Finally, we invoke the file upload widget from our *Utils.py* file and store the uploaded Pandas dataframes in the session state, making them accessible on demand.

Listing 11-15. main.py

```python
import streamlit as st
from Utils import *
import streamlit_authenticator as stauth
import yaml
from yaml.loader import SafeLoader
import config # config.py not to be mixed with config.yaml
with open('../config.yaml') as file:
    config = yaml.load(file, Loader=SafeLoader)

authenticator = stauth.Authenticate(
    config['credentials'],
    config['cookie']['name'],
    config['cookie']['key'],
    config['cookie']['expiry_days']
)
```

```python
# Importing pages
from lr import lr_main
def main(engine):
    # Creating pages dictionary
    pages_ml_classifier = {
        'Logistic Regression Classifier': lr_main
        }
    # Creating pages menu
    st.sidebar.subheader('Menu')
    ml_module_selection = st.sidebar.selectbox('Select
    Classifier',
    ['Logistic Regression Classifier'])
    # Creating dataset uploader widgets
    if 'df_train' not in st.session_state:
        st.session_state['df_train'] = None
    if 'df_real' not in st.session_state:
        st.session_state['df_real'] = None
    st.sidebar.subheader('Training Dataset')
    _, st.session_state['df_train'] = file_upload('Please
    upload a training dataset')
    st.sidebar.subheader('Test Dataset')
    _, st.session_state['df_real'] = file_upload('Please upload
    a test dataset')
    # Running selected page
    pages_ml_classifier[ml_module_selection](engine)
if __name__ == '__main__':
    # Creating PostgreSQL client for insights database
    username = config.database_credentials['username']
    password = config.database_credentials['password']
    port = config.database_credentials['port']
    engine = db_engine(username, password, port)
```

```
# Creating user authentication object
authenticator = stauth.Authenticate(config.user_
credentials['names'],
config.user_credentials['usernames'], config.user_
credentials['passwords'],
'some_cookie_name','some_signature_key', cookie_expiry_
days=30)
# Displaying login bar
try:
    authenticator.login()
except Exception as e:
    st.error(e)
if st.session_state['authentication_status']:
    authenticator.logout('Logout', 'main')
    st.write(f'Welcome *{st.session_state["name"]}*')
    main(engine)
elif st.session_state['authentication_status'] == False:
    st.sidebar.error('Username/password is incorrect')
elif st.session_state['authentication_status'] == None:
    st.sidebar.warning('Please enter your username and
    password')
```

Logistic Regression Classifier

The final and undoubtedly most impactful step is to create the script
for our logistic regression classifier page. As mentioned earlier, this
application will provide machine learning-as-a-service, enabling users
to train a logistic regression model on an uploaded training dataset and
then use the trained model to classify a test dataset. The beauty of such
an application lies in its plug-and-play nature, where users do not need
to install any libraries or manage a server. To enable this functionality,
we have a set of functions, as shown in Listing 11-16, that will provide the
following:

1. Visualize a Confusion Matrix: Display the confusion matrix to evaluate the performance of the model, showing the true positive, false positive, true negative, and false negative results.

2. Visualize an ROC Curve: Generate and visualize the Receiver Operating Characteristic (ROC) curve to evaluate the model's classification performance across different threshold values.

3. Create an Expandable Entry Form for Model Hyperparameters: Allow users to customize the logistic regression model's hyperparameters via an expandable form, making the model more flexible and adaptable.

4. Train the Logistic Regression Model: Train the model using the uploaded training dataset and cache the function using `st.cache_resource` to optimize performance on subsequent runs.

5. Classify Test Data Using the Trained Model: Use the trained logistic regression model to classify the provided test data.

6. Visualize Accuracy Metrics of Classified Data: Display various accuracy metrics (e.g., accuracy score, precision, recall, F1 score) to assess the model's performance on the test data.

In addition to the core machine learning functionality, we will integrate a traffic insights feature to track and record user interactions at each step of the application. Specifically, as users progress through various stages of the application, the following actions will be logged:

1. Tracking User Progress: At each step of the application, traffic insight functions imported from the Utils.py file will be invoked to record the exact date and time when the user reaches a specific step. This will help provide insights into user behavior and engagement with the application.

2. Data Size Recording: The size of the uploaded datasets will be logged. This information can be helpful for understanding the scale of data the user is working with and optimizing future data handling strategies.

3. Saving Insights into PostgreSQL Database: All the recorded insights (such as timestamps, dataset sizes, and user actions) will be saved into a PostgreSQL database. This information can later be used for analytics or improving the application's performance.

4. Download Hyperparameters and Predictions: After completing the model training and prediction steps, the user will have the option to download their model hyperparameters and predicted data. This will enable users to retain and further utilize their machine learning models outside the platform.

The various steps of this process, from uploading the dataset to viewing the results and downloading the predictions, are visualized in Figure 11-14, providing an overview of the workflow.

Listing 11-16. lr.py

```python
import streamlit as st
import pandas as pd
from sklearn.model_selection import train_test_split
from sklearn.linear_model import LogisticRegression
from sklearn import metrics
import plotly.express as px
import plotly.graph_objects as go
import plotly.figure_factory as ff
from datetime import datetime
from Utils import *
# Plotly confusion matrix visualization
def confusion_matrix_plot(y_test, y_pred):
    cnf_matrix = metrics.confusion_matrix(y_test, y_pred)
    z = cnf_matrix.tolist()[::-1]
    x = ['Negative', 'Positive']
    y = ['Positive', 'Negative']
    z_text = z
    fig = ff.create_annotated_heatmap(z, x, y, annotation_
    text=z_text, text=z,
    hoverinfo='text', colorscale='Blackbody')
    st.write(fig)
# Plotly receiver operating characteristic visualization
function
def roc_plot(X_test, logreg, y_test):
    y_pred_proba = logreg.predict_proba(X_test)[::,1]
    fpr, tpr, _ = metrics.roc_curve(y_test, y_pred_proba)
    roc_data = pd.DataFrame([])
    roc_data['True positive'] = tpr
    roc_data['False positive'] = fpr
    fig = px.line(roc_data, x='False positive', y='True positive')
```

```
    st.write(fig)
    auc = metrics.roc_auc_score(y_test, y_pred_proba)
    st.info(f'Area Under Curve: **{ round(auc,3)}**')
# Hyperparameters expander function
def lr_hyperparameters():
    with st.expander('Advanced Parameters'):
        col2_1, col2_2 = st.columns(2)
        with col2_1:
            penalty = st.selectbox('Penalty', ['l2','l1','elast
            icnet','none'])
            tol = st.number_input('Tolerance (1e-4)',
            value=1)/10000
            fit_intercept = st.radio('Intercept', [True,False])
            class_weight = st.radio('Class weight',
            [None,'balanced'])
            solver = st.selectbox('Solver', ['lbfgs','newton-
            cg','liblinear','sag',
            'saga'])
            multi_class = st.selectbox('Multi class',
            ['auto','ovr','multinomial'])
            warm_start = st.radio('Warm start', [False,True])
        with col2_2:
            dual = st.radio('Dual or primal formulation',
            [False,True])
            C = st.number_input('Inverse regularization
            strength', 0.0, 99.0, 1.0, 0.1)
            intercept_scaling = st.number_input('Intercept
            scaling', 0.0, 99.0, 1.0, 0.1)
            random_state = st.radio('Random state',
            [None,'Custom'])
            if random_state == 'Custom':
```

```
                random_state = st.number_input('Custom random
                state', 0, 99, 1, 1)
            max_iter = st.number_input('Maximum iterations', 0,
            100, 100, 1)
            verbose = st.number_input('Verbose', 0, 99, 0, 1)
            l1_ratio = st.radio('L1 ratio', [None,'Custom'])
            if l1_ratio == 'Custom':
                l1_ratio = st.number_input('Custom l1 ratio',
                0.0, 1.0, 1.0, 0.01)
        #Download hyperparameters feature
        hyperparameters = {'penalty':[penalty], 'dual':[dual],
        'tol':[tol], 'C':[C],
        'fit_intercept':[fit_intercept], 'intercept_
        scaling':[intercept_scaling],
        'class_weight':[class_weight],
        'random_state':[random_state],
        'solver':[solver], 'max_iter':[max_iter], 'multi_
        class':[multi_class],
        'verbose':[verbose],'warm_start':[warm_start], 'l1_
        ratio':[l1_ratio]}
        st.download_button(
            label='Download hyperparameters',
            data=pd.DataFrame(hyperparameters).to_
            csv(index=False).encode('utf-8'),
            file_name='Hyperparameters.csv',
        )
    return (penalty, tol, fit_intercept, class_weight, solver,
    multi_class, warm_start, dual, C, intercept_scaling,
    random_state, max_iter, verbose, l1_ratio)
# Logistic regression training function
@st.cache_resource
```

```python
def log_train(df, feature_cols, label_col, test_size, penalty,
tol, fit_intercept, class_weight, solver, multi_class,
    warm_start, dual, C, intercept_scaling, random_state,
    max_iter, verbose, l1_ratio):
    x = df[feature_cols]
    y = df[label_col]
    x_train,x_test,y_train,y_test=train_test_split(x, y, test_
    size=test_size, random_state=0)
    logreg = LogisticRegression(penalty=penalty, dual=dual,
    tol=tol, C=C, fit_intercept=fit_intercept, intercept_
    scaling=intercept_scaling, class_weight=class_weight,
    random_state=random_state, solver=solver, max_
    iter=max_iter,
    multi_class=multi_class, verbose=verbose, warm_start=
    warm_start, l1_ratio=l1_ratio)
    logreg.fit(x_train,y_train)
    y_pred = logreg.predict(x_test)
    return x_train, x_test, y_train, y_test, y_pred, logreg
# Logisitic regression predictor function
def log_real(logreg, df_real, feature_cols, label_col):
    x_test_real = df_real[feature_cols]
    y_pred_real = logreg.predict(x_test_real)
    x_pred_real = df_real.copy()
    x_pred_real[label_col] = y_pred_real
    return x_pred_real.sort_index()
# Prediction statistics function
def stats(y_test, y_pred):
    accuracy = metrics.accuracy_score(y_test, y_pred)
    precision = metrics.precision_score(y_test, y_pred)
    recall = metrics.recall_score(y_test, y_pred)
    f1 = metrics.f1_score(y_test, y_pred)
```

```
col2_1, col2_2, col2_3, col2_4 = st.columns(4)
with col2_1:
    st.info(f'Accuracy: **{round(accuracy,3)}**')
with col2_2:
    st.info(f'Precision: **{round(precision,3)}**')
with col2_3:
    st.info(f'Recall: **{round(recall,3)}**')
with col2_4:
    st.info(f'F1 Score: **{round(f1,3)}**')
def lr_main(engine):
    _, session_id = get_session()
    insert_row(session_id, engine)
    update_row('lr1',datetime.now().strftime('%H:%M:%S
    %d/%m/%Y'), session_id, engine)
    if st.session_state['df_train'] is not None:
        df = st.session_state['df_train']
        update_row('data1_rows',len(df),session_id,engine)
        update_row('lr2',datetime.now().strftime('%H:%M:%S
        %d/%m/%Y'), session_id,
         engine)
        st.title('Training')
        st.subheader('Parameters')
        col1, col2, col3 = st.columns((3,3,2))
        with col1:
            feature_cols = st.multiselect('Please select
            features', df.columns)
        with col2:
            label_col = st.selectbox('Please select label',
            df.columns)
        with col3:
```

```
    test_size = st.number_input('Please enter test
    size', 0.01, 0.99, 0.25, 0.05)
(penalty, tol, fit_intercept, class_weight, solver,
multi_class,
warm_start, dual, C, intercept_scaling, random_state,
max_iter, verbose,
l1_ratio) = lr_hyperparameters()
try:
    x_train, x_test, y_train, y_test, y_pred, logreg =
    log_train(df, feature_cols, label_col, test_size,
    penalty, tol, fit_intercept, class_weight, solver,
    multi_class, warm_start, dual, C, intercept_scaling,
    random_state, max_iter, verbose, l1_ratio)
    st.subheader('Confusion Matrix')
    confusion_matrix_plot(y_test, y_pred)
    st.subheader('Metrics')
    stats(y_test, y_pred)
    st.subheader('ROC Curve')
    roc_plot(x_test, logreg, y_test)
    update_row('lr3',datetime.now().strftime('%H:%M:%S
    %d/%m/%Y'),
    session_id, engine)
    if st.session_state['df_real'] is not None:
        try:
            df_real = st.session_state['df_real']
            st.title('Testing')
            update_row('data2_rows',len(df_real),
            session_id, engine)
            st.subheader('Predicted Labels')
            x_pred_real = log_real(logreg, df_real,
            feature_cols, label_col)
```

```
                        st.write(x_pred_real)
                        update_row('lr4',datetime.now().
                        strftime('%H:%M:%S %d/%m/%Y'),
                        session_id, engine)
                        st.download_button(
                                label='Download predicted labels',
                                data=pd.DataFrame(x_pred_real).to_
                                csv(index=False)
                                .encode('utf-8'),
                                file_name='Predicted labels.csv',
                        )
                    except:
                        st.warning('Please upload a test dataset with
                        the same feature
                        set as the training dataset')
                elif st.session_state['df_real'] is None:
                        st.sidebar.warning('Please upload a test dataset')
        except:
            st.warning('Please select at least one feature, a
            suitable binary
            label and appropriate advanced parameters')
elif st.session_state['df_train'] is None:
    st.title('Welcome      ')
    st.subheader('Please use the left pane to upload your dataset')
    st.sidebar.warning('Please upload a training dataset')
```

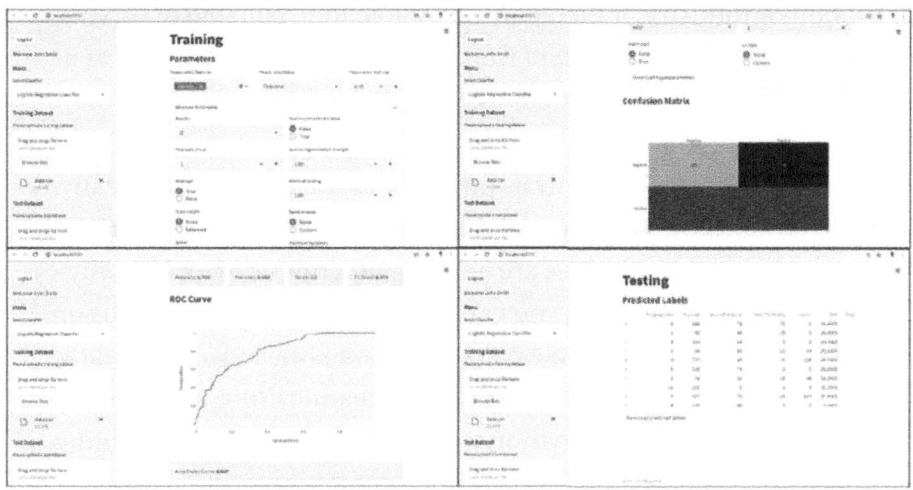

Figure 11-14. Output of Listing 11-16, with Pima Indians Diabetes training dataset [21]

11.4. Summary

As you near the end of this chapter and approach the completion of the entire book, it is becoming clear just how versatile and impactful Streamlit can be in solving real-world problems. What started as a simple Python tool for creating web applications has evolved into a powerful framework capable of addressing a wide range of use cases. From data visualization and time-series analysis to specialized applications like SCADA data loggers and motor control dashboards, Streamlit has proven its flexibility. Its ability to integrate with external systems, such as Arduino microcontrollers, sensors, and other peripherals, shows its potential to scale into embedded systems, bridging the gap between software and hardware in practical, real-world applications. A key takeaway from this chapter is the realization that Streamlit isn't limited to just one type of application or industry. It's a highly adaptable tool, capable of serving diverse needs—whether for data warehousing, machine learning as a service, or more specialized areas like industrial automation and IoT systems.

Ultimately, Streamlit is only as powerful as the developer's creativity and the tech stack they choose. As you continue exploring and building with Streamlit, the possibilities are endless, and this chapter has only scratched the surface of what you can accomplish. Congratulations on reaching this point! You now have the tools and knowledge to tackle a wide range of real-world challenges using Streamlit. Your journey toward creating efficient, impactful Python web applications is just beginning.

CHAPTER 12

Testing in Streamlit

Testing is a vital quality assurance process that verifies software functionality, detects issues early, and ensures reliability. By validating requirements and promoting best practices, testing enhances stability, maintainability, and user satisfaction—especially in dynamic platforms like Streamlit.

12.1. Principles of Testing

Testing is the process of verifying and validating that software behaves as intended, aiming to identify defects, errors, or missing requirements early in the development cycle. It involves creating test cases that check the code's output against expected results, ensuring reliability and consistency across scenarios. More than just finding bugs, testing also confirms that software meets requirements and follows best practices, contributing to its robustness and maintainability. In platforms like Streamlit, where rapid prototyping and interactive features are common, thorough testing is crucial to ensure accurate and dependable functionality. Ultimately, testing is a key aspect of quality assurance that supports software stability and user satisfaction.

© Mohammad Khorasani, Mohamed Abdou, Javier Hernández Fernández 2025
M. Khorasani et al., *Streamlit for Web Development*,
https://doi.org/10.1007/979-8-8688-1826-4_12

12.1.1. What Is Testing?

Testing, at its core, is the process of verifying and validating that software performs as intended. It is a systematic approach to identifying defects, errors, or missing requirements in a piece of code. Rather than relying solely on manual observation or user feedback after deployment, code testing aims to uncover issues early in the development lifecycle. This proactive strategy significantly reduces the risk of costly and disruptive bugs in production environments.

From a theoretical perspective, code testing can be seen as an exercise in building confidence in the correctness and reliability of software. It involves creating a set of conditions, or test cases, that evaluate different aspects of the code by comparing actual outputs with expected results. The goal is to ensure the code behaves predictably and consistently across various scenarios.

It is important to recognize that testing is not merely about finding bugs. It also involves validating that the code meets specified requirements and adheres to best practices. A well-tested application reflects robustness, maintainability, and a higher degree of user satisfaction. In the context of Streamlit, which supports rapid prototyping and deployment of data-driven web applications, thorough testing helps ensure that analytical insights and interactive elements remain accurate and dependable.

Ultimately, code testing is a key component of quality assurance, offering tangible evidence of a software's functionality and stability. It is an essential part of the development process, regardless of the application's complexity.

12.1.2. Benefits of Testing

Incorporating code testing into your general development workflow— not just in Streamlit projects—is essential and can significantly enhance the quality and longevity of your applications. It helps detect bugs early, allowing you to identify and fix issues before they propagate through the system and become more complex and difficult to resolve. This reduces debugging time and effort, enabling faster development cycles. Additionally, writing tests encourages developers to produce cleaner, more modular, and maintainable code.

Creating test cases also promotes a deeper understanding of the code's functionality and potential edge cases, leading to better design decisions. When collaborating with other developers, well-written tests allow fresh eyes to quickly grasp the behavior of the code, making it easier to build upon existing components. In this way, tests act as an additional form of documentation.

Testing also enhances reliability. Well-tested code is less likely to fail in production, minimizing downtime and reducing user frustration. This is particularly important for Streamlit applications, which often involve critical data analysis and visualizations. Thorough testing ensures that interactive elements and visual outputs behave as expected across different browsers and user inputs—an essential factor when your application is intended for a broad audience.

12.1.3. Types of Testing

There are numerous types of code testing, each serving a specific purpose and targeting different aspects of a software system. For Streamlit applications, two fundamental categories are especially relevant: unit testing and integration testing.

Unit testing focuses on verifying individual components or units of code in isolation. A unit is typically the smallest testable part of an application, such as a function or method. The goal is to ensure that each unit performs its intended task correctly, independent of other parts of the system. In the context of Streamlit, this might involve testing functions that process data, generate plots, or handle user inputs. Unit tests are usually automated and run frequently during development, providing quick feedback on the correctness of individual code units.

351

Integration testing, on the other hand, examines how different units or components interact with one another. It verifies that the interfaces between these components function properly and that the application behaves as expected when the parts are combined. For Streamlit applications, integration testing might involve checking the interaction between input widgets and output displays, or ensuring seamless communication between the app and external data sources or APIs. Integration tests help confirm that the application works as a cohesive whole, not just as isolated pieces.

Beyond these two types, other testing methods exist—such as system testing, which evaluates the entire application against specified requirements, and acceptance testing, which confirms that the application meets user expectations. However, for the scope of this chapter, a solid understanding of unit and integration testing provides a strong foundation for building robust and reliable Streamlit applications.

By understanding the principles, benefits, and various types of code testing, developers can build Streamlit applications that are not only functional, but also reliable, maintainable, and user-friendly. This chapter will explore practical examples and techniques for implementing effective testing strategies in your Streamlit projects.

12.2. Why Test in Streamlit?

Streamlit applications have evolved beyond demos to support real production use cases, making thorough testing essential as they grow in scope. A well-structured, modular codebase—with separate folders for APIs, logic, and utilities—ensures a reliable user experience. Because of this modularity, each component can and should be independently verified using unit tests.

12.2.1. Behavioral and Logical Testing

Streamlit applications are no longer limited to demo purposes—they can now evolve to support real production use cases. As the scope of an application grows, it becomes increasingly important to test its underlying components to ensure a correct and seamless end user experience.

Since Streamlit applications are more than just UI components—as discussed in previous chapters—a well-structured Streamlit project should follow an extensible and modular folder organization. This typically includes directories for API invocations, logical components, and utility functions. These modules directly influence the application's behavior and user experience, making thorough testing essential.

Given the modular nature of these components, each file can—and should—be tested individually using unit tests. This ensures that every part of the system functions correctly in isolation, contributing to the overall reliability and maintainability of the application.

12.2.2. User Interface Testing

Once the application is rendered and presented to the user, it is important to ensure that the user interface behaves as expected. This includes verifying that actions like button clicks are properly registered and that text inputs correctly update their outputs to reflect user interactions.

This process is known as *App Testing*, a specific type of testing focused on user interface components. It is especially useful for custom components to ensure the UI behaves as intended. For example, this can be applied to the Tab Bar from the *Extra-Streamlit-Components* package. Since this component is built using React and wrapped for use in Streamlit—rather than being a built-in feature—it's a good candidate for app testing to confirm its behavior aligns with user expectations.

12.3. Testing Streamlit Applications

Streamlit facilitates testing, by providing its own native App Testing framework *streamlit.testing.v1*. This enables developers to build and conduct headless tests without rendering their applications on a browser. It can even be used to simulate user input and examine rendered outputs. This framework can be run using PyTest and can even be automated in a CI environment such as GitHub Actions.

12.3.1. Setting Up Testing Environment

Firstly, we need an application to test. Listings 12-1 and 12-2 display the code for a simple calculator app that supports basic mathematical operations between two numbers. Figure 12-1 displays the associated application for this test.

Listing 12-1. *main.py*

```
import streamlit as st
from utility import calculate

st.title('Simple Calculator')
num1 = st.number_input('Enter first number', value=0.0,
key='INPUT_1')
num2 = st.number_input('Enter second number', value=0.0,
key='INPUT_2')
operation = st.selectbox('Select operation', ['+', '-', '*',
'/'], key='OPERATION')

result = None
if st.button('Calculate', key='BUTTON'):
    result = calculate(operation, num1, num2)
    if result is None:
```

```
        st.error('Error: Cannot divide by zero')
    else:
        st.write(f'Result: {result}')
```

Listing 12-2. *utility.py*

```python
def calculate(operation: str, num1: float, num2: float):
    if operation == '+':
        return num1 + num2
    elif operation == '-':
        return num1 - num2
    elif operation == '*':
        return num1 * num2
    elif operation == '/':
        if num2 != 0:
            return num1 / num2
    return None
```

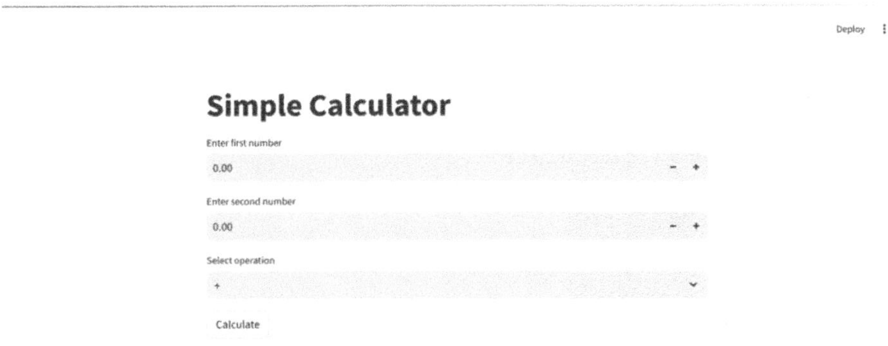

Figure 12-1. *Simple Calculator app*

To test the application, we need to install a Python package called PyTest, which will assist in constructing unit tests. You can install it using the command `pip install pytest`.

12.3.2. Writing Tests

Tests such as the one shown in Listing 12-4 should typically be placed in a separate folder at the root level of the project, such as *my_project/tests/*. They should follow the naming convention with a *test_* prefix, which allows testing tools like PyTest to recognize and execute them. Below is an example of a test file for a utility method. This is a unit test, as it targets specific parts of the application's code based on expected use cases.

Since the utility file is used as a module in the main application, we will need to expose it in the test folder by adding Listing 12-3.

Listing 12-3. *tests/__init__.py*

```
import utility
```

Listing 12-4. *tests/test_utility.py*

```
import pytest
from utility import calculate

@pytest.mark.parametrize(
    'operation, num1, num2, expected',
    [
        ('+', -2, 7, 5),
        ('+', 5.5, 2.5, 8.0),
        ('-', 10, 4, 6),
        ('-', 0, 0, 0),
        ('*', 2, 6, 12),
        ('*', -3, 4, -12),
```

```
        ('*', 2.5, 4, 10.0),
        ('/', 1, 2, 0.5),
        ('/', 10.0, 2.0, 5.0),
    ],
)
def test_calculate_basic_operations(operation, num1, num2,
expected):
    assert calculate(operation, num1, num2) == expected

@pytest.mark.parametrize(
    'operation, num1, num2',
    [
        ('/', 1, 0),
        ('/', 10.0, 0),
        ('/', 0, 0),
    ],
)
def test_division_by_zero(operation, num1, num2):
    assert calculate(operation, num1, num2) is None

# Test invalid operations
@pytest.mark.parametrize(
    'operation, num1, num2',
    [
        ('%', 5, 3),
        ('abc', 5, 3),
    ],
)
def test_invalid_operations(operation, num1, num2):
    assert calculate(operation, num1, num2) is None
```

Another type of test is *App Testing*, which verifies that the entire application reacts to user interactions as expected. This testing package is included by default with Streamlit, so no additional packages are required. The app test should involve manipulating the number inputs, clicking the button, and verifying that the output contains the expected result. Listing 12-5 below is an example of the App Test.

Listing 12-5. *tests/test_main.py*

```
from streamlit.testing.v1 import AppTest

def test_main():
    at = AppTest.from_file('../main.py').run()

    at.number_input[0].set_value(10).run()
    at.number_input[1].set_value(4).run()
    at.selectbox[0].set_value('-').run()
    at.button[0].click().run()
    assert at.markdown[0].value == 'Result: 6.0'

    at.number_input[0].set_value(2).run()
    at.number_input[1].set_value(6).run()
    at.selectbox[0].set_value('*').run()
    at.button[0].click().run()
    assert at.markdown[0].value == 'Result: 12.0'

    at.number_input[0].set_value(10).run()
    at.number_input[1].set_value(2).run()
    at.selectbox[0].set_value('/').run()
    at.button[0].click().run()
    assert at.markdown[0].value == 'Result: 5.0'

    at.number_input[0].set_value(10).run()
    at.number_input[1].set_value(0).run()
    at.selectbox[0].set_value('/').run()
```

```
at.button[0].click().run()
assert at.error

at.number_input[0].set_value(-5).run()
at.number_input[1].set_value(3).run()
at.selectbox[0].set_value('+').run()
at.button[0].click().run()
assert at.markdown[0].value == 'Result: -2.0'
```

To run these tests, open a terminal session and type *pytest*. PyTest will automatically begin by looking in the test folder, searching for files prefixed with *test_* while ignoring *__init__.py* files. It will then execute the methods that are also prefixed with *test_*, ensuring that only actual tests are run and not helper methods.

It is worth noting that *AppTest* as of Streamlit 1.47.x is limited in controlling specific native components and not everything. Components like *st.data_editor* and *st.dialog* are not supported in this type of test.

For unit tests, PyTest will use parameterized tests, which involve invoking the test method multiple times with different inputs and comparing the results. For the App Test, only one method will be run, simulating interactions within a single session. These tests will also be recognized by an IDE, allowing you to run them easily with a mouse click on the green triangles. However, if you choose to run them from the terminal, the output will be the same as shown in Figure 12-2.

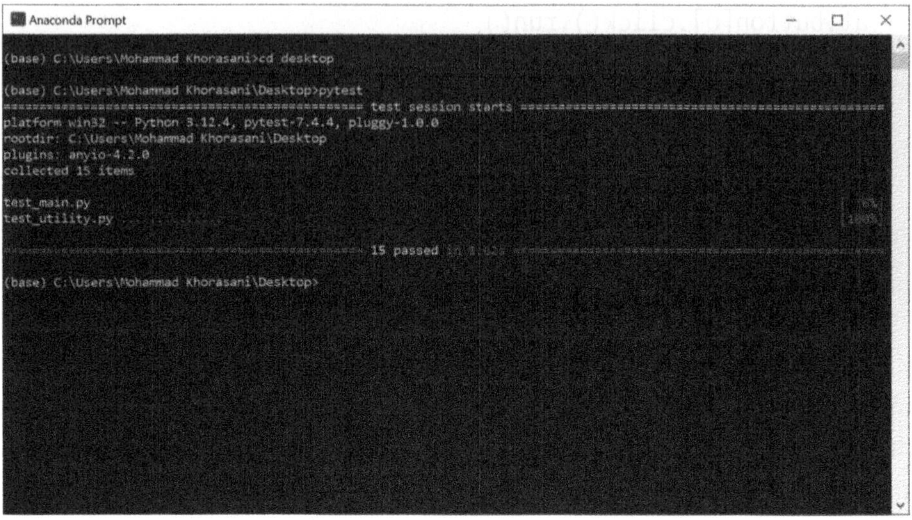

Figure 12-2. *PyTest output*

12.4. Automated Testing with GitHub Actions

Testing Streamlit applications can be automated with GitHub Actions, ensuring that whenever a push is made to a remote repository, automated test is implemented and the result immediately displayed. This ensures that all pushes comply with any testing requirements you have and also eliminates the need for manually conducting such tests. You may also use the same testing script created using PyTest and the Streamlit testing framework detailed in Section 12.2. The steps to implement automated testing with GitHub Actions is detailed in the following sections.

12.4.1. Setting Up the Workflow

To implement a GitHub Action through a repository, you must first create a workflow. This can be done by creating the folder structure shown in Figure 12-3. You must then create a *test.yaml* file that will tell GitHub how to execute the test explained in Section 12.4.2, and finally you must place a *requirements.txt* file in your root directory listing all the dependencies required for the Streamlit application.

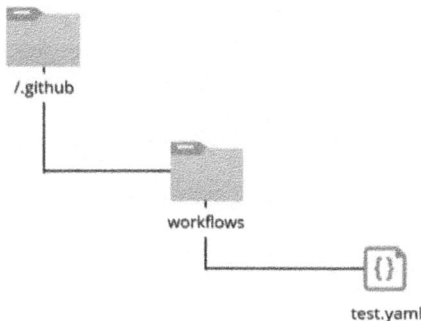

Figure 12-3. GitHub Actions workflow folder structure

12.4.2. Creating the Test Script

To configure GitHub Actions, you will need to create a *test.yaml* script that tells GitHub how to execute the test. This file must be placed in the folder structure detailed in Section 12.4.1. Please note that in the *test.yaml* file, you must include the path to two files, namely, the Streamlit application, i.e., *tests/app.py* and the PyTest file, i.e., *tests/test.py*. You may use the test script shown in Listing 12-6 as a sample.

Listing 12-6. *test.yaml*

```
name: Streamlit Testing

on:
  push:
    branches:
      - main
  pull_request:
    branches:
```

```
      - main

jobs:
  test:
    runs-on: ubuntu-latest

    steps:
    - name: Checkout repository
      uses: actions/checkout@v4

    - name: Set up Python
      uses: actions/setup-python@v5
      with:
        python-version: '3.9'

    - name: Install dependencies
      run: |
        python -m pip install --upgrade pip
        pip install -r requirements.txt
        pip install pytest

    - name: Run Streamlit app and tests
      run: |
        nohup streamlit run <path to applicaton> &
        pytest <path to PyTest script> --maxfail=1 --disable-
        warnings -q
```

Subsequently, when you make a push to the main branch of your repository, a test will be automatically conducted and the results displayed in the *Actions* tab of your GitHub repository. Should the test fail, you can access the logs as shown in Figure 12-4.

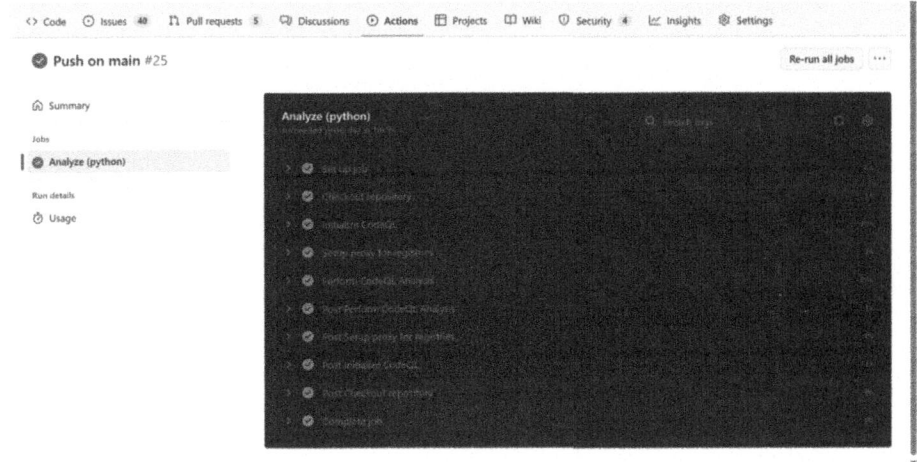

Figure 12-4. *GitHub Actions automated testing tab*

12.5. Summary

This chapter emphasized the crucial role of testing in Streamlit development, progressing from simple demos to robust applications. We covered core testing principles, focusing on early bug detection, code quality, and reliability. We specifically explored unit and integration testing, which are particularly relevant for Streamlit. We highlighted the importance of testing behavior, logic, and UI rendering in Streamlit applications. Practical examples were provided to demonstrate how to set up testing environments and write effective unit and App tests. PyTest was used for unit testing, while streamlit.testing.v1 was introduced for simulating user interactions, with parameterized tests for efficiency. *Test early and often* is the key takeaway. Integrating testing into CI/CD pipelines using GitHub Actions ensures that Streamlit applications remain reliable and maintainable. We encourage further exploration of testing tools and the refinement of strategies, especially for more complex projects. This chapter serves as a foundation for building high-quality Streamlit applications through consistent testing.

CHAPTER 13

Streamlit for AI

Streamlit's nature as a web framework opens doors for web developers to use it with any type of business or technology. Artificial Intelligence, particularly in the generative domain—including Large Language Models (LLMs) and Retrieval-Augmented Generation (RAG) models—is now more accessible than ever. Companies and corporations are competing to deliver better, faster, and more accessible models by providing a wide range of LLMs through APIs. This approach frees end users from relying solely on official portals to harness the immense capabilities of an LLM. In this chapter, we will explore LLMs, learn how to use them programmatically, and build a demo application in Streamlit that functions as a personal web information agent.

13.1. What Are LLMs and How Are They Useful?

LLMs are large-scale deep learning models, typically consisting of billions of parameters. Their purpose is not restricted to a single task; they can be applied to a variety of use cases. LLMs are trained on massive amounts of data from diverse domains, providing them with broad general intelligence across numerous areas. Fundamentally, LLMs are predictive models, meaning their outputs are shaped by the nature and quality of the data they were trained on.

© Mohammad Khorasani, Mohamed Abdou, Javier Hernández Fernández 2025
M. Khorasani et al., *Streamlit for Web Development*,
https://doi.org/10.1007/979-8-8688-1826-4_13

LLMs operate on the concept of tokens. Tokens are the building blocks of sentences and can include words, numbers, or symbols. A sequence of tokens is used as input to the LLM, which then produces a sequence of output tokens. The input tokens establish a context about a specific topic within the LLM. Based on the data it was trained on, the output tokens are generated statistically, reflecting the model's previously acquired knowledge.

The architecture of an LLM typically begins with a transformer layer, which processes the input text and converts it into a mathematical representation of the context. This means that no matter how sophisticated an LLM appears, its performance ultimately depends on the model's size, architecture, and the quality and quantity of the training data. Conversely, poor-quality data—whether misleading, poorly written, or inaccurate—can negatively affect the output, leading to grammatical errors, spelling mistakes, or even factual inaccuracies in the final result.

Real-world use cases of LLMs range from using the models independently to integrating them with other software to assist in performing specific tasks. Some examples include the following.

13.1.1. Summarization

A vast number of parameters in LLMs fundamentally store the information they were trained on in the form of statistical relationships and patterns. This allows them to summarize the information they were exposed to during training. Since the same topics can appear in various forms across different sources within the training data, an LLM can serve as a data summarizer when queried about these topics.

For example, we asked Gemini 1.5 Flash why the sky is blue, and it provided the following output:

The sky is blue due to a phenomenon called Rayleigh scattering. Sunlight is made up of all the colors of the rainbow. When sunlight enters the Earth's atmosphere, it collides with tiny air molecules (mostly nitrogen and oxygen). These molecules are much smaller than the wavelengths of visible light.

The output was likely influenced by the data the model was trained on, as the input consisted only of a question without any additional details. Additionally, a pre-trained LLM can accept varying input sizes depending on its architecture. Generally, larger models have a greater capacity to handle bigger inputs without losing significant context. This enables LLMs to build a detailed understanding of the input, which can then be used for tasks like rephrasing or summarization. For example, Chapter 3 was provided as an input prompt to Gemini 1.5 Flash, with a request to summarize it in less than 80 words. The following is the summary:

Chapter 3 details Streamlit's UI architecture. It explains how to customize the interface (themes, colors, layout) using both code and configuration files. The chapter covers page organization with sidebars, columns, and expanders, and shows how to create multi-page and sub-page applications. Dynamic content display using placeholders and progress bars is also demonstrated, along with best practices for modular application development.

We can observe that the LLM's summary primarily draws information from the abstract and summary sections of the chapter. This is because these sections typically contain the most relevant information related to the input prompt. We can also experiment with a different type of input to obtain the LLM's summarized opinion on a specific aspect of the same chapter. The following input prompt was provided to the same model:

The following is a chapter which is part of a book about Streamlit. What UI component discussed in that chapter can be useful to most applications and why:

[Chapter 3 content]

And the output was this:

Based on Chapter 3, the UI component most useful to most Streamlit applications is the placeholder (st.empty or st.sidebar.empty). The reason is its versatility and power in handling dynamic content. The chapter highlights its use for: Displaying content out of order or on demand: This is crucial for applications that need to update information asynchronously or based on user interactions without a complete page reload. This improves responsiveness and user experience significantly. Creating dynamic elements: The example of a real-time clock demonstrates how a placeholder can be used to update content repeatedly within a loop, creating dynamic visualizations. This extends to any dynamic element, such as charts updating with new data or progress bars showing the status of long-running tasks. While other components like sidebars, columns, and expanders are important for page organization and structure, the placeholder's ability to handle dynamic updates makes it a uniquely valuable tool applicable across a wide range of Streamlit applications, from simple dashboards to complex interactive tools. The other components enhance the presentation of data; placeholders handle the dynamic updating of the data itself.

The model built a context around the entire chapter and offered an opinion on a specific Streamlit component, highlighting it as the most useful due to its versatility. It also provided examples to support this viewpoint.

13.1.2. Content Generation

We have seen examples where large inputs are used to generate smaller outputs, mostly in text form. This is because LLMs fundamentally operate on tokens. However, with additional components and fine-tuning for content types beyond text, a model can generate new content and earn the label of a *Generative LLM*. The content that can be generated is not limited to images; it also depends on the training data used for fine-tuning the model. LLMs can be modified and fine-tuned to generate videos, audio, or specific types of text, such as poetry or code.

The quality of the content it produces will align with the quality of its input data. The well-known concept of *garbage in, garbage out*, frequently cited in machine learning domains, applies to LLMs as well. One reason LLMs are more widely used for image and video generation is the abundance of high-quality visual content. Additionally, the standard for generated images and videos is relatively low, and these outputs are generally accepted by most.

LLMs can certainly speed up coding and save developers time by generating repeated or well-known code snippets. However, they still lack the ability to write sophisticated, high-quality code. This is partly because much of the code available in the open source domain does not meet a specific standard, and the quality tends to be skewed toward the lower end due to the large amount of poorly written code used to train LLMs.

13.1.3. Retrieval Augmented Generation

LLMs, on their own, are highly capable. Allowing LLMs access to other software and data stores to perform actions can significantly expand their capabilities. This fundamentally enables LLMs to cross-check live data from various sources, whether from the Internet or local data, both before and during the output token generation process. This built-in power of retrieving and augmenting information during content generation is

369

known as Retrieval-Augmented Generation (RAG). Not every LLM is a RAG model, but those that are extended in this way possess enhanced and more accurate capabilities than standard LLMs. Both LlamaIndex and LangChain enable RAG systems. LlamaIndex streamlines search-and-retrieval, while LangChain is a modular platform supporting many use cases. Popular RAG platforms include Langchain with a Pinecone vector database and LlamaIndex (which contains its own vector DB), which have become essential tools for developers building knowledge-enhanced AI applications. RAG represents an architectural model rather than a single product , and it is indispensable and intricate in real-world applications across industries from customer support to financial analysis.

13.2. Different Ways to Interact with LLMs

LLMs can be accessed in various ways, depending on your use case, budget, and required level of privacy. Some of these methods include interacting with the official web page of the model, calling APIs over the Internet, or even self-hosting the model on a machine or a cluster of , machines for local access.

13.2.1. Official Web Pages

Creators of LLMs typically build web pages to allow people to use their models. They tailor the user interface (UI) to the capabilities of the model they provide, making it clear to users that they can input various content types, not just text prompts. Figure 13-1 shows the prompt window of Gemini, demonstrating the ability to attach voice, images, or videos as part of the prompt. This additional content helps formulate the overall context and can influence the final output.

Figure 13-1. *Gemini prompt on Google AI Studio*

13.2.2. Application Program Interfaces

The average user typically interacts with a final product, but LLMs accessible through a web page might not suit the needs of some, such as developers. Those who want to integrate the power of LLMs into their software products, either on a pay-per-use basis or for free, can leverage APIs that expose LLMs to developers.

The method of invocation for these models remains the same—by tokens—regardless of the medium used. When APIs are utilized, they can be scaled to handle billions of calls, making free usage of LLMs unsustainable. This is where token monitoring and billing come into play. LLM hosts track API calls by grouping usage according to the API token used. The total input and output tokens processed by the LLM can then be used to calculate the bill, if applicable. A new cost-efficiency mechanism, *tokens per dollar per watt*, helps assess the financial feasibility of processing a given token using a specific amount of electrical power.

APIs for LLMs can also be created by those who offer LLMs for use over a web page. For instance, Google allows the creation of API keys at `https://aistudio.google.com/app/apikey`, which can be used to invoke Gemini models. The following figure shows how multiple API keys can be created and used in a Curl command to make an HTTP call to Gemini 1.5 Flash with a sample input as shown in Figure 13-2 below.

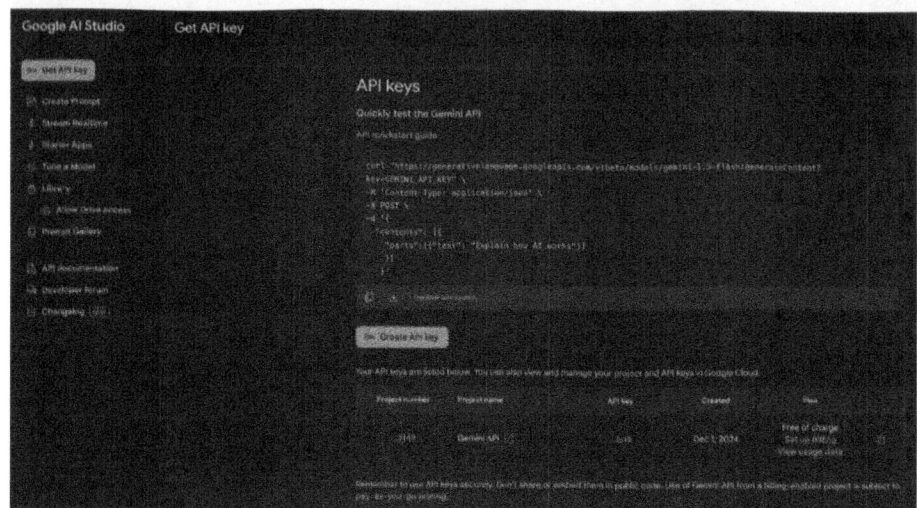

Figure 13-2. *Google API Studio API key generation*

13.2.3. Self-Hosting and Deployment

Using APIs and web pages to interact with LLMs means submitting your prompts to a server before invoking the LLM itself. For most use cases, this is convenient, as it removes the hassle of managing and hosting an LLM on your own. However, if privacy is a key requirement, the safest option is to deploy the LLM on your own infrastructure. Self-hosting LLMs comes with its own costs, such as the initial investment in hardware, ensuring a reliable energy supply, and managing clusters of machines to support heavy traffic to the model.

Many LLMs are available for download and can be run on your machine. One example is Llama, created by Meta. An easy way to get started with Llama is by downloading it from *https://ollama.com/ download*, which installs a desktop application that, in turn, installs command-line tools to manage different Llama models and run them as shown in Figure 13-3.

The following Figures 13-4 and 13-5 show the process of installing Llama 3.2 on a MacBook Pro i9. Performance may vary depending on the machine, but smaller models with fewer than three billion parameters can even run on mobile phones.

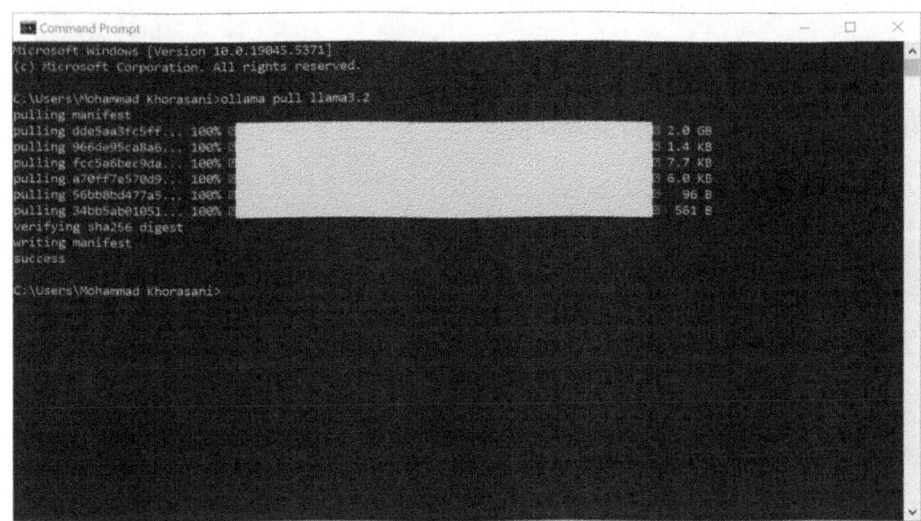

Figure 13-3. *Installing Llama3.2*

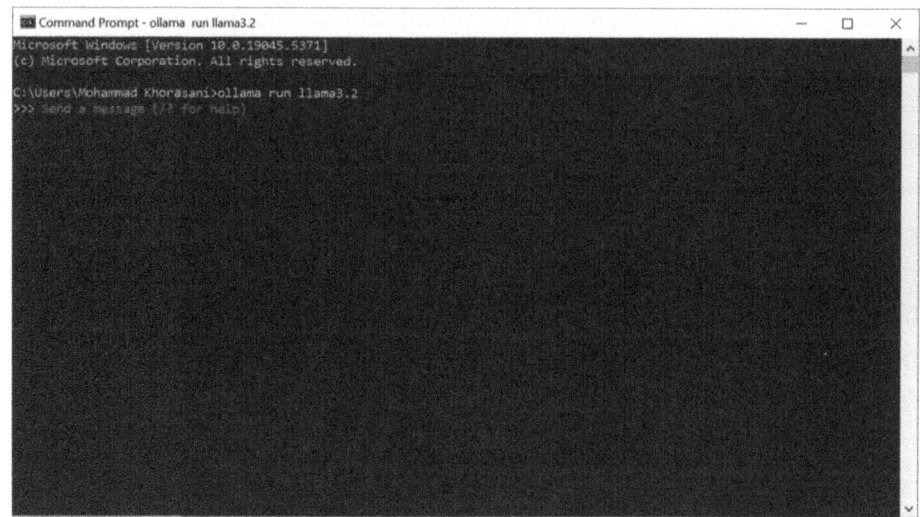

Figure 13-4. *Running Llama3.2*

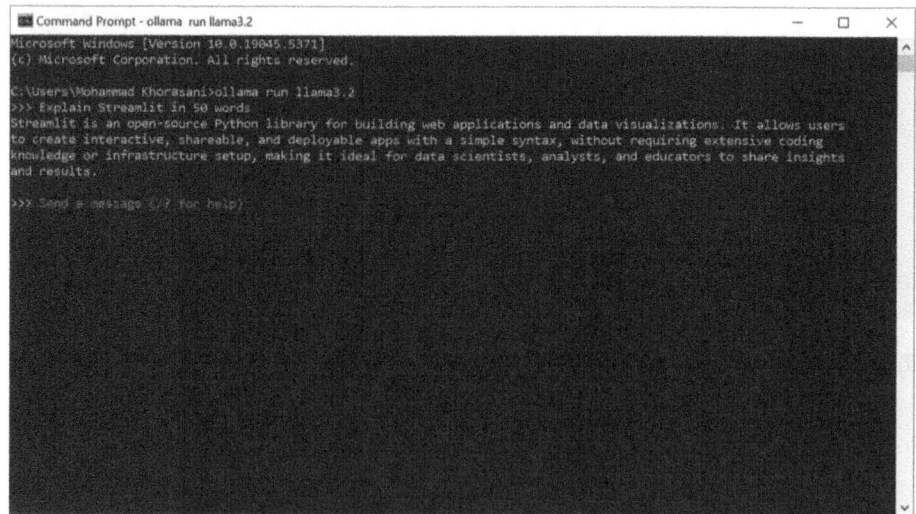

Figure 13-5. *Prompting Llama3.2*

If you want to prompt the model programmatically, you can do so by calling an endpoint on the local host, which is exposed when the model is run through the terminal. For more information, visit https://github. com/ollama/ollama/blob/main/docs/api.md.

13.3. Integrating LLMs with Streamlit

Streamlit is a web framework, and LLMs are typically deployed as independent services to avoid tight coupling with other software. This means LLMs can be used in Streamlit as if they were any other service, and their method of invocation can be done via network calls. This setup works whether the Streamlit server and LLM server are on the same machine or different machines.

The following steps outline how to replicate the behavior of LLM websites, where users supply prompts, call the LLM with the prompt, wait for the response, and render the output in a stream UI format.

13.3.1. Building an Input User Interface

A basic LLM website typically requires three main UI components: a text input, a send button, and an output area. Listing 13-1 takes in an input and displays dummy text when the send button is clicked as shown in Figure 13-6.

Listing 13-1. sample_text_input.py

```
import streamlit as st

st.title('LLMs in Streamlit')
text = st.text_area('Write prompt here')
sent = st.button('Send')
if sent:
    output = 'Dummy Output' # Replace with LLM call
    st.text(output)
```

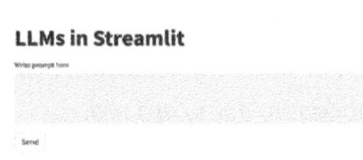

Figure 13-6. *LLM sample text input user interface (output of Listing 13-1)*

13.3.2. Setting Up an HTTP Connection

For demonstration purposes, we will use an LLM through an API. We can build on top of Gemini's API, for which we generated an API key earlier. To start, let us generate the key using the steps mentioned in previous sections of this chapter. Since API keys are sensitive data, they should not be hardcoded into your application. Instead, we will add the key to our environment variables. This can be done by adding Listing 13-2 to a file named .env, located in the same directory as your Streamlit application's main file.

Listing 13-2. .env

```
API_KEY=<YOUR_API_KEY_HERE>
```

The API key can then be read in Python as shown in Listing 13-3. First, you need to install the python-dotenv package by running pip install python-dotenv to use a method called load_env. This method reads the *.env* file and adds the key-value pairs to the system environment, making them easily accessible from your code.

Listing 13-3. read_variables.py

```
import os
from dotenv import load_dotenv

load_dotenv()
API_KEY = os.getenv('API_KEY')
print(f'{API_KEY=}')
```

For this example, we are using Gemini's API from Google AI Studio. The curl command provided on the API key generation page is more suited for usage in the terminal or CMD. To recreate it in Python, we can apply the knowledge learned in previous chapters and use the *requests* package in Python as shown in Listing 13-4 below.

Listing 13-4. gemini_input.py

```
import os
import requests
import json

API_KEY = os.getenv('API_KEY')
URL = 'https://generativelanguage.googleapis.com/v1beta/models/
gemini-1.5-flash-latest:generateContent'

def call_llm(text: str) -> str:
    body = {
        'contents': [{
            'parts': [{'text': text}]
        }]
    }
```

```
response = requests.post(
    URL, params={'key': API_KEY}, headers={'Content-Type':
    'application/json'},
    data=json.dumps(body)
)
return response.json().get('candidates', [{}])[0].
get('content', {}).get('parts', [{}])[0].get('text')
```

13.3.3. Creating the Stream Effect

Now that we have a method for calling an LLM in code, we need a way to present its output. For our API use case, there is only an HTTP method, and no WebSocket method. A WebSocket could have streamed the LLM's output to our Streamlit app token by token, allowing us to render the output word by word and create the famous LLM-streamed output experience.

Since this is not the case, we can circumvent this limitation and simulate our own stream effect. This is possible because Streamlit has a method called *write_stream*, which takes in an iterable of strings and renders the output in a stream-like fashion. Fortunately, we can not only convert the LLM's block output into an iterable of strings, but also adjust the speed at which each string appears in the iterable.

To start, we need to create a method that takes in a string and returns an iterable of strings. The iterable should introduce a delay between each element to mimic the behavior of LLM stream output. This can be achieved by pausing the Python interpreter for a few milliseconds. The following method as shown in Listing 13-5 accomplishes this.

Listing 13-5. string_iterable_converter.py

```python
import time
from typing import Iterable

def yield_text(text: str) -> Iterable:
    for word in text.split(' '):
        yield  word + ' '
        time.sleep(0.01)
```

13.3.4. Building an LLM Application with Streamlit

To bring everything together, this section combines the concepts from previous sections to build a fully-fledged LLM Streamlit application. This application takes text input from the user, invokes the Gemini 1.5 Flash API, and displays the output in a streamed fashion. Listing 13-6 displays the complete code for the application.

Listing 13-6. streamlit_llm_application.py

```python
import os
import time
import requests
import json
import streamlit as st
from dotenv import load_dotenv
from typing import Iterable

def call_llm(text: str) -> str:
    """Call LLM using direct requests to Google API"""
    body = {
        'contents': [{
            'parts': [{'text': text}]
```

```
        }]
    }

    try:
        response = requests.post(
            URL,
            params={'key': API_KEY},
            headers={'Content-Type': 'application/json'},
            data=json.dumps(body),
            timeout=30
        )
        response.raise_for_status()  # Raise an exception for
        bad status codes

        response_data = response.json()
        response_text = response_data.get('candidates',
        [{}])[0].get('content', {}).get('parts', [{}])[0].
        get('text', '')

        if not response_text:
            return "No response generated. Please try again."

        return response_text

    except requests.exceptions.RequestException as e:
        return f"Error calling API: {str(e)}"
    except (KeyError, IndexError) as e:
        return f"Error parsing response: {str(e)}"

def yield_text(text: str) -> Iterable[str]:
    """Yield text word by word for streaming effect"""
    for word in text.split(' '):
        yield word + ' '
```

```python
        time.sleep(0.02)  # Slightly slower for better
        readability

def main():
    load_dotenv()

    st.title('LLM Chat with Streamlit')

    # Main interface
    st.write("Enter your prompt below and click Send to get a
    response from Gemini.")

    text = st.text_area(
        'Your prompt:',
        height=120,
        placeholder="Ask me anything..."
    )

    sent = st.button('Send', type="primary")

    # Handle submission
    if sent:

        response_text = call_llm(text)
        st.write_stream(yield_text(response_text))

if __name__ == '__main__':
    API_KEY = os.getenv('API_KEY')
    URL = 'https://generativelanguage.googleapis.com/v1beta/
    models/gemini-1.5-flash-latest:generateContent'

    main()
```

The output is as expected: we can prompt the model with any text and
see the result displayed in a streamed effect. Check the difference between
Figures 13-7 and 13-8.

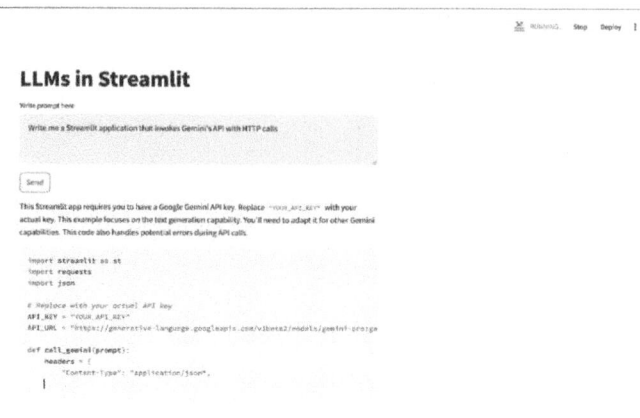

Figure 13-7. *LLM stream response midway through rendering*

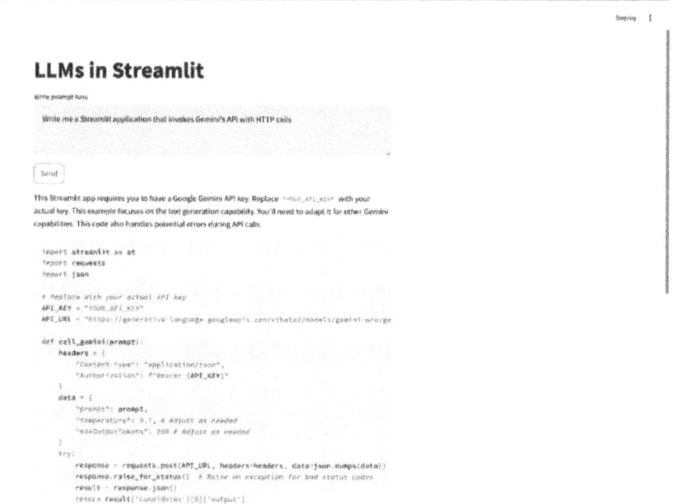

Figure 13-8. *LLM response after rendering*

Another way to invoke hosted LLM models is via official pip packages as shown in Listing 13-7. In our previous example, this can be done by using *genai* module from the pip package *google*. This comes with multiple benefits, like encapsulating the HTTP invocation in one line, as well as support streaming of the response live, token by token—or batch by batch—from Gemini directly instead of waiting for the whole response to be ready before receiving it. Using it will give a more appealing user experience as shown in Figure 13-9 below.

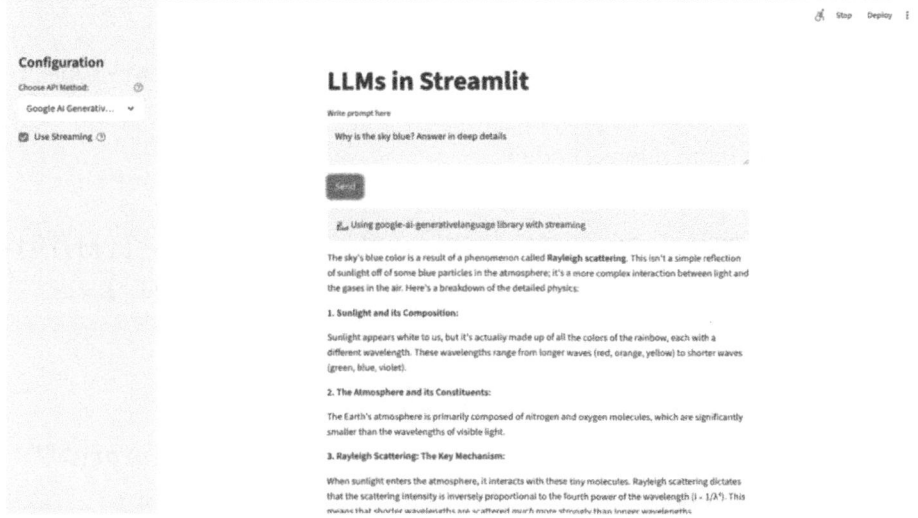

Figure 13-9. *LLM response streaming*

Listing 13-7. streamlit_llm_streaming_application.py

```
import os
import time
import requests
import json
import streamlit as st
from dotenv import load_dotenv
from typing import Iterable
```

```python
from google import genai

def call_llm_requests(text: str) -> str:
    """Call LLM using direct requests to Google API"""
    body = {
        'contents': [{
            'parts': [{'text': text}]
        }]
    }

    response = requests.post(
        URL, params={'key': API_KEY}, headers={'Content-Type':
        'application/json'},
        data=json.dumps(body)
    )
    response_text = response.json().get('candidates', [{}])[0].
    get('content', {}).get('parts', [{}])[0].get('text')

    return response_text

def call_llm_genai(text: str) -> str:
    """Call LLM using google-ai-generativelanguage library"""
    try:
        # Create client
        client = genai.Client(api_key=API_KEY)

        # Generate content
        response = client.models.generate_content(
            model='gemini-1.5-flash-latest',
            contents={'parts': [{'text': text}]}
        )

        return response.candidates[0].content.parts[0].text
    except Exception as e:
```

```
        return f"Error calling LLM with google-ai-
        generativelanguage: {str(e)}"

def call_llm_genai_stream(text: str) -> Iterable[str]:
    """Call LLM using google-ai-generativelanguage library with
    streaming"""

    try:
        # Create client
        client = genai.Client(api_key=API_KEY)

        # Generate content with streaming
        response = client.models.generate_content_stream(
            model='gemini-1.5-flash-latest',
            contents={'parts': [{'text': text}]}
        )

        for chunk in response:
            if chunk.candidates and chunk.candidates[0].
            content.parts:
                text_chunk = chunk.candidates[0].content.
                parts[0].text
                if text_chunk:
                    yield text_chunk
                    time.sleep(0.01)  # Small delay for
visual effect
    except Exception as e:
        yield f"Error calling LLM with streaming: {str(e)}"

def yield_text(text: str) -> Iterable[str]:
    """Yield text word by word for streaming effect"""
    for word in text.split(' '):
        yield word + ' '
        time.sleep(0.01)
```

```python
def main():
    load_dotenv()

    st.title('LLMs in Streamlit')

    # API method selection
    st.sidebar.title("Configuration")

    api_options = ["Direct Requests", "Google AI
GenerativeLanguage Library"]

    api_method = st.sidebar.selectbox(
        "Choose API Method:",
        api_options,
        help="Select how to call the Google Gemini API"
    )

    # Streaming option for google-ai-generativelanguage
    use_streaming = False
    if api_method == "Google AI GenerativeLanguage Library":
        use_streaming = st.sidebar.checkbox(
            "Use Streaming",
            value=True,
            help="Stream the response in real-time (only
            available with google-ai-generativelanguage library)"
        )

    # Main interface
    text = st.text_area('Write prompt here', height=100)
    sent = st.button('Send', type="primary")

    if not sent or not text.strip():
        return

    if not API_KEY:
```

```
    st.error("API_KEY not found. Please set it in your
    .env file.")
    return

# Show which method is being used
if api_method == "Direct Requests":
    st.info("🔗 Using direct HTTP requests to Google API")
    with st.spinner("Generating response..."):
        response_text = call_llm_requests(text)
    st.write_stream(yield_text(response_text))

elif api_method == "Google AI GenerativeLanguage Library":
    st.info("🔵 Using google-ai-generativelanguage library
    with streaming")
    st.write_stream(call_llm_genai_stream(text))
else:
    st.error("Selected API method is not available. Please
    install the required library or choose a different
    method.")

if __name__ == '__main__':
    API_KEY = os.getenv('API_KEY')
    URL = 'https://generativelanguage.googleapis.com/v1beta/
    models/gemini-1.5-flash-latest:generateContent'

    main()
```

13.4. Summary

LLMs have become the new focus of the technology community due to the unique benefits they provide. Using an LLM can be the final solution, but not always. Artificial intelligence can serve as a tool to create even greater products, like Streamlit. Both LLMs and Streamlit can work together to enhance a good product and make it even better. In this chapter, we learned an overview of LLMs and how they operate, along with the various ways they can be interacted with. We then used one of these interaction methods to build clones of a generic AI assistant that takes text input and provides text output. The beauty of the product we built in this chapter lies in its modularity. As a developer, you can experiment with, or even run in parallel, different types of models from various API providers, or opt for a self-hosted solution.

CHAPTER 14

Streamlit at Work

This final chapter presents two real-world cases demonstrating the use of Streamlit. The first example highlights an analysis tool developed by Iberdrola, a renewable energy company, for solar farms. This tool evaluates the operational conditions of photovoltaic (PV) power plants, enhancing the understanding of current PV plants and informing future development decisions. The second case examines the use of Streamlit in industrial environments with maxon Group, a producer of high-precision electronic motors. Streamlit is used to create a command & control dashboard application, enabling both local and remote management of maxon motors in a surgical scope adapter system.

14.1. Streamlit in Clean Energy: *Iberdrola*

Iberdrola is a global electric utility company operating in over 30 countries. Since its founding, the company has prioritized a clean and reliable business model through renewable energy investments, establishing itself as one of the largest renewable energy operators worldwide by installed capacity. Sustainable generation is a key business unit for Iberdrola, alongside networks and retail solutions [Ref: The Iberdrola Group is today a global energy leader—Iberdrola].

© Mohammad Khorasani, Mohamed Abdou, Javier Hernández Fernández 2025
M. Khorasani et al., *Streamlit for Web Development*,
https://doi.org/10.1007/979-8-8688-1826-4_14

The company generates electrical energy from clean sources such as wind (onshore and offshore), hydro, photovoltaic, and others. Over the next three years, Iberdrola plans to invest €41 billion in renewable energy and other projects [Ref: Iberdrola Strategic Plan 2024-2026—Iberdrola]. Of this, €15.5 billion will be allocated to renewables, with a target capacity of 60 GW. By 2030, the company expects its installed renewable capacity to reach 95 GW [Ref: Renewable Energies—Iberdrola]. To get a glimpse of the numbers associated with one solar plant, please see Figure 14-1.

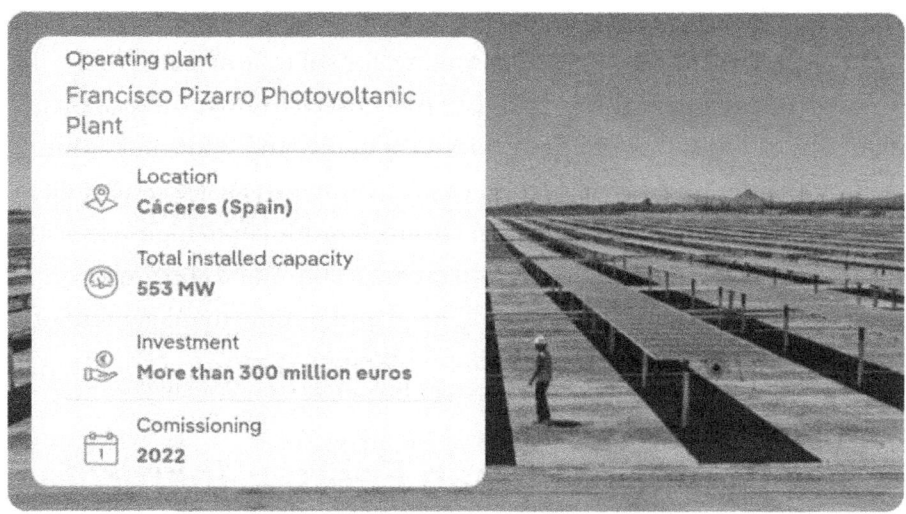

Figure 14-1. *Francisco Pizarro Photovoltaic Plant [Ref: `https://www.iberdrola.com/about-us/what-we-do/solar-photovoltaic-energy/francisco-pizarro-photovoltaic-plant`].*

14.1.1. Visualizing Operational Performance of Solar Farms

Nuria Sanchez, Daniel Paredes, and Brenno Teixeira Martins from the Energy Resource Department have spent years developing algorithms and custom software to analyze Iberdrola's solar and wind farms. The specific use case highlighted here is a software tool designed to assess the performance of PV (Photovoltaic) farms and identify operational losses. The program collects data from field devices, various databases, and models to calculate the efficiency and losses of the power plants. This information is then used to study the plants and their components, as well as to detect deviations.

To meet the needs of operational performance analysis, an innovative in-house software solution was developed. This software automates and streamlines computations that would otherwise be performed manually. Initially created as a series of Python scripts, the tool effectively met the operational analysis requirements but was limited in scalability, accessibility, and interaction with other systems. As a result, transitioning to a cloud-based deployment would enhance its potential and enable additional features and integration for end-users. Since all algorithms were already implemented in Python, a web framework was needed to interface with the web browser. Streamlit was chosen for this purpose due to its pure Pythonic nature, which required minimal learning and eliminated the need for HTML or CSS knowledge.

In collaboration with Iberdrola Innovation Middle East, a research center focused on smart grids and the integration of distributed renewable energy, the solar analysis tool was redesigned, and its functionality enhanced. The following sections will discuss some of the Streamlit-based graphical representations used by Iberdrola's solar engineers.

14.1.2. Wind and Solar Production

Hybrid farms, which combine wind and solar energy production, are a popular approach to maximizing renewable energy output. These farms capitalize on the complementary nature of wind and solar resources, as wind tends to be stronger at night and during the winter months, while solar energy is abundant during the day and in summer. By integrating both energy sources, hybrid farms can offer a more stable and continuous power supply, reducing reliance on fossil fuels and enhancing grid stability.

Figure 14-2 presents the hourly production profile of a hybrid farm, generated using synthetic data to highlight the dynamic interaction between wind and solar energy throughout the day. The Y-axis represents hourly production in megawatts (MW), while the X-axis shows the hours of the day.

In the graph, wind energy production is depicted in blue, showing how wind power fluctuates throughout the day, typically peaking during the night and early morning hours. Photovoltaic (PV) production is shown in green, illustrating the increase in solar energy generation as the sun climbs higher in the sky, reaching its peak at midday, and tapering off toward the evening.

PV loss, represented in red, indicates the amount of potential solar energy that is not captured due to the Point of Interconnection (POI) limit. The yellow curve represents the percentage of PV loss, providing a clear visual of how these losses correlate with levels of PV production. Notably, the PV loss percentage tends to increase with higher PV production, mainly due to the POI limit, which restricts the amount of energy that can be fed into the grid.

This detailed visualization effectively demonstrates the complementary nature of wind and solar energy in a hybrid farm setup, highlighting how these renewable sources can work together to provide a more stable and continuous power supply throughout the day.

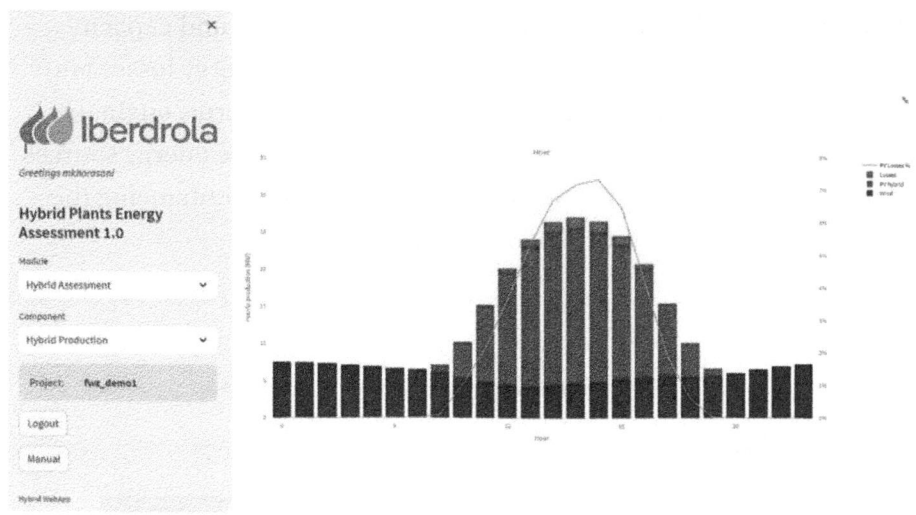

Figure 14-2. *Hourly profile of a hybrid farm production*

14.1.3. Heat Maps

A heat map (or heatmap) is a visual tool that uses colors to represent data values, making it easier to identify patterns and trends. The heat map in Figure 14-3 shows the percentage of PV loss and the probability of exceeding the POI limit for simulated hybrid farm production, broken down by month and hour. In this heat map, red cells indicate a higher percentage of PV losses and a greater probability of exceeding the POI limit, while blue cells represent periods of no production. This visualization provides engineers with a comprehensive overview of energy loss patterns, which is crucial for optimizing the sizing and dimensioning of renewable energy systems.

Moreover, this data is invaluable for integrating battery storage into hybrid farms. For instance, the heat map shows that February and March experience higher PV losses. Additionally, the probability of exceeding the POI limit is generally higher between 10 AM and 3 PM from February

393

to July. These insights can guide the strategic placement and capacity planning of battery storage systems, helping mitigate energy losses and enhance overall efficiency. By understanding these patterns, engineers can make informed decisions about the mix of renewable energy sources and the implementation of storage solutions, ultimately enhancing the performance and reliability of hybrid farms.

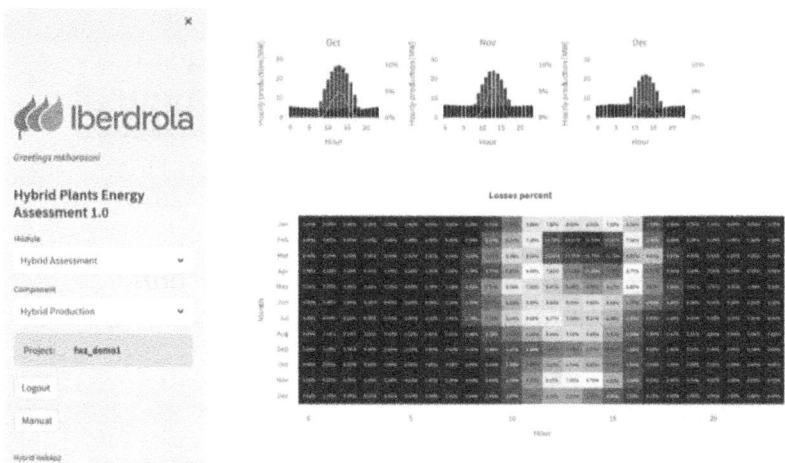

Figure 14-3. *Heatmap of the PV loss percentage for hybrid farm production on a monthly and hourly basis*

14.1.4. Closing Remarks

Beyond its visualization capabilities, Streamlit has shown remarkable versatility for Iberdrola Renewables. One of its key advantages is the ability to render multiple datasets on demand. Users can easily select the data they wish to display through an interactive interface, eliminating the need for manual programming in the source code. This feature greatly enhances user experience and efficiency.

Another valuable aspect of Streamlit is its support for two-way communication with charts using pure Python. This functionality enables dynamic and interactive data visualizations, allowing users to engage with the data more effectively. Additionally, Streamlit offers the ability to render charts as HTML on a website. This means the charts can be made interactive and integrated with other widgets, providing a seamless user experience. This is a significant improvement over running the application locally without third-party interactions, as it offers greater flexibility and interactivity in data presentation. Overall, Streamlit's features make it an indispensable tool for Iberdrola Renewables, facilitating advanced data visualization, user interaction, and integration with web-based platforms.

> *This publication is supported by Iberdrola S.A. as part of its innovation department research studies. Its contents are solely the responsibility of the authors and do not necessarily represent the official views of Iberdrola Group.*

14.2. Streamlit in Industry: *maxon Group*

maxon

maxon Group, a Swiss company, manufactures and distributes industrial-scale electronic motors for high-precision and advanced applications. Their products are widely used in various industries, including healthcare, aerospace, automotive, and packaging. The combination of versatile products, exceptional build quality, and excellent customer service allows developers to meet and exceed stringent performance requirements, both on Earth and in space. maxon's product range includes brushed, brushless, AC, and DC motors, along with gearboxes, encoders, hall effect sensors, and motor controllers that can be operated via RS232, USB, CANopen, and EtherCAT communication protocols. Additionally, maxon offers extensive customization options, enabling precise adjustments to dimensions, mechanical interfaces, cables, bearings, and other drive features to meet specific needs. Please see Figures 14-4 and 14-5 for examples of a brushless motor and motor controller developed by maxon.

Figure 14-4. *Disposition of a maxon GPX Speed 13 reduction gearbox, ECX Speed 13M brushless motor, and ENX13 encoder*

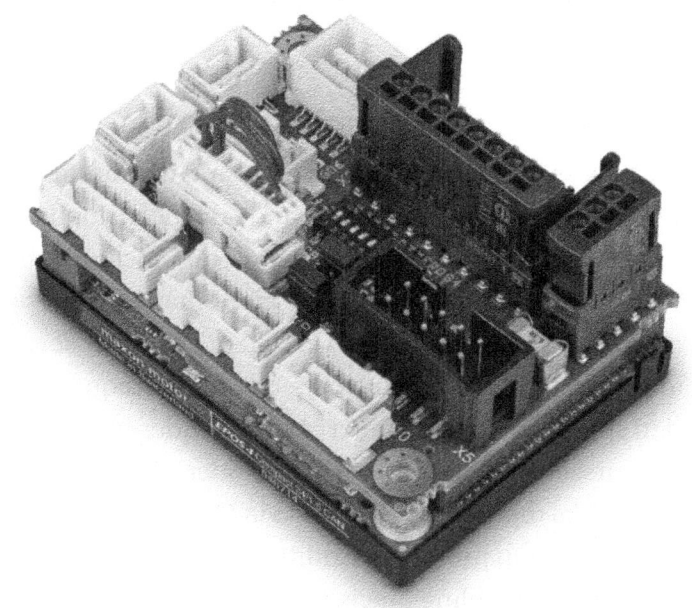

Figure 14-5. *maxon EPOS4 Compact 24/1.5 CAN motor controller*

14.2.1. Developing a Novel Surgical Scope Adapter System for Minimally Invasive Laparoscopy

Laparoscopy, a form of minimally invasive surgery, is increasingly becoming the preferred method for abdominal procedures. This technique involves making small incisions, leading to quicker recovery times and a lower risk of complications for patients. Currently, these procedures are performed manually, with a surgical assistant responsible for holding and maneuvering the endoscope inserted into the abdomen to provide real-time visuals of the surgical area Figure 14-6. This setup requires the operator to have excellent dexterity and hand-eye coordination, as even slight inaccuracies can lead to errors during surgery. [Ref: https://onlinelibrary.wiley.com/doi/10.1002/rcs.2475]

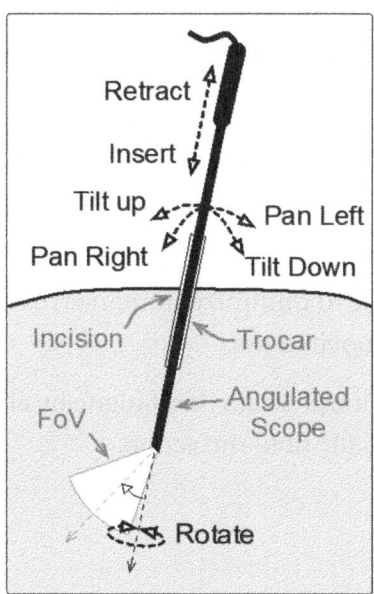

Figure 14-6. *Schematic of an endoscope inserted into the abdomen*

To address the limitations of having a human operator in the feedback loop, Dr. Nikhil Navkar and Mohammad Khorasani developed and prototyped an innovative scope adapter (illustrated in Figures 14-7 and 14-9). In this design, the endoscope and its camera head are mounted and controlled by a UR5 robotic arm, which provides six degrees of freedom. Additionally, the adapter itself offers two more degrees of freedom, allowing for the rotation of the scope and camera head around its axis and the angulation of the scope tip.

The rotation mechanism is driven by a maxon ECX brushless motor, while the angulation is powered by a maxon brushed DCX motor. Each motor is paired with a reduction gearbox, achieving top speeds of 20 RPM for rotation and 16 RPM for angulation. Furthermore, a three-channel optical encoder is used, providing resolutions of 4,096 steps per revolution for rotation and 2,048 steps per revolution for angulation.

Additional benefits of the surgical scope adapter include the following:

- Compatible with various endoscopes, camera heads, and robotic arms.

- Operable through multiple input methods, such as a joystick or by tracking optical markers on the surgeon's head.

- Programmable to minimize human error and prevent unintended movements.

- Alleviates operator strain and fatigue by eliminating the need to manually hold the scope.

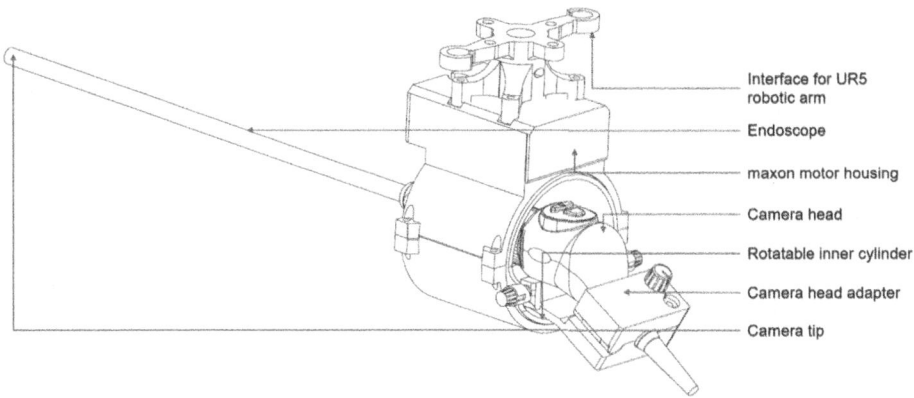

Interface for UR5
robotic arm

Endoscope

maxon motor housing

Camera head

Rotatable inner cylinder

Camera head adapter

Camera tip

Figure 14-7. *Engineering drawing of the maxon-powered surgical scope adapter*

14.2.2. Streamlit Command and Control Dashboard

After completing the mechanical prototype of the surgical scope adapter, a Streamlit application was developed to display a real-time dashboard showing the speed and position of the rotation and angulation motors (as illustrated in Figure 14-8). This application was also integrated with a three-axis joystick, allowing for precise control of each maxon motor (as shown in Figure 14-9). Additionally, by port forwarding the Streamlit application, remote control of the motors over the Internet became possible. This feature is particularly valuable for tele-surgery, enabling an operator to participate in a surgery without being physically present at the hospital. However, it is important to note that remote control over long distances can introduce latency, which may affect the device's performance.

Figure 14-8. *Streamlit command & control dashboard for the surgical scope adapter*

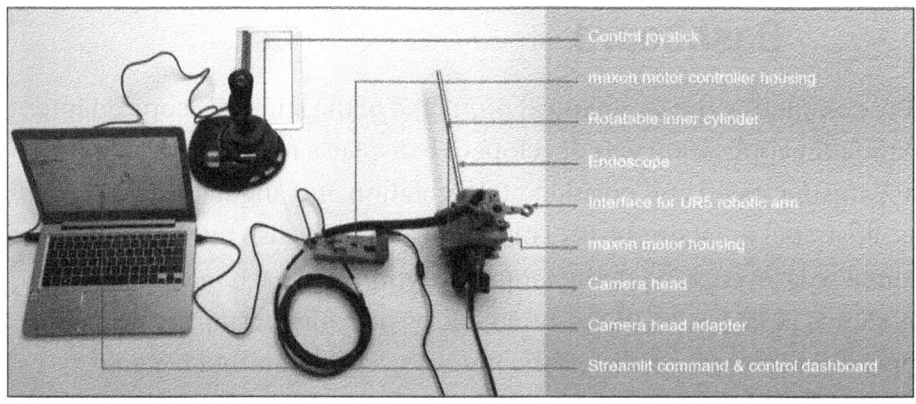

Figure 14-9. *Prototype of the surgical scope adapter with the Streamlit command & control dashboard*

14.2.3. Closing Remarks

While Streamlit is branded as a framework for machine learning and data science applications, it offers enough versatility to be used for various purposes. As demonstrated in this case, Streamlit was effectively used to integrate several non-trivial subsystems into one contiguous system. Specifically, Streamlit was used to interface the maxon motors with a joystick, enable remote control over both the local area network and the Internet, and provide a real-time dashboard displaying the motors' position and speed, all in just a few lines of code.

This work was supported by National Priority Research Program (NPRP) award (NPRP13S-0116-200084) from the Qatar National Research Fund (a member of The Qatar Foundation) and IRGC-04-JI-17-138 award from Medical Research Center (MRC) at Hamad Medical Corporation (HMC). All opinions, findings, conclusions or recommendations expressed in this work are those of the authors and do not necessarily reflect the views of our sponsors.

14.3. Summary

In this final chapter, we have explored two real-world instances of Streamlit being effectively utilized for commercial and industrial activities. The first case demonstrates how Iberdrola, a renewable energy firm, is using Streamlit to create a corporate data management application for their wind farms to estimate electrical losses during production. The second case expands on an industrial use case, where high-precision electronic motors manufactured by maxon Group are controlled via a Streamlit application for use within a surgical scope adapter system. Both examples highlight the utility that Streamlit offers to the corporate world and beyond.

Bibliography

[1] A. A. Sutchenkov and A. I. Tikhonov, "Active Investigation and Publishing of Calculation Web Based Applications for Studying Process," *Journal of Physics* 7 (2020).

[2] D. Karade and V. Karade, "AIDrugApp: Artificial Intelligence-Based Web-App for Virtual Screening of Inhibitors against SARS-COV-2," ChemRxiv, preprint (2021).

[3] D. M. A. Raheem, S. Tabassum, S. K. Nahid, and S. A. Anzer, "A Deep Learning Approach for the Automatic Analysis and Prediction of Breast Cancer for Histopathological Images Using A Webapp," *International Journal of Engineering Research*, vol. 10, no. 6, pp. 439–443, (2021).

[4] A. N. Habowski, T. J. Habowski, and M. L. Waterman, "GECO: Gene Expression Clustering Optimization App for Non-Linear Data Visualization of Patterns," *BMC Bioinformatics* 22, 29 (2021).

[5] F. M. Torun, S. V. Winter, S. Doll, F. M. Riese, A. Vorobyev, J. B. Mueller-Reif, P. E. Geyer, and M. T. Strauss, "Transparent Exploration of Machine Learning for Biomarker Discovery from Proteomics and Omics Data," Journal of Proteome Research, vol. 22, no. 11, pp. 2953–2966, (2023).

© Mohammad Khorasani, Mohamed Abdou, Javier Hernández Fernández 2025
M. Khorasani et al., *Streamlit for Web Development*,
https://doi.org/10.1007/979-8-8688-1826-4

[6] R. Shigapov, P. Zumstein, J. Kamlah, L. Oberländer, J. Mechnich, and I. Schumm, "Bbw: Matching CSV to Wikidata via Meta-Lookup," CEUR Workshop Proceedings, vol. 2775, pp. 17–26, (2020).

[7] A. R. Kashyap and M.-Y. Kan, "SciWING – A Software Toolkit for Scientific Document Processing," arXiv preprint, arXiv:2004.03807, (2020).

[8] J. Vig, W. Kryściński, K. Goel, and N. F. Rajani, "SummVis: Interactive Visual Analysis of Models, Data, and Evaluation for Text Summarization," arXiv preprint, arXiv:2104.07605 (2021).

[9] A. Pournaki, F. Gaisbauer, S. Banisch, and E. Olbrich, "The Twitter Explorer: A Framework for Observing Twitter Through Interactive Networks," arXiv preprint, arXiv:2003.03599 (2020).

[10] A. Saxena, M. Dhadwal, and M. Kowsigan, "Indian Crop Production: Prediction and Model Deployment Using ML and Streamlit," Academia. edu preprint, (2021).

[11] S. F. N. Islam, A. Sholahuddin, and A. S. Abdullah, "Extreme Gradient Boosting (XGBoost) Method in Making Forecasting Application and Analysis of USD Exchange Rates against Rupiah," *J. Phys.: Conf. Ser.* 1722, 012016 (2021).

[12]   A. Aboah, M. Boeding, and Y. Adu-Gyamfi, "Mobile Sensing for Multipurpose Applications in Transportation," Journal of Big Data Analytics in Transportation, vol. 4, pp. 171–183 (2022).

[13]   J. Tang, T. Ma, and Q. Luo, "Trends Prediction of Big Data: A Case Study based on Fusion Data," Procedia Computer Science, vol. 174, pp. 181–190, (2020).

Index

© Mohammad Khorasani, Mohamed Abdou, Javier Hernández Fernández 2025
M. Khorasani et al., *Streamlit for Web Development*,
https://doi.org/10.1007/979-8-8688-1826-4

The manufacturer's authorised representative in the EU is Springer
Nature Customer Service Centre GmbH, Europaplatz 3, 69115 Heidelberg,
Germany. If you have any concerns regarding our products, please
contact ProductSafety@springernature.com

Printed and bound by CPI Group (UK) Ltd, Croydon, CR0 4YY

23/04/2026

02095592-0014